Java Programming: Introductory

Java Programming: Introductory

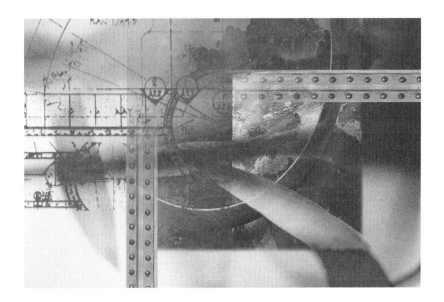

Joyce Farrell

McHenry County College

COURSE
TECHNOLOGY

ONE MAIN STREET, CAMBRIDGE, MA 02142

an International Thomson Publishing company I(T)P®

Cambridge • Albany • Bonn • Boston • Cincinnati • London • Madrid • Melbourne • Mexico City
New York • Paris • San Francisco • Singapore • Tokyo • Toronto • Washington

Java Programming: Introductory is published by Course Technology.

Managing Editor	Kristen Duerr
Product Manager	Cheryl Ouellette
Developmental Editor	Jessica Evans
Production Editor	Jean Bermingham
Text Designer	Doug Goodman
Cover Designer	Efrat Reis

© 1999 by Course Technology— I(T)P®

For more information contact:

Course Technology, Inc.
One Main Street
Cambridge, MA 02142

International Thomson Editores
Seneca, 53
Colonia Polanco
11560 Mexico D.F. Mexico

ITP Europe
Berkshire House 168-173
High Holborn
London WCIV 7AA
England

ITP GmbH
Königswinterer Strasse 418
53227 Bonn
Germany

Nelson ITP, Australia
102 Dodds Street
South Melbourne, 3205
Victoria, Australia

ITP Asia
60 Albert Street, #15-01
Albert Complex
Singapore 189969

ITP Nelson Canada
1120 Birchmount Road
Scarborough, Ontario
Canada M1K 5G4

ITP Japan
Hirakawacho Kyowa Building, 3F
2-2-1 Hirakawacho
Chiyoda-ku, Tokyo 102
Japan

ISBN 0-7600-1069-2

Printed in Canada

2 3 4 5 6 7 8 9 WC 02 01 00 99

Preface

Java Programming: Introductory is designed to guide the beginning programmer in developing applications and applets using the Java programming language. This textbook assumes that students have no programming language experience.

Organization and Coverage

Java Programming: Introductory introduces students to object-oriented programming concepts along with the Java syntax to implement them. Object-oriented techniques are introduced in Chapter 1 and explored extensively in Chapters 2 and 3, which is earlier than in many other texts. Chapters 4 and 5 teach students the fundamentals of structured logic using decisions, loops, and array manipulation. In Chapter 6, students write Java applets that use GUI components.

Java Programming: Introductory combines text explanation with step-by-step exercises that illustrate the concepts being explained, reinforcing students' understanding and retention of the material. Java applications are introduced prior to applets, so the student has a more thorough understanding of the programming process, and testing of the student's programs is simplified.

The student using *Java Programming: Introductory* builds applications and applets from the bottom up rather than using prewritten objects. This facilitates a deeper understanding of the concepts used in object-oriented programming. When students complete this book, they will know how to create and modify simple Java language applications and applets, and they will have the tools to create more complex examples. Students will also have a fundamental knowledge of object-oriented programming concepts that will be useful whether they continue to learn more about the Java language or go on to other object-oriented languages, such as C++ and Visual Basic.

Java Programming: Introductory distinguishes itself from other Java language books in the following ways:

- It is written and designed specifically for students with no previous programming experience.

- The code examples are short; one concept is featured in each code example.

- Object-oriented techniques are covered earlier than in many other texts.

- Text explanation is interspersed with step-by-step exercises.

- Java applications are introduced prior to applets, so the student has a more thorough understanding of the programming process, and testing is simplified.

- Java applications are built from the bottom up; the student gains a clear picture of how complex programs are built.

After completing this textbook, students will be able to write simple applications and applets using the Java programming language. Further instruction is available in *Java Programming: Comprehensive*, which contains eight additional chapters to those included in this book. After completing the Comprehensive book, students will be familiar with the topics covered in the Sun Certified Programmer Examination. After practicing and applying those topics to writing professional business applications, they will be ready to take the certification exam.

Features

Java Programming: Introductory is a superior textbook because it also includes the following features:

- **"Read This Before You Begin" Page** This page is consistent with Course Technology's unequaled commitment to helping instructors introduce technology into the classroom. Technical considerations and assumptions about hardware, software, and default settings are listed in one place to help instructors save time and eliminate unnecessary aggravation.

- **Case Approach** Each chapter addresses a programming-related problem that students could reasonably expect to encounter in business. Many of the cases are followed by a demonstration of an application that could be used to solve the problem. Showing students the completed application before they learn how to create it is motivational and instructionally sound. By allowing students to see the type of application they will create after completing the chapter, students will be more motivated to learn because they can see how the programming concepts that follow can be used and, therefore, why the concepts are important.

- **Step-by-Step Methodology** The unique Course Technology methodology keeps students on track. They write program code always within the context of solving the problems posed in the chapter. The text constantly guides students and lets them know where they are in the process of solving a problem. The numerous illustrations guide students in creating useful, working programs.

- **HELP?** These paragraphs anticipate problems students are likely to encounter and help them resolve these problems on their own. This feature facilitates independent learning and frees the instructor to focus on substantive issues rather than on common procedural errors.

- **Tips** Tips provide additional information—for example, an alternative method of performing a procedure, background information on a technique, a commonly-made error to watch out for, or the name of a Web site the student can visit to gather more information.

- **Summaries** Following each chapter is a Summary that recaps the programming concepts and commands covered in each section.

- **Review Questions** Each chapter concludes with meaningful, conceptual Review Questions that test students' understanding of what they learned in the chapter.

- **Exercises** Programming Exercises provide students with additional practice using the skills and concepts they learned in the lesson. These exercises increase in difficulty and are designed to allow students to explore the language and programming environment independently.

■ **Debugging Exercises** Each chapter contains four programs that contain the types of errors students are likely to make in their own programs. By debugging these files, students learn to recognize the source of errors and learn how to fix them. These exercises also expose students to errors that they might never make, but that other programmers do make. The ability to modify existing programs is an important programming skill.

The Java Programming Environment

This book was written using Sun Microsystem's Java Development Kit (JDK) version 1.1.6 installed on a Windows personal computer. Later and earlier versions of the JDK might have slightly different capabilities, but the core functionality is the same. Specific instructions for installing the JDK are provided in the Instructor's Manual.

The Supplements

All of the supplements for this text are found in the Instructor's Resource Kit, which is available on Course Technology's Web site or on a CD-ROM.

■ **Instructor's Manual** The author wrote the Instructor's Manual and it was quality assurance tested. It is available through the Course Technology Faculty Online Companion on the World Wide Web at www.course.com. (Call your customer service representative for the specific URL and your password.) The Instructor's Manual contains the following items:

■ Complete instructions for downloading the Java Development Kit from the Sun Web site or installing it from the CD-ROM included with the book.

■ Answers to all of the Review Questions and solutions to all of the Programming Exercises in the book.

■ Teaching notes to help introduce and clarify the material presented in the chapters.

■ Technical notes that include troubleshooting tips.

■ **Course Test Manager Version 1.2 Engine and Test Bank** Course Test Manager (CTM) is a cutting-edge Windows-based testing software program, developed exclusively for Course Technology, that helps instructors design and administer examinations and practice tests. This full-featured program allows instructors to randomly generate practice tests that provide immediate on-screen feedback and detailed study guides for incorrectly answered questions. Instructors can also use Course Test Manager to create printed and online tests over a network. Tests on any or all chapters of this textbook can be created, previewed, and administered entirely over a local area network. Course Test Manager can grade the tests automatically at the computer and can generate statistical information on individual as well as group performance. A CTM test bank has been written to accompany this textbook and is included on the CD-ROM. The test bank includes multiple-choice, true/false, short answer, and essay questions.

- **Solutions Files** Solutions Files contain possible solutions to all programs students are asked to create or modify in the chapters and cases. (Due to the nature of programming, students' solutions might differ from these solutions and still be correct.)

- **Student Files** Student Files, containing all of the data that students will use for the chapters and exercises in this textbook, are provided through Course Technology's Online Companion, on the Instructor's Resource Kit CD-ROM, and on the Student Resource Kit CD-ROM. A Help file includes technical tips for lab management. See the inside front cover of this textbook and the "Read This Before You Begin" page preceding Chapter 1 for more information on Student Files.

Acknowledgments

I would like to thank all of the people who helped to make this book a reality, especially Jessica Evans, Developmental Editor, who worked day and night, found all my typos, improved my grammar, and generally made working on this book a pleasure. Thanks also to Kristen Duerr, Managing Editor; Cheryl Ouellette, Product Manager; Jean Bermingham, Production Editor; and Alex White and Jon Greacen, Quality Assurance testers.

I am grateful to the many reviewers who provided helpful and insightful comments during the development of this book, including Thomas Alhborn, West Chester University; Jim Dunne, Arapahoe Community College; John Humphrey, Asheville-Buncombe Technical College; Joe Kozlevcar, Lakeland Community College; Keith Morneau, Computer Learning Center; and Arland Richmond, Computer Learning Center. I extend special thanks to Jim Dunne for providing additional student exercises for the end of each section in each chapter.

Thanks, too, to my husband, Geoff, whose constant support makes everything I do possible, and whose presence makes it all fun. Thanks to my daughters, Andrea and Audrey, who are managing to age me as well as keep me young at the same time.

Finally, I would like to dedicate this book to my mother, Colleen Bussell.

Joyce Farrell

Contents

chapter 4

INPUT, SELECTION, AND REPETITION *133*

Previewing the ChooseManager Program Using the Event Class *134*

c h a p t e r   6

Read This Before You Begin

To the Student

Student Disks

To complete the chapters and exercises in this book, you need Student Disks. Your instructor will provide you with Student Disks or ask you to make your own.

If you are asked to make your own Student Disks, you will need two blank, formatted high-density disks. You will need to copy a set of folders from a file server or standalone computer onto your disks. Your instructor will tell you which computer, drive letter, and folders contain the files you need. The following table shows you which folders go on each of your disks, so that you will have enough disk space to complete all the chapters and exercises:

Student Disk	Write this on the disk label	Put these folders on the disk
1	Chapters 1, 2, and 3	Chapter.01, Chapter.02, and Chapter.03
2	Chapters 4, 5, and 6	Chapter.04, Chapter.05, and Chapter.06

When you begin each chapter, make sure you are using the correct Student Disk. See the inside front cover of this book for more information on Student Disk files, or ask your instructor or technical support person for assistance.

Using Your Own Computer

You can use your own computer to complete the chapters and exercises in this book. To use your own computer, you will need the following:

- **Software** You can download the JDK compiler from the CD-ROM that came with this book or by going to Sun's Web site (http://java.sun.com/products/jdk/). This download is approximately 15 MB of software, so it could take up to one hour to complete using a modem with a regular telephone line. To install the downloaded JDK compiler, double-click the downloaded file, and then follow the on-screen instructions.

- **Hardware** You must have a computer running Windows or Windows NT workstation, 100 MB of free disk space, and a minimum of 32 MB of memory (64 MB is recommended for Windows NT).

- **Student Disks** You can get the Student Disk files from your instructor or from the CD-ROM that comes with this book. You will not be able to complete all of the chapters and exercises in this book using your own computer until you have Student Disks. The student files may also be obtained electronically through the Internet. See the inside front cover of this book for more details.

Starting the JDK Compiler

The steps in this book assume that you can compile *.java files from any path, and that the current path will be the drive that contains the Student Disk and the folder for the current tutorial, such as A:\Chapter.06>. To configure Java to work in this manner, do the following:

1   Go to the command prompt.

2   Type **path = *drive*:*pathname*\bin**, where *drive* is the drive letter that contains your JDK installation, and *pathname* is the complete pathname of the JDK folder. For example, your command might be **C:\JDK1.1.6\bin** if your installation is on drive C in the JDK1.1.6 folder.

3   Press the **Enter** key. Now you can compile Java files from any folder. However, you must type this path command every time you start Java. If you prefer, you can add the path line to your computer's autoexec.bat file so that Java will start automatically.

Visit Our World Wide Web Site

Additional materials designed especially for your course might be available on the World Wide Web. Go to **www.course.com**. Search for this book title periodically on the Course Technology Web site for more details.

To the Instructor

To complete all of the exercises and chapters in this book, your students must use a set of Student Files. These files are included in the Instructor's Resource Kit, as well as on the CD-ROM that accompanies this book. They may also be obtained electronically through the Internet. See the inside front cover of this book for more details. Follow the instructions in the Help file to copy the Student Files to your server or standalone computer. You can view the Help file using a text editor, such as WordPad or Notepad.

Once the files are copied, you can make Student Disks for the students yourself, or tell students where to find the files so they can make their own Student Disks. Make sure the files get copied correctly onto the Student Disks by following the instructions in the Student Disks section, which will ensure that students have enough disk space to complete all of the chapters and exercises in this book.

Course Technology Student Files

You are granted a license to copy the Student Files to any computer or computer network used by students who have purchased this book.

A First Program Using Java

case ▶ As you read your e-mail, a sinking feeling descends on you. There's no denying the message: "Please see me in my office as soon as you are free—Lynn Greenbrier." Lynn Greenbrier is the head of programming for Event Handlers Incorporated, and you have worked for her as an intern for only two weeks. Event Handlers manages the details of private and corporate parties; every client has different needs, and the events are interesting and exciting.

"Did I do something wrong?" you ask as you enter her office. "Are you going to fire me?"

Almost like a mind reader, Lynn stands to greet you and says, "Please wipe that worried look off your face! I want to see if you are interested in a new challenge. Our programming department is going to create several new programs in the next few months. We've decided that the Java programming language is the way to go. It's object-oriented, platform independent, and perfect for applications on the World Wide Web, which is where we want to expand our marketing efforts."

"I'm not sure what 'object-oriented' and 'platform independent' mean," you say, "but I've always been interested in computers, and I'd love to learn more about programming."

"Based on your aptitude tests, you're perfect for programming," Lynn says. "Let's get started now. I'll describe the basics to you."

SECTION A
objectives

In this section you will learn
- About programming tasks
- Object-oriented programming concepts
- About the Java programming language
- How to write a Java program
- How to add comments to a Java program
- How to run a Java program
- How to modify a Java program

Creating a Program

Programming

A computer **program** is simply a set of instructions that you write to tell a computer what to do. Computers are constructed from circuitry that consists of small on/off switches, so you *could* write a computer program by writing something along the following lines:

first switch—on
second switch—off
third switch—off
fourth switch—on

Your program could go on and on, for several thousand switches. A program written in this style is written in **machine language**, which is the most basic circuitry-level language. The problems with this approach lie in keeping track of the many switches involved in programming any worthwhile task, and in discovering the errant switch or switches if the program does not operate as expected. Additionally, the number and location of switches varies from computer to computer, which means that you would need to customize a machine language program for every type of machine on which you want the program to run.

Fortunately, programming has evolved into an easier task because of the development of high-level programming languages. A **high-level programming language** allows you to use a vocabulary of reasonable terms like "read," "write," or "add" instead of the sequences of on-off switches that perform these tasks. High-level languages also allow you to assign intuitive names to areas of computer memory, like "hoursWorked" or "rateOfPay," rather than having to remember the memory locations (switch numbers) of those values.

Each high-level language has its own **syntax**, or rules of the language. For example, depending on the specific high-level language, you might use the verb "print" or "write" to produce output. All languages have a specific, limited vocabulary and a specific set of rules for using that vocabulary. Programmers use a computer program called a **compiler** (or **interpreter** or **assembler**) to translate their high-level language statements into machine code. The compiler issues an error message each time the programmer uses the programming language incorrectly; subsequently, the programmer can correct the error and attempt another translation by compiling the program again. When you are learning a computer programming language such as the Java programming language, C++, or COBOL, you really are learning the vocabulary and syntax rules for that language.

In addition to learning the correct syntax for a particular language, a programmer also must understand computer programming logic. The **logic** behind any program involves executing the various statements and procedures in the correct order to produce the desired results. For example, you might be able to execute perfect individual notes on a musical instrument, but if you do not execute them in the proper order (or execute a B flat when an F sharp was expected), you will not produce an enjoyable musical performance. Similarly, you might be able to use a computer language's syntax correctly, but be unable to execute a logically constructed, workable program. Examples of logical errors include multiplying two values when you meant to divide them, or producing output prior to obtaining the appropriate input.

Object-Oriented Programming

There are two popular approaches to writing computer programs: procedural programming and object-oriented programming.

Procedural programming involves using your knowledge of a programming language to create computer memory locations that can hold values and writing a series of steps or operations that manipulate those values. The computer memory locations are called **variables** because they hold values that might vary. For example, a payroll program written for a company might contain a variable named `rateOfPay`. The memory location referenced by the name `rateOfPay` might contain different values (a different value for every employee of the company) at different times. During the execution of the payroll program, each value stored under the name `rateOfPay` might have many **operations** performed on it—for example, reading the value from an input device, multiplying the value by another variable representing hours worked, and printing the value on paper. For convenience, the individual operations used in a computer program often are grouped into logical units called **procedures**. For example, a series of four or five comparisons and calculations that together determine an individual's federal withholding tax value might be grouped as a procedure named `calculateFederalWithholding`. A procedural program defines the variable memory locations, and then **calls** or **invokes** a series of procedures to input, manipulate, and output the values stored in those locations. A single procedural program often contains hundreds of variables and thousands of procedure calls.

Object-oriented programming is an extension of procedural programming in which you take a slightly different approach to writing computer programs. Thinking in an object-oriented manner involves envisioning program components as objects that are similar to concrete objects in the real world. Then you manipulate the objects to achieve a desired result. Writing object-oriented programs involves both creating objects and creating applications that use those objects.

If you've ever used a computer that uses a command-line operating system (such as DOS), and if you've also used a GUI (graphical user interface, such as Windows), then you already have an idea of the difference between procedural and object-oriented programs. If you want to move several files from a floppy disk to a hard disk, you can use either a typed command at a prompt or command line or use a mouse in a graphical environment to accomplish the task. The difference lies in whether you issue a series of commands, in sequence, to move the three files, or you drag icons representing the files from one screen location to another, much as you would physically move paper files from one file cabinet to another in your office. You can move the same three files using either operating system, but the GUI system allows you to manipulate the files like their real-world paper counterparts. In other words, the GUI system allows you to treat files as objects.

Objects in both the real world and in object-oriented programming are made up of states and methods. The **states** of an object also are known as its **attributes**. For example, some of your automobile's attributes are its make, model, year, and purchase price. Other attributes include whether the automobile is currently running, its gear, its speed, and whether it is dirty. All Automobiles possess the same attributes, but not, of course, the same values for those attributes. Similarly, your Dog has the attributes breed, name, age, and whether or not his or her shots are current. Your red Chevrolet automobile with the dent is an **instance** of the **class** that is made up of all automobiles, and your Golden Retriever Dog named Goldie is an instance of the class that is made up of all dogs. Thinking of items as instances of a class allows you to apply your general knowledge of the class to individual members of the class. Your particular instances of these objects **inherit** their attributes from the general category. If your friend purchases an Automobile, you know it has a model name, and if your friend gets a Dog, you know the dog has a breed. You might not know the exact contents or current state of your friend's Automobile's speed or her Dog's shots, but you do know what attributes exist for the Automobile and Dog classes. Similarly, in a GUI operating environment, you expect each component to have specific, consistent attributes, such as a menu bar and a title bar, because each component inherits these attributes as a member of the general class of GUI components.

· ·

By convention, programmers using the Java programming language begin their class names with an uppercase letter. Thus the class that defines the attributes and methods of an automobile would probably be named Automobile, **and the class for dogs would probably be named** Dog. **However, following this convention is not required to produce a workable program.**

· ·

Besides attributes, objects can use **methods** to accomplish tasks. Automobiles, for example, can move forward and backward. They also can be filled with gasoline or be washed, both of which are methods that change some of their attributes. Methods exist for ascertaining certain attributes, such as the current speed of an Automobile and the current status of its gas tank. Similarly, a Dog can walk or run, eat food, and get a bath, and there are methods for determining how hungry the Dog is. GUI operating system components can be maximized, minimized, and dragged. Like procedural programs, object-oriented programs have variables (attributes) and procedures (methods), but the attributes and methods are encapsulated into objects that are then used much like real-world objects. **Encapsulation** is the technique of packaging an object's attributes into a cohesive unit that you can use as an undivided entity. Programmers sometimes refer to encapsulation as using a "black box," or a device that you can use without regard to the internal mechanisms.

If an object's methods are well written, the user is unaware of the low-level details of how the methods are executed, in which case the user must simply understand the **interface** or interaction between the method and the object. For example, if you are able to fill your Automobile with gasoline, it is because you understand the interface between the gas pump nozzle and the vehicle's gas tank opening. You don't need to understand how the pump works mechanically or where the gas tank actually is located inside your vehicle. If you can read your speedometer, it does not matter how the display figure is calculated. As a matter of fact, if someone produces a superior, more accurate speed-determining device and inserts it in your Automobile, you don't have to know or care how it operates, as long as your interface remains the same. The same principles apply to well-constructed objects used in object-oriented programs.

The Java Programming Language

The **Java programming language** was developed by Sun Microsystems as an object-oriented language that is used both for general-purpose business programs and interactive World Wide Web-based Internet programs. Some of the advantages that have made the Java programming language so popular in recent years are its security features, and the fact that it is **architecturally neutral**, which means that you can use the Java programming language to write a program that will run on any platform. A machine that runs a program written in the Java programming language only needs to have a special program called an **interpreter** to translate the program for the host machine. In contrast, when using other programming languages, software vendors usually have to produce multiple versions of the same product (a DOS version, Windows 3.1 version, Windows 95 version, Windows 98 version, Macintosh version, and so on) so all users can use the program. With the Java programming language, one program version will run on all these platforms. A program written in the Java programming language is compiled into Java Virtual Machine code, called **bytecode**. The compiled bytecode is subsequently interpreted on the machine where the program is executed. Any compiled program will run on any machine that has a Java programming language interpreter.

For simplicity, the terms "Java program" and "program for the Java programming language" are used interchangeably throughout this text.

Another advantage of the Java programming language is that it is simpler to use than many other object-oriented languages. The Java programming language is modeled after the C++ programming language. Although neither language qualifies as "simple" to read or understand on first exposure, the Java programming language eliminates some of the most difficult features to understand in C++.

Starting a Program

At first glance, even the simplest Java program involves a fair amount of confusing syntax. Consider the following simple program. This program is written on seven lines, and its only task is to print "First Java program" on the screen.

```java
public class First
{
  public static void main(String[] args)
  {
    System.out.println("First Java program");
  }
}
```

The statement that does the actual work in this program is `System.out.println("First Java program");`. All Java programming language statements end with a semicolon.

The text "First Java program" is a **literal string** of characters; that is, it is a series of characters that will appear exactly as entered. Any literal string in Java appears between double quotation marks.

The string "First Java program" appears within parentheses because the string is an argument to a method, and arguments to methods always appear within parentheses. **Arguments** consist of information that a method requires to perform its task. For example, you might place a catalog order with a company that sells sporting goods. Processing a catalog order is a method that consists of a set of standard procedures. However, each catalog order requires information—such as which item number you are ordering and the quantity of the item desired—and this information can be considered as the order's argument. If you order two of item 5432 from a catalog, you expect different results than if you order 1,000 of item 9008. Likewise, if you pass the argument "Happy Holidays" to a method, you expect different results than if you pass the argument "First Java program".

Within the statement `System.out.println("First Java program");`, the method to which you are passing "First Java program" is named println(). The println() method prints a line of output on the screen, positions the cursor on the next line, and stands ready for additional output.

Within the statement System.out.println("First Java program");, out is an object. The out object represents the screen. Several methods, including println(), are available with the out object. Of course, not all objects have a println() method (for instance, you can't print to a keyboard, to your Automobile, or to your Dog), but the creators of the Java platform assumed you frequently would want to display output on a screen. Therefore the out object was created and endowed with the method named println(). In this section, you will create your own objects and endow them with your own methods.

> The print() method is very similar to the println() method. With println(), after the message prints, the cursor appears on the following line. With print(), the cursor does not advance to a new line; it remains on the same line as the output.

Within the statement System.out.println("First Java program");, System is a class. Therefore, System defines the attributes of a collection of similar "System" objects just as the Dog class defines the attributes of a collection of similar Dog objects. One of the System objects is out. (You can probably guess that another is the object in, and that it represents an input device.)

> The Java programming language is case sensitive—the class named System is a completely different class from one named system, SYSTEM, or even sYsTeM.

The dots (periods) in the statement System.out.println("First Java program"); are used to separate the names of the class, object, and method. You will use this same class-dot-object-dot-method format repeatedly in your Java programs.

The statement that prints the string "First Java program" is embedded in the program shown in Figure 1-1.

```
public class First

{

   public static void main(String[] args)

   {

     System.out.println("First Java program");

   }

}
```

Figure 1-1: Printing a string

Everything that you use within a Java program must be part of a **class**. When you write public class First, you are defining a class named First. You can define a Java class using any name or identifier you need, as long as it meets the following requirements:

- A class name must begin with a letter of the alphabet (which includes any non-English letter, such as α or π), an underscore, or a dollar sign.
- A class name can contain only letters, digits, underscores, or dollar signs.
- A class name cannot be a Java programming language reserved keyword, such as `public` or `class` (see Figure 1-2 for a list of reserved keywords).
- A class name cannot be one of the following values: `true`, `false`, or `null`.

....

The Java programming language is based on Unicode, which is an international system of character representation. The term *letter* indicates English-language letters, as well as characters from Arabic, Greek, and other alphabets. See Section B of this chapter for more information on Unicode.

....

abstract	float	private
boolean	for	protected
break	future	public
byte	generic	rest
byvalue	goto	return
case	if	short
cast	implements	static
catch	import	super
char	inner	switch
class	instanceof	synchronized
const	int	this
continue	interface	throw
default	long	throws
do	native	transient
double	new	try
else	null	var
extends	operator	void
final	outer	volatile
finally	package	while

Figure 1-2: Java programming language reserved keywords

It is a Java programming language standard to begin class names with an uppercase letter and employ other uppercase letters as needed to improve readability.

Figure 1-3 lists some valid and conventional class names for the Java programming language.

Class Name	Description
Employee	Begins with an uppercase letter
UnderGradStudent	Begins with an uppercase letter, contains no spaces, and emphasizes each new word with an initial uppercase letter
InventoryItem	Begins with an uppercase letter, contains no spaces, and emphasizes the second word with an initial uppercase letter
Budget2001	Begins with an uppercase letter and contains no spaces

Figure 1-3: Some valid class names in the Java programming language

Figure 1-4 lists some class names that are valid, but unconventional.

You should follow established conventions for the Java programming languages so your programs will be easy for other programmers to interpret and follow. This book uses established Java programming conventions.

Class Name	Description
employee	Begins with a lowercase letter
Undergradstudent	New words are not indicated with initial uppercase letters; difficult to read
Inventory_Item	The underscore is not commonly used to indicate new words
BUDGET2001	Appears as all uppercase letters

Figure 1-4: Some unconventional class names in the Java programming language

Figure 1-5 lists some illegal class names.

Class Name	Description
an employee	Space character is illegal
Inventory Item	Space character is illegal

Figure 1-5: Some illegal class names in the Java programming language (continues on next page)

Class Name	Description
class	class is a reserved word
2001Budget	Class names cannot begin with a digit
phone#	The # symbol is not allowed

Figure 1-5: Some illegal class names in the Java programming language (continued)

In Figure 1-1, the line `public class First` contains the keyword `class`, which identifies `First` as a class. The reserved word `public` is an access modifier. An **access modifier** defines the circumstances under which a class can be accessed. Public access is the most liberal type of access; you will learn about public and other types of access in Chapter 2.

You enclose the contents of all classes within curly brackets ({ and }). A class can contain any number of data items and methods. In Figure 1-1, the class First contains only one method within its curly brackets. The name of the method is main(), and the main() method contains its own set of brackets and only one statement—the println() statement.

> In general, whitespace is optional in the Java programming language. Whitespace is any combination of spaces, tabs, and carriage returns (blank lines). However, you cannot use whitespace within any identifier or keyword. You can insert whitespace between words or lines in your program code by typing spaces, tabs, or blank lines, because the compiler will ignore these extra spaces. You use whitespace to organize your program code and make it easier to read.

For every opening curly bracket ({) in a Java program, there must be a corresponding closing curly bracket (}). The placement of the opening and closing curly brackets is not important to the compiler. For example, the following method is executed exactly the same as the one shown in Figure 1-1. The only difference is that the method is organized differently. Usually, code in which you vertically align each pair of opening and closing curly brackets is easier to read. You should strive to type your code so it is easy to read.

```
public static void main(String[] args) {
System.out.println("First Java program"); }
```

The **method header** for the main() method is quite complex. The meaning and purpose of each of the terms used in the method header will become clearer as you complete this textbook; a brief explanation will suffice for now.

In the method header `public static void main(String[] args)`, the word `public` is an access modifier, just as it is when you define the First class. In the English language, the word *static* means showing little change, or stationary. In the Java programming language, the reserved keyword **static** also means unchanging, and indicates that every member created for the First class will have an identical, unchanging main() method. Within the Java programming language, static also implies uniqueness. Only one main() method for the First class will ever be stored in the memory of the computer. Of course, other classes eventually might have their own, different main() methods.

In English, the word *void* means empty. When the keyword **void** is used in the main() method header, it does not indicate that the main() method is empty, but rather, that the main() method does not return any value when it is called. This doesn't mean that main() doesn't produce output—in fact, the method does. The main() method does not send any value back to any other method that might use it. You will learn more about return values in Chapter 2.

All Java applications must include a method named main(), and most Java applications have additional methods. When you execute a Java application, the compiler always executes the main() method first.

In the method header public static void main(String[] args), you already might recognize that the contents between the parentheses, (String[] args), must represent an argument passed to the main() method, just as the string "First Java program" is an argument passed to the println() method. String represents a Java class that can be used to represent character strings. The identifier args is used to hold any Strings that might be sent to the main() method. The main() method *could* do something with those arguments, such as printing them, but in Figure 1-1 the main() method does not actually use the args identifier. Nevertheless, you must place an identifier within the main() method's parentheses. The identifier does not need to be named args—it could be any legal Java identifier—but the name args is traditional.

When you refer to the String class in the main() method header, the square brackets indicate an array of String objects. You will learn more about arrays and the String class in Chapter 5.

The simple program shown in Figure 1-1 has many pieces to remember. However, for now, you can use the program shown in Figure 1-6 as a shell, where you replace the line /******/ with any statements that you want to execute.

```
public class First
{
  public static void main(String[] args)
  {
    /******/
  }
}
```

Figure 1-6: Shell output program

Now that you understand the basic framework of a program written in the Java programming language, you are ready to enter your first Java program into a text editor. It is a tradition among programmers that the first program you write in any language produces "Hello, world!" as its output. You will create such a program now. You can use any text editor, such as Notepad, WordPad, or any other word processing program.

To write your first Java program:

1 Start any text editor (such as Notepad, WordPad, or any other word processing program), and then open a new document, if necessary. (Notepad is the easiest program to use to write your programs.)

2 Type the class header **public class Hello**. In this example, the class name is Hello. You can use any valid name you want for the class. If you choose Hello, you must refer to the class as Hello, and not as hello, because the Java programming language is case sensitive.

3 Press the **Enter** key once, type **{**, press the **Enter** key again, and then type **}**. You will add the main() method between the curly brackets. Although it is not required, it is a good practice to place each curly bracket on its own line. This practice will make your code easier to read.

4 As shown in Figure 1-7, add the main() method header between the curly brackets and then type a set of curly brackets for main().

```
public class Hello

{

   public static void main(String[] args)

   {

   }

}
```

Figure 1-7: The main() method shell for the Hello class

Next add the statement within the main() method's brackets that will produce the output, "Hello, world!".

5 Use Figure 1-8 to add a println() statement to the main() method.

```
public class Hello

{

  public static void main(String[] args)

  {

    System.out.println("Hello, world!");

  }

}
```

Figure 1-8: Complete main() method for the Hello class

6 Save the program as **Hello.java** in the Chapter.01 folder on your Student Disk. It is important that the file extension is `.java`. If it is not, the compiler for the Java programming language will not recognize the program.

help

Many text editors attach their own filename extension (such as .txt or .doc) to a saved file. Double-check your saved file to ensure that it does not have a double extension (such as Hello.java.txt). If the file has a double extension, rename the file. If you explicitly type quotes surrounding a filename (such as "Hello.java"), most editors will save the file as you specify, without adding their own extensions. Make sure that you save your .java files as text documents. The default for Notepad is to save all documents as text.

Adding Comments to a Program

As you can see, even the simplest Java program takes several lines of code, and contains somewhat perplexing syntax. Large programs that perform many tasks include much more code, and as you write longer programs, it becomes increasingly difficult to remember why you included steps, or how you intended to use particular variables. **Program comments** are nonexecuting statements that you add to a program for the purpose of documentation. Programmers use comments to leave notes for themselves and for others who might read their programs in the future. At the very least, your programs should include comments indicating the program's author, the date, and the program's name or function.

tip

It is suggested that as you work through this book you add comments as the first three lines of every program. The comments should contain the program name, your name, and the date. Your instructor might ask you to include additional comments.

Comments also can serve a useful purpose when you are developing a program. If a program is not performing as expected, you can comment out various statements and subsequently run the program to observe the effect. When you **comment out** a statement, you turn it into a comment so the compiler will not execute its command. This helps you pinpoint the location of errant statements in malfunctioning programs.

There are three types of comments in the Java programming language:

- **Line comments** start with two forward slashes (//) and continue to the end of the current line. Line comments can appear on a line by themselves or at the end of a line following executable code.
- **Block comments** start with a forward slash and an asterisk (/*) and end with an asterisk and a forward slash (*/). Block comments can appear on a line by themselves, on a line before executable code, or after executable code. Block comments also can extend across as many lines as needed.
- A special case of block comments are **javadoc** comments. They begin with a forward slash and two asterisks (/**) and end with an asterisk and a forward slash (*/). You can use javadoc comments to generate documentation with a program named javadoc.

The forward slash (/) and the backslash (\) characters often are confused, but they are two distinct characters. You cannot use them interchangeably.

The Java Development Kit (JDK) includes the javadoc tool, which contains classes that you can use when writing programs in the Java programming language.

Figure 1-9 shows how comments are used in code.

```
// Demonstrating comments
/* This shows
   that these comments
       don't matter  */
System.out.println("Hello"); // This line executes
     // up to where the comment started
/** Everything but the println() line
 is a comment. */
```

Figure 1-9: Using comments in a program

Next you will add comments to your Hello.java program.

To add comments to your program:

1 Position your cursor at the top of the file, press the **Enter** key to insert a new line, press the **Up** arrow key to go to that line, and then type the following comments at the top of the file. Press the Enter key after typing each line. Insert your name and today's date where indicated.

```
// Filename Hello.java
// Written by <your name>
// Written on <today's date>
```

2 Scroll to the end of the line that reads `public class Hello`, press the **Enter** key, and then type the following block comment in the program:

```
/*  This program demonstrates the use of the println()
    method to print the message Hello, world!  */
```

3 Save the file, replacing the old Hello.java file with this new, commented version.

Running a Program

After you write and save your program, there are two steps that must occur before you can view the program output.

1. You must compile the program you wrote (called the source code) into bytecode.
2. You must use the Java interpreter to translate the bytecode into executable statements.

To compile your source code from the command line, you type `javac` followed by the filename of the file that contains the source code. For example, to compile a file named First.java, you would type `javac First.java` and then press the Enter key. There will be one of three outcomes:

- You receive a message such as "Bad command or file name."
- You receive one or more program language error messages.
- You receive no messages, which means that the program compiled successfully.

 tip

When compiling, if the source code file is not in the current path, you can type a full path with the filename—for example, `javac c:\java\myprograms\First.java`.

If you receive a message such as "Bad command or file name," it might mean one of the following:

- You misspelled the command `javac`.
- You misspelled the filename.
- You are not within the correct subfolder or subdirectory on your command line.
- The Java programming language was not installed properly.

If you receive a programming language error message, then there are one or more syntax errors in the source code. A **syntax error** is a programming error that occurs when you introduce typing errors into your program. For example, if your class name is "first" (with a lowercase *f*) in the source code, but you saved the file as First.java, you will get an error message, such as `public class first should not be defined in First.java`, after compiling the program because "first" and "First" are not the same in a case-sensitive language. If this error occurs, you must reopen the text file that contains the source code and make the necessary corrections.

If you receive no error messages after compiling the code in a file named First.java, then the program compiled successfully and a file named First.class was created and saved in the same folder as the program text file. After a successful compile, you can run the class file on any computer that has a Java language interpreter.

To run the program from the command line, you type `java First`. Figure 1-10 shows the program's output. Next, you will compile and interpret your Hello.java program.

Figure 1-10: Output of the First program

To compile and interpret your Hello.java program:

1 Go to the command-line prompt for the drive and folder or subdirectory in which you saved Hello.java.

2 At the command line, type **javac Hello.java**.

If you receive an error message, look in the section "Running a Program" to find its cause and then make the necessary corrections. Save the file again, and then repeat Steps 1 and 2 until your program compiles successfully.

3 When the compile is successful, execute your program by typing **java Hello** at the command line. The output should appear on the next line, as shown in Figure 1-11 on the following page.

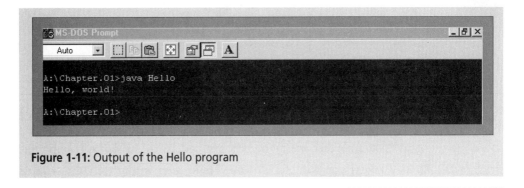

Figure 1-11: Output of the Hello program

When you run a Java program using the `java` command, do not add the .class extension to the filename. If you type `java  First`, the interpreter will look for a file named **First.class**. If you type `java First.class`, the interpreter will incorrectly look for a file named **First.class.class**.

Modifying a Program

After viewing the program output, you might decide to modify the program to get a different result. For example, you might decide to change the First program's output from `First Java program` to the following:

```
My new and improved
Java program
```

To produce the new output, first you must modify the text file that contains the existing program. You want to change the literal string that currently prints and then add an additional text string. Figure 1-12 shows the program to change the output.

```
public class First
{
  public static void main(String[] args)
  {
    System.out.println("My new and improved");
    System.out.println("Java program");
  }
}
```

Figure 1-12: Changing a program's output

The two changes are the addition of the statement `System.out.println("My new and improved");` and the removal of the word "First" from the string in the statement `System.out.println("Java  program");`. However, if you type `java First` at the command line right now, you will not see the new output—you will see the old output. Before the new source code will execute, you must do the following:

- Save the file with the changes using the same filename (First.java).
- Compile the First class with the `javac` command.
- Interpret the First.class bytecode with the `java` command.

Next you will change your Hello class and rerun your program.

To change the Hello class and rerun the program:

1 Open the file **Hello.java** in your text editor.

2 Add the following statement below the statement that prints "Hello, world!": **`System.out.println("I'm ready for Java programming!");`**. Make sure to type the semicolon at the end of the statement and use the correct case.

3 Save the file as **Hello.java** in the Chapter.01 folder on your Student Disk. You will replace the Hello.java file that is already saved there.

4 At the command line, compile the file by typing the command **javac Hello.java**.

help

If you receive compile errors, return to the Hello.java file in the text editor, fix the errors, and then repeat Steps 3 and 4 until the program compiles successfully.

5 Interpret and execute the class by typing the command **java Hello**. Your output should look like Figure 1-13.

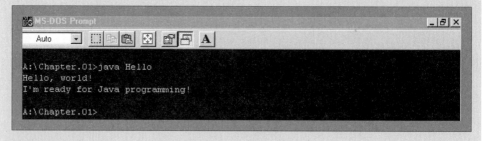

Figure 1-13: Output of the revised Hello program

S U M M A R Y

- A computer program is a set of instructions. To write a program in machine language, you must keep track of thousands of on-off switches.

- High-level programming languages allow you to use a vocabulary of English-like terms. Each high-level computer language has its own syntax, or rules of the language. A software program called an interpreter (or compiler or assembler) translates high-level language statements into machine code.

- To program correctly, you must learn the syntax of a language, as well as programming logic.

- Procedural programming involves creating computer memory locations to hold values, and then writing a series of steps or operations that manipulate those values.

- Variables represent memory locations that hold values.

- Computer program operations often are grouped into logical units called procedures.

- Object-oriented programming involves creating program components as objects that are similar to concrete objects in the real world that are manipulated to achieve a desired result.

- Objects are made up of states and methods. The states of an object also are known as its attributes. An individual object is an instance of a class; the object inherits its attributes from the class. The user of an object does not need to understand the details of any method, but must understand the interface with the object.

- The Java programming language is an object-oriented language that is used both for Web-based Internet and general-purpose programs. Key attributes of the Java programming language are its security features and the fact that it is architecturally neutral.

- A program written in Java is compiled into bytecode, which is subsequently interpreted on the machine where the program is executed.

- All Java programming language statements end with a semicolon.

- A series of characters that appears between double quotation marks is a literal string.

- Java programming language methods might require arguments or messages to perform the appropriate task.

- Periods (called dots) are used to separate classes, objects, and methods in program code. Everything that you use within a Java program must be part of a class. A Java programming language class might take any name or identifier that begins with either an uppercase or lowercase letter of the alphabet, and contains only uppercase and lowercase letters, digits, and underscores. A class name cannot be a reserved keyword of the Java programming language.

- The reserved word `public` is an access modifier that defines the circumstances under which a class can be accessed.

- The contents of all classes are contained within opening and closing curly brackets.

■ The keyword static in a method header indicates that every member of a class will have an identical, unchanging method.

■ The keyword void in a method header indicates that the method does not return any value when it is called.

■ All Java application programs must have a method named main(). Most Java applications have additional methods.

■ Program comments are nonexecuting statements that you add to a program for the purpose of documentation. There are three types of comments in the Java programming language: Line comments begin with two forward slashes (//), block comments begin with a forward slash and an asterisk (/*) and end with an asterisk and a forward slash (*/), and javadoc comments begin with a forward slash and two asterisks (/**) and end with an asterisk and a forward slash (*/).

■ To compile your source code from the command line, type javac followed by the filename of the file that contains the source code. If the file resides in a different path from the command prompt, use the full path and filename. When you compile your source code, the compiler creates a file with a .class extension. You can run the .class file on any computer that has a Java language interpreter by entering the java command followed by the name of the class file. Do not type the .class extension with the filename.

■ If you modify a program's source code file, you must save and recompile the program before executing it again.

Q U E S T I O N S

1. The most basic circuitry-level computer language, which consists of on and off switches, is _____.
   a. a high-level language
   b. machine language
   c. the Java programming language
   d. C++

2. Languages that let you use a vocabulary of descriptive terms like "read," "write," or "add" are known as _____ languages.
   a. high-level
   b. machine
   c. procedural
   d. object-oriented

3. The rules of a programming language constitute its _____.
   a. objects
   b. logic
   c. format
   d. syntax

4. A _____ translates high-level language statements into machine code.
   a. programmer
   b. syntax detector
   c. compiler
   d. decipherer

5. Programmer-named computer memory locations are called _____.
   a. compilers
   b. variables
   c. addresses
   d. appellations

6. For convenience, the individual operations used in a computer program often are grouped into logical units called _____.
   a. procedures
   b. variables
   c. constants
   d. logistics

7. Envisioning program components as objects that are similar to concrete objects in the real world is the hallmark of _____.
   a. command-line operating systems
   b. procedural programming
   c. object-oriented programming
   d. machine languages

8. An object's attributes also are known as its _____.
   a. states
   b. orientations
   c. methods
   d. procedures

9. An instance of a(n) _____ inherits its attributes from it.
   a. object
   b. procedure
   c. method
   d. class

10. The Java programming language is architecturally _____.
    a. specific
    b. oriented
    c. neutral
    d. abstract

11. You must compile programs written in the Java programming language into _____.
    a. bytecode
    b. source code
    c. javadoc statements
    d. object code

12. All Java programming language statements must end with a _____.
    a. period
    b. comma
    c. semicolon
    d. closing parenthesis

13. Arguments to methods always appear within _____.
    a. parentheses
    b. double quotation marks
    c. single quotation marks
    d. curly brackets

14. In a Java program, you must use _____ to separate classes, objects, and methods.
    a. commas
    b. semicolons
    c. periods
    d. forward slashes

15. All Java programs must have a method named _____.
    a. method()
    b. main()
    c. java()
    d. Hello()

16. Nonexecuting program statements that provide documentation are called _____.
    a. classes
    b. notes
    c. comments
    d. commands

17. The Java programming language supports three types of comments: _____, _____, and javadoc.
    a. line, block
    b. string, literal
    c. constant, variable
    d. single, multiple

18. After you write and save a program file, you _____ it.
    a. interpret and then compile
    b. interpret and then execute
    c. compile and then resave
    d. compile and then interpret

19. The command to execute a compiled program is _____.
    a. run
    b. execute
    c. javac
    d. java

20. You save text files containing Java language source code using the file extension _____.
    a. .java
    b. .class
    c. .txt
    d. .src

E X E R C I S E S

1. For each of the following Java programming language identifiers, note whether they are legal or illegal:
   a. weeklySales _____
   b. last character _____
   c. class _____
   d. MathClass _____
   e. myfirstinitial _____
   f. phone# _____
   g. abcdefghijklmnop _____
   h. 23jordan _____
   i. my_code _____
   j. 90210 _____
   k. year2000problem _____
   l. αβφfraternity _____

2. Name some attributes that might be appropriate for each of the following classes:
   a. TelevisionSet: _____
   b. EmployeePaycheck: _____
   c. PatientMedicalRecord: _____

3. Write, compile, and test a program that prints your first name on the screen. Save the program as Name.java in the Chapter.01 folder on your Student Disk.

4. Write, compile, and test a program that prints your full name, street address, city, state, and zip code on three separate lines on the screen. Save the program as Address.java in the Chapter.01 folder on your Student Disk.

5. Write, compile, and test a program that displays the following pattern on the screen:
   ```
       X
      XXX
     XXXXX
   XXXXXXX
       X
   ```
   Save the program as Tree.java in the Chapter.01 folder on your Student Disk.

6. Write, compile, and test a program that prints your initials on the screen. Compose each initial with six lines of small initials, as in the following example:
   ```
        J     FFFFFF
        J     F
        J     FFFF
   J    J     F
   JJJJJJ     F
   ```
   Save the program as Initial.java in the Chapter.01 folder on your Student Disk.

7. Write, compile, and test a program that prints the learning objectives listed at the beginning of Section A of this chapter. Save the program as Objectives.java in the Chapter.01 folder on your Student Disk.

8. Write, compile, and test a program that displays the following pattern on the screen:

```
    *
  *   *
*   *   *
  *   *
    *
```

Save the program as Diamond.java in the Chapter.01 folder on your Student Disk.

9. Write, compile, and test a program that displays the following statement about comments:

Program comments are non-executing statements you add to a program for the purpose of documentation.

Also include the same statement in three different comments in the program; each comment uses one of the three different methods of including comments in a Java program. Save the program as Comments.java in the Chapter.01 folder on your Student Disk.

SECTION B

objectives

In this section you will learn

■ How to use variables and constants

■ About the int data type

■ How to write arithmetic statements

■ About the boolean data type

■ About floating-point data types

■ About numeric type conversion

■ About the char data type

Using Data

Variables and Constants

You can categorize data as variable or constant. Data is **constant** when it cannot be changed after a program is compiled; data is **variable** when it might change. For example, if you include the statement System.out.println(459); in a Java program, the number 459 is a constant. Every time the program containing the constant 459 is executed, the value 459 will print. You can refer to the number 459 as a **literal constant** because its value is taken literally at each use.

> Besides using literal constants, you can use symbolic constants, which you will learn about in Chapter 3.

On the other hand, if you create a variable named ovenTemperature, and include the statement System.out.println(ovenTemperature); within a Java program, then different values might display when the program is executed multiple times, depending on what value is stored in ovenTemperature during each run of the program.

Variables are named memory locations that your program can use to store values. The Java programming language provides for eight **primitive types** of data:

- boolean
- byte
- char
- double
- float
- int
- long
- short

> The eight primitive data types are called primitive types because they are simple and uncomplicated. Primitive types also serve as the building blocks for more complex data types, called reference types. The objects you will begin to create in Chapter 2 are examples of reference types.

You name variables using the same naming rules for legal class identifiers described in Section A. Basically, that means variable names must start with a letter and cannot be any reserved keyword. You must declare all variables you want to use in a program. A **variable declaration** includes the following:

- A data type that identifies the type of data that the variable will store
- An identifier that is the variable's name
- An optional assigned value, when you want a variable to contain an initial value
- An ending semicolon

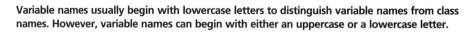

Variable names usually begin with lowercase letters to distinguish variable names from class names. However, variable names can begin with either an uppercase or a lowercase letter.

For example, the variable declaration `int myAge = 25;` declares a variable of type int named myAge and assigns it an initial value of 25. This is a complete statement that ends in a semicolon. The equals sign (=) is the **assignment operator**. Any value to the right of the equals sign is assigned to the variable on the left of the equals sign. An assignment made when you declare a variable is an **initialization**; an assignment made later is simply an **assignment**. Thus, `int myAge = 25;` initializes myAge to 25, and a subsequent statement `myAge = 42;` might assign a new value to the variable. You should note that the expression `25 = myAge` is illegal.

The variable declaration `int myAge;` also declares a variable of type int named myAge, but no value is assigned at the time of creation.

You can declare multiple variables of the same type in separate statements on different lines. For example, the following statements declare two variables—the first variable is named myAge and its value is 25. The second variable is named yourAge and its value is 19.

```
int myAge = 25;
int yourAge = 19;
```

You also can declare two variables of the same type in a single statement by separating the variable declarations with a comma, as shown in the following statement:

```
int myAge = 25, yourAge = 19;
```

However, if you want to declare variables of different types, you must use a separate statement for each type. The following statements declare two variables of type int (myAge and yourAge) and two variables of type double (mySalary and yourSalary):

```
int myAge, yourAge;
double mySalary, yourSalary;
```

The int Data Type

In the Java programming language, you use variables of type int to store (or hold) **integers**, or whole numbers. An integer can hold any whole number value from -2,147,483,648 to 2,147,483,647. When you assign a value to an int variable, you do not type any commas; you type only digits and an optional plus or minus sign to indicate a positive or negative integer.

The legal integer values are -2^{31} through $2^{31}-1$. These are the highest and lowest values that you can store in four bytes of memory, which is the size of an int.

The types **byte, short,** and **long** are all variations of the integer type. You use byte or short if you know a variable will need to hold only small values so you can save space in memory. You use a long if you know you will be working with very large values. Figure 1-14 shows the upper and lower value limits for each of these types. It is important to choose appropriate types for the variables you will use in a program. If you attempt to assign a value that is too large for the data type of the variable, the compiler will issue an error message and the program will not execute. If you choose a data type that is larger than you need, you waste memory. For example, a personnel program might use a byte variable for number of dependents (because a limit of 127 is more than enough), a short for hours worked in a month (because 127 isn't enough), and an integer for an annual salary (because even though a limit of 32,000 might be large enough for your salary, it isn't enough for the CEO).

If your program uses a literal constant integer, such as 932, the integer is an int by default. If you need to use a constant higher than 2,147,483,647, you must follow the number with the letter *L* to indicate long. For example, `long mosquitosInTheNorthWoods = 2444555888L;` stores a number that is greater than the maximum limit for the int type. You can type either an uppercase or lowercase *L* to indicate the long type, but the uppercase *L* is preferred to avoid confusion with the number one.

Type	Minimum Value	Maximum Value	Size in Bytes
byte	-128	127	1
short	-32,768	32,767	2
int	-2,147,483,648	2,147,483,647	4
long	-9,223,372,036,854,775,808	9,223,372,036,854,775,807	8

Figure 1-14: Limits on integer values by type

Next, you will write a program to declare and display numeric values.

To declare and display values in a program:

1 Open a new document in your text editor.

2 Create a class header and an opening and closing curly bracket for a new class named DemoVariables by typing the following:

```
public class DemoVariables
{
}
```

3 Position the cursor after the opening curly bracket, press the **Enter** key, press the **Spacebar** several times to indent the line, and then type the following main() method and its curly brackets:

```
public static void main(String[] args)
{
}
```

4 Position the cursor after the opening curly bracket in the main() method, press the **Enter** key, press the **Spacebar** several times to indent the line, and then type **int oneInt = 315;** to declare a variable of type int named oneInt with a value of 315.

> You can declare variables at any point within a method prior to their first use. However, it is common practice to declare variables first and place method calls second.

5 Press the **Enter** key at the end of the oneInt declaration statement, indent the line, and then type the following two output statements. The first statement uses the print() method to output "The int is " and leaves the cursor on the same output line. The second statement uses the println() method to output the value of oneInt and advances the cursor to a new line.

```
System.out.print("The int is ");
System.out.println(oneInt);
```

> When your output contains a literal string such as "The int is ", you should type a space before the closing quotation mark so there is a space between the end of the literal and the value that prints.

6 Save the file as **DemoVariables.java** in the Chapter.01 folder on your Student Disk.

7 Compile the file from the command line by typing **javac DemoVariables.java**. If necessary, correct any errors, save the file, and then compile again.

8 Execute the program from the command line by typing **java DemoVariables**. The output should be The int is 315.

Even though you intend to add additional statements to the DemoVariables program, by compiling and executing the program at this point, you are assured that it is working exactly as intended. Sometimes it is a good idea to write and compile your programs in steps, so you can identify any syntax or logical errors as you go, instead of waiting until you finish writing the entire program. Next, you will declare two more variables in your program.

To declare two more variables in the program:

1 Return to the **DemoVariables.java** file in the text editor.

2 Position the cursor at the end of the line that contains the oneInt declaration, press the **Enter** key, and then type the following variable declarations on separate lines:

```
short oneShort = 23;
long oneLong = 123456789876543L;
```

3 Position the cursor at the end of the line that contains the println() method that displays the oneInt value, press the **Enter** key, and then type the following statements to display the values of the two new variables:

```
System.out.print("The short is ");
System.out.println(oneShort);
System.out.print("The long is ");
System.out.println(oneLong);
```

4 Save the program using the same filename.

5 Compile the program by typing **javac DemoVariables.java**. If necessary, correct any errors, save the file, and then compile again.

6 Execute the program by typing **java DemoVariables**. Your output should match Figure 1-15.

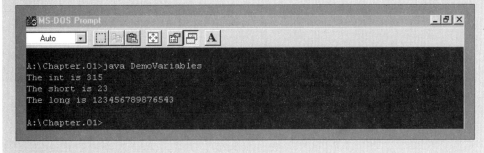

Figure 1-15: Output of the DemoVariables program

In the previous program, you used two print methods to print a compound phrase with the following code:

```
System.out.print("The long is ");
System.out.println(oneLong);
```

To reduce the amount of typing, you can use one method and combine the arguments with a plus sign using the following statement: `System.out.println("The long is " + oneLong);`. It doesn't matter which format you use—the result is the same, as you will see next.

To change the two print methods into a single statement:

1 Open the **DemoVariables.java** text file.

2 Use the mouse to select the two statements that print "The int is " and the value of oneInt, and then press the **Delete** key to delete them. In place of the deleted statements, type the following println() statement: **`System.out.println("The int is " + oneInt);`**.

3 Select the two statements that produce output for the short variable, press the **Delete** key to delete them, and then type the statement **`System.out.println("The short is " + oneShort);`**.

4 Finally, select the two statements that produce output for the long variables, delete them, and replace them with **`System.out.println("The long is " + oneLong);`**.

5 Save, compile, and test the program. The output should be the same as that shown in Figure 1-15.

Arithmetic Statements

Figure 1-16 describes the five standard arithmetic operators for integers. You use the arithmetic operators to manipulate values in your programs.

You will learn about the shortcut arithmetic operators for the Java programming language in Chapter 4.

Operator	Description	Example
+	Addition	45 + 2, the result is 47
-	Subtraction	45 - 2, the result is 43
*	Multiplication	45 * 2, the result is 90
/	Division	45 / 2, the result is 22 (not 22.5)
%	Modulus (remainder)	45 % 2, the result is 1 (that is, 45 / 2 = 22 with a remainder of 1)

Figure 1-16: Integer arithmetic operators

You do not need to perform a division operation before you can perform a modulus operation. A modulus operation can stand alone.

The operators / and % deserve special consideration. When you divide two integers, whether they are integer constants or integer variables, the result is an *integer*. In other words, any fractional part of the result is lost. For example, the result of 45 / 2 is 22, even though the result is 22.5 in a mathematical expression. When you use the modulus operator with two integers, the result is an integer with the value of the remainder after division takes place—so the result of 45 % 2 is 1 because 2 "goes into" 45 twenty-two times with a remainder of 1.

You can use modulus (%) only with integers. You can use the other four operators with floating-point data.

Next, you will add some arithmetic statements to the DemoVariables.java program.

To use arithmetic statements in a program:

1 Open the **DemoVariables.java** file in your text editor.

2 Position the cursor on the last line of the current variable declarations, press the **Enter** key, and then type the following declarations:

```
int value1 = 43, value2 = 10, sum, difference,
    product, quotient, modulus;
```

3 Position the cursor after the statement that prints the oneLong variable, press the **Enter** key, and then type the following statements on separate lines:

```
sum = value1 + value2;
difference = value1 - value2;
product = value1 * value2;
quotient = value1 / value2;
modulus = value1 % value2;
```

4 Press the **Enter** key, and then type the following output statements:

```
System.out.println("Sum is " + sum);
System.out.println("Difference is " + difference);
System.out.println("Product is " + product);
System.out.println("Quotient is " + quotient);
System.out.println("Modulus is " + modulus);
```

5   Save the program using the same filename (DemoVariables.java).

6   Compile and run the program. Your output should look like Figure 1-17. Analyze the output and confirm that the arithmetic is correct.

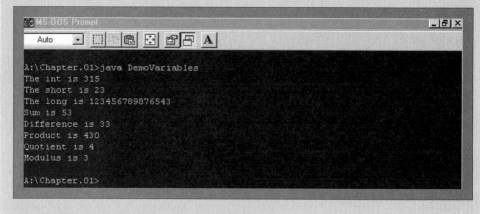

Figure 1-17: Output of the revised DemoVariables program

When you combine mathematical operations in a single statement, you must understand **operator precedence**, or the order in which parts of a mathematical expression are evaluated. Multiplication, division, and modulus always take place prior to addition or subtraction in an expression. For example, the expression `int result = 2 + 3 * 4;` results in 14, because the multiplication (3 * 4) occurs before adding 2. You can override normal operator precedence by putting the operation to perform first in parentheses. The statement `int result = (2 + 3) * 4;` results in 20, because the addition within the parentheses takes place first, and then that result (5) is multiplied by 4.

You will learn more about operator precedence in Chapter 4.

The boolean Data Type

Boolean logic is based on true-or-false comparisons. Whereas an int variable can hold millions of different values (at different times), a **boolean variable** can hold only one of two values—`true` or `false`. The following statements declare and assign appropriate values to boolean variables:

```
boolean isItPayday = false;
boolean areYouBroke = true;
```

You also can assign values based on the result of comparisons to boolean variables. The Java programming language supports six comparison operators. A **comparison operator** compares two items; an expression containing a comparison operator has a boolean value. Figure 1-18 describes the comparison operators.

tip

You will learn about other boolean operators in Chapter 4.

Operator	Description	true **Example**	false **Example**
<	Less than	3 < 8	8 < 3
>	Greater than	4 > 2	2 > 4
==	Equal to	7 == 7	3 == 9
<=	Less than or equal to	5 <= 5	8 <= 6
>=	Greater than or equal to	7 >= 3	1 >= 2
!=	Not equal to	5 != 6	3 != 3

Figure 1-18: Comparison operators

When you use any of the operators that have two symbols (==, <=, >=, or !=), you cannot place any whitespace between the two symbols.

Legal, but somewhat useless, declaration statements might include the following statements, which compare two values directly:

```
boolean isSixBigger = (6 > 5);
  // Value stored would be true
boolean isSevenSmallerOrEqual = (7 <= 4);
  // Value stored would be false
```

tip

Variable names are easily identified as boolean if you use a form of "to be" (such as "is" or "are") as part of the variable name.

The Boolean expressions are more meaningful when variables (that have been assigned values) are used in the comparisons, as in the following examples. In the first statement, the hours variable is compared to a constant value of 40. If the hours variable is not greater than 40, then the expression evaluates to false. In the second statement, the income variable must be greater than 100000 for the expression to evaluate to true.

```
boolean overtime = (hours > 40);
boolean highTaxBracket = (income > 100000);
```

Next, you will add two boolean variables to the DemoVariables.java file.

To add boolean variables to a program:

1 Open the **DemoVariables.java** file in your text editor.

2 Position the cursor at the end of the line with the integer variable declarations, press the **Enter** key, and then type **boolean isProgrammingFun = true, isProgrammingHard = false;** on one line to add two new boolean variables to the program.

Next, add some print statements to display the values.

3 Press the **Enter** key, and then type the following statements:

```
System.out.println("The value of isProgrammingFun is "
    + isProgrammingFun);
System.out.println("The value of isProgrammingHard is "
    + isProgrammingHard);
```

4 Save the file, compile it, and then test the program.

Floating-point Data Types

A **floating-point** number contains decimal positions. The Java programming language supports two floating-point data types: float and double. A **float** data type can hold values up to six or seven significant digits of accuracy. A **double** data type can hold 14 or 15 significant digits of accuracy. The term **significant digits** refers to the mathematical accuracy of a value. For example, a float given the value 0.324616777 will display as 0.324617 because the value is only accurate to the sixth decimal position. Figure 1-19 shows the minimum and maximum values for each data type.

A float given the value 324616777 will display as 3.24617e+008, which means approximately 3.24617 times 10 to the 8th power, or 324617000. The e stands for *exponent*; the format is called scientific notation. The large value contains only six significant digits.

Type	Minimum	Maximum	Size in Bytes
Float	$-3.4 * 10^{38}$	$3.4 * 10^{38}$	4
Double	$-1.7 * 10^{308}$	$1.7 * 10^{308}$	8

Figure 1-19: Limits on floating-point values

A value written as $-3.4 * 10^{38}$ indicates that the value is -3.4 multiplied by 10 to the 38th power, or 10 with 38 trailing zeros—a very large number.

Just as an integer constant, such as 178, is an int by default, a floating-point number constant such as 18.23 is a double by default. To store a value explicitly as a float, you can type the letter *F* after the number, as in `float pocketChange = 4.87F;`. You can type either a lowercase or an uppercase *F*. You also can type *D* (or *d*) after a floating-point value to indicate it is a double, but even without the *D*, the value will be stored as a double by default.

As with ints, you can perform the mathematical operations of addition, subtraction, multiplication, and division with floating-point numbers; however, you cannot perform modulus operations using floating-point values. (Floating-point division yields a floating-point result, so there is no remainder.)

Next, you will add some floating-point variables to the DemoVariables.java file and perform arithmetic with them.

To add floating-point variables to the program:

1 Open the **DemoVariables.java** file in your text editor.

2 Position the cursor after the line that declares the boolean variables, press the **Enter** key, and then type **double doubNum1 = 2.3, doubNum2 = 14.8, doubResult;** on one line to add some new floating-point variables.

3 Press the **Enter** key, and then type the following statements to perform arithmetic and produce output:

```
doubResult = doubNum1 + doubNum2;
System.out.println("The sum of the doubles is "
   + doubResult);
doubResult = doubNum1 * doubNum2;
System.out.println("The product of the doubles is "
   + doubResult);
```

4 Save the file, compile it, and then run the program.

Numeric Type Conversion

When you are performing arithmetic with variables or constants of the same type, the result of the arithmetic retains the same type. For example, when you divide two integers, the result is an integer, and when you subtract two doubles, the result is a double. Often, you might want to perform mathematical operations on unlike types. For example, in the following example, you multiply an integer by a double:

```
int hoursWorked = 37;
double payRate = 6.73;
grossPay = hoursWorked * payRate;
```

When you perform arithmetic operations with operands of unlike types, the Java programming language chooses a **unifying type** for the result. The Java programming language then **implicitly** (or automatically) converts nonconforming operands to the unifying type. The unifying type is the type of the involved operand that appears first in the following list:

1. double
2. float
3. long
4. int
5. short
6. byte

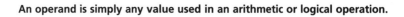

An operand is simply any value used in an arithmetic or logical operation.

In other words, grossPay is the result of multiplication of an int and a double, so grossPay itself must be a double. Similarly, the addition of a short and an int results in an int.

You can **explicitly** (or purposely) override the unifying type imposed by the Java programming language by performing a type cast. **Type casting** involves placing the desired result type in parentheses followed by the variable or constant to be cast. For example, two casts are performed in the following code:

```
double bankBalance = 189.66;
float weeklyBudget = (float) bankBalance / 4;
  // weeklyBudget is 47.40, one-fourth of bankBalance
int dollars = (int) weeklyBudget;
  // dollars is 47, the integer part of weeklyBudget
```

It is easy to lose data when performing a cast. For example, the largest byte value is 127 and the largest int value is 2,147,483,647, so the following statements produce distorted results:

```
int anOkayInt = 200;
byte aBadByte = (byte)anOkayInt;
```

A byte is constructed from eight 1s and 0s, or binary digits. The first binary digit, or bit, holds a 0 or 1 to represent positive or negative. The remaining seven bits store the actual value. When the integer value 200 is stored in the byte variable, its large value consumes the eighth bit, turning it to a 1, and forcing the aBadByte variable to appear to hold the value -56, which is inaccurate and misleading.

The double value `bankBalance / 4` is converted to a float before it is stored in weeklyBudget, and the float value weeklyBudget is converted to an int before it is stored in dollars. When the float value is converted to an int, the decimal place values are lost.

The char Data Type

You use the **char** data type to hold any single character. You place constant character values within single quotation marks because the computer stores characters and integers differently. For example, the statements char aCharValue = '9'; and int aNumValue = 9; are legal. The statements char aCharValue = 9; and int aNumValue = '9'; are illegal. A number can be a character, in which case it must be enclosed in single quotation marks and declared as a char type. However, you cannot store an alphabetic letter in a numeric type. The following code shows how you can store any character string using the char data type:

```
char myInitial = 'J';
char percentSign = '%';
char numThatIsAChar = '9';
```

A variable of type char can hold only one character. To store a string of characters, such as a person's name, you must use a data structure called a **String**. Unlike single characters, which use single quotation marks, string constants are written between double quotation marks. For example, the expression that stores the name Audrey as a string in a variable named firstName is firstName = "Audrey";.

tip

You will learn more about Strings in Chapter 5.

You can store any character—including nonprinting characters such as a backspace or a tab—in a char variable. To store these characters, you must use an **escape sequence**, which always begins with a backslash. For example, the following code stores a backspace character and a tab character in the char variables aBackspaceChar and aTabChar:

```
char aBackspaceChar = '\b';
char aTabChar = '\t';
```

In the preceding code, the escape sequence indicates a unique value for the character, instead of the letters *b* or *t*. Figure 1-20 describes some common escape sequences that are used in the Java programming language.

Escape Sequence	Description
\b	Backspace
\t	Tab
\n	Newline or linefeed
\f	Form feed
\r	Carriage return

Figure 1-20: Common escape sequences (continues on next page)

Escape Sequence	Description
\"	Double quotation mark
\'	Single quotation mark
\\	Backslash

Figure 1-20: Common escape sequences (continued)

The characters used in the Java programming language are represented in **Unicode**, which is a 16-bit coding scheme for characters. For example, the letter *A* actually is stored in computer memory as a set of 16 zeros and ones as 0000 0000 0100 0001 (the spaces inserted after every set of four digits are for readability). Because 16-digit numbers are difficult to read, programmers often use a shorthand notation called **hexadecimal**, or **base 16**. In hexadecimal shorthand, 0000 becomes 0, 0100 becomes 4, and 0001 becomes 1, so the letter *A* is represented in hexadecimal as 0041. You tell the compiler to treat the four-digit hexadecimal 0041 as a single character by preceding it with the \u escape sequence. Therefore, there are two ways to store the character *A*:

```
char letter = 'A';
char letter = '\u0041';
```

For more information about Unicode, go to http://www.unicode.org.

The second option using hexadecimal obviously is more difficult and confusing than the first method, so it is not recommended that you store letters of the alphabet using the hexadecimal method. However, there are some interesting values you can produce using the Unicode format. For example, the sequence '\u0007' is a bell that produces a noise if you send it to output. Letters from foreign alphabets that use characters instead of letters (Greek, Hebrew, Chinese, and so on) and other special symbols (foreign currency symbols, mathematical symbols, geometric shapes, and so on) are available using Unicode, but not on a standard keyboard, so it is important that you know how to use Unicode characters.

Next, you will add statements to your DemoVariables.java file to use the \n and \t escape sequences.

To use escape sequences in a program:

1 Open the **DemoVariables.java** file in your text editor.

2 Position the cursor after the last method line in the program, press the **Enter** key, and then type the following:

```
System.out.println("\nThis is on one line\nThis on another");
System.out.println("This shows\thow\ttabs\twork");
```

3 Save, compile, and test the program. Your output should look like Figure 1-21.

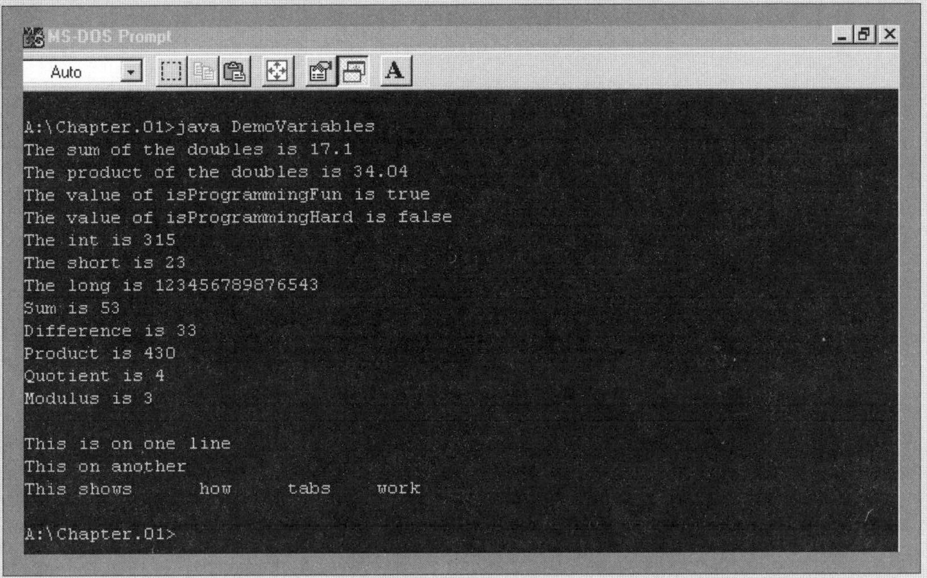

Figure 1-21: Output of the DemoVariables program demonstrating escape sequences

S U M M A R Y

- Data is constant when it cannot be changed after a program is compiled; data is variable when it might change.

- Variables are named memory locations that your program can use to store values. You can name a variable using any legal identifier. A variable name must start with a letter and cannot be any reserved keyword. You must declare all variables you want to use in a program. A variable declaration requires a type and a name; it also can include an assigned value.

- The Java programming language provides for eight primitive types of data: boolean, byte, char, double, float, int, long, and short.

- The equals sign (=) is the assignment operator. Any value to the right of an equals sign is assigned to the variable on the left of the equals sign.

- You can declare multiple variables of the same type in separate statements or in a single statement, separated by commas.

- Variables of type int are used to hold integers, or whole numbers. An integer can hold any whole number value from -2,147,483,648 to 2,147,483,647. The types byte, short, and long are all variations of the integer type.

- There are five standard arithmetic operators for integers: + - * / and %.

- Operator precedence is the order in which parts of a mathematical expression are evaluated. Multiplication, division, and modulus always take place prior to addition or subtraction in an expression.

- A boolean type variable can hold `true` or `false`.

- There are six comparison operators: > < == >= <= and !=.

- A floating-point number contains decimal positions. The Java programming language supports two floating-point data types: float and double.

- When you perform mathematical operations on unlike types, Java implicitly converts the variables to a unifying type. You can explicitly override the unifying type imposed by the Java programming language by performing a type cast.

- You use the char data type to hold any single character. You type constant character values in single quotation marks. You type String constants that store more than one character between double quotation marks.

- You can store some characters using an escape sequence, which always begins with a backslash.

- The characters used in Java programming are represented in the 16-bit Unicode scheme.

QUESTIONS

1. When data cannot be changed after a program is compiled, the data is _____.
   a. constant
   b. variable
   c. volatile
   d. mutable

2. Which of the following is *not* a primitive data type in the Java programming language?
   a. boolean
   b. byte
   c. int
   d. sector

3. Which of the following elements is *not* required in a variable declaration?
   a. a type
   b. an identifier
   c. an assigned value
   d. a semicolon

4. The assignment operator in the Java programming language is _____.
   a. =
   b. ==
   c. :=
   d. ::

5. Which of the following values can you assign to a variable of type int?
   a. 0
   b. 98.6
   c. 'S'
   d. 5,000,000,000,000

6. Which of these data types can store a value in the least amount of memory?
   a. short
   b. long
   c. int
   d. byte

7. The modulus operator _____.
   a. is represented by a forward slash
   b. provides the remainder of integer division
   c. provides the remainder of floating-point division
   d. two of the preceding answers are correct

8. According to the rules of operator precedence, division always takes place prior to _____.
   a. multiplication
   b. modulus
   c. subtraction
   d. two of the preceding answers are correct

9. A boolean variable can hold _____.
   a. any character
   b. any whole number
   c. any decimal number
   d. the values true or false

10. The "equal to" comparison operator is _____.
    a. =
    b. ==
    c. !=
    d. !!

11. The value 137.68 can be held by a variable of type _____.
    a. int
    b. float
    c. double
    d. two of the preceding answers are correct

12. When you perform arithmetic with values of diverse types, the Java programming language _____.
    a. issues an error message
    b. implicitly converts the values to a unifying type
    c. requires you to explicitly convert the values to a unifying type
    d. requires you to perform a cast

13. If you attempt to add a float, an int, and a byte, the result will be a(n) _____.
   a. float
   b. int
   c. byte
   d. error message

14. Explicitly overriding an implicit type is a _____.
   a. mistake
   b. type cast
   c. format
   d. type set

15. Which assignment is correct?
   a. `char aChar = 5;`
   b. `char aChar = "W";`
   c. `char aChar = '*';`
   d. two of the preceding answers are correct

16. An escape sequence always begins with a(n) _____.
   a. 'e'
   b. forward slash
   c. backslash
   d. equals sign

17. The 16-bit coding scheme employed by the Java programming language is

   _____.

   a. Unicode
   b. ASCII
   c. EBCDIC
   d. hexadecimal

E X E R C I S E S

1. What is the numeric value of each of the following expressions as evaluated by the Java programming language?
   a. 4 + 6 * 3   _____
   b. 6 / 3 * 7   _____
   c. 18 / 2 + 14 / 2   _____
   d. 16 / 2   _____
   e. 17 / 2   _____
   f. 28 / 5   _____
   g. 16 % 2   _____
   h. 17 % 2   _____
   i. 28 % 5   _____
   j. 28 % 5 * 3 + 1   _____
   k. (2 + 3) * 4   _____
   l. 20 / (4 + 1)   _____

2. What is the value of each of the following boolean expressions?
   a. 4 > 1   _____
   b. 5 <= 18   _____
   c. 43 >= 43   _____
   d. 2 == 3   _____
   e. 2 + 5 == 7   _____
   f. 3 + 8 <= 10   _____
   g. 3 != 9   _____
   h. 13 != 13   _____
   i. -4 != 4   _____
   j. 2 + 5 * 3 == 21 _____

3. Which of the following expressions are illegal? For the legal expressions, what is the numeric value of each of the following statements as evaluated by the Java programming language?
   a. 2.3 * 1.2
   b. 5.67 - 2
   c. 25.0 / 5.0
   d. 7.0 % 3.0
   e. 8 % 2.0

4. Choose the best data type for each of the following, so that no memory storage is wasted. Give an example of a typical value that would be held by the variable and explain why you chose the type you did.
   a. your age
   b. the U.S. national debt
   c. your shoe size
   d. your middle initial

5. Use a text editor to write a Java program that declares variables to represent the length and width of a room in feet. Use Room as the class name. Assign appropriate values to the variables—for example, length = 15 and width = 25. Compute and display the floor space of the room in square feet (area = length * width). Do not display only a value as output; display explanatory text with the value—for example, The floor space is 375 square feet. Save the program as Room.java in the Chapter.01 folder on your Student Disk.

6. Use a text editor to write a Java program that declares variables to represent the length and width of a room in feet, and the price of carpeting per *square foot* in dollars and cents. Use Carpet as the class name. Assign appropriate values to the variables. Compute and display, with explanatory text, the cost of carpeting the room. Save the program as Carpet.java in the Chapter.01 folder on your Student Disk.

7. Write a program that declares variables to represent the length and width of a room in feet, and the price of carpeting per *square yard* in dollars and cents. Use Yards as the class name. Assign the value 25 to the length variable and the value 42 to the width variable. Compute and display the cost of carpeting the room. There are nine square feet in one square yard. Save the program as Yards.java in the Chapter.01 folder on your Student Disk.

8. Write a program that declares a minutes variable that represents minutes worked on a job and assign a value. Use Time as the class name. Display the value in hours and minutes. For example, 197 minutes becomes 3 hours and 17 minutes. Save the program as Time.java in the Chapter.01 folder on your Student Disk.

9. Write a program that declares variables to hold your three initials. Display the three initials with a period following each one, as in J.M.F. Save the program as Initials.java in the Chapter.01 folder on your Student Disk.

10. Write a program that contains variables that hold your tuition fee and your book fee. Display the sum of the variables. Save the program as Fees.java in the Chapter.01 folder on your Student Disk.

11. Write a program that contains variables that hold your hourly rate and number of hours that you worked. Display your gross pay, your withholding tax, which is 15 percent of your gross pay, and your net pay (gross pay – withholding). Save the program as Payroll.java in the Chapter.01 folder on your Student Disk.

12. a. Write a program that calculates and displays the conversion of $57 into 20's, 10's, 5's, and 1's. Create a separate method to do the calculation and display. Pass 57 as a variable to this method. Save the program as Dollars.java in the Chapter.01 folder on your Student Disk.

    b. In the Dollars.java program, alter the value of the variable that holds the amount of money. Run the program and confirm that the amount of each denomination calculates correctly.

13. Write a program that calculates and displays the amount of money you would have if you invested $1,000 at 5 percent interest for one year. Create a separate method to do the calculation and return the result to be displayed. Save the program as Interest.java in the Chapter.01 folder on your Student Disk.

14. Write a program that calculates and displays the weekly salary for an employee who earns $25 an hour, works 40 regular hours, 13 overtime hours, and earns time and one-half (wage * 1.5) for overtime hours worked. Create a separate method to do the calculation and return the result to be displayed. Save the program as Salary.java in the Chapter.01 folder on your Student Disk.

15. Each of the following files in the Chapter.01 folder on your Student Disk has syntax and/or logical errors. In each case, determine the problem and fix the program. After you correct the errors, save each file using the same filename preceded with *Fix*. For example, DebugOne1.java will become FixDebugOne1.java.
    a. DebugOne1.java
    b. DebugOne2.java
    c. DebugOne3.java
    d. DebugOne4.java

Using Methods, Classes, and Objects

case ▶ "How do you feel about programming so far?" asks Lynn Greenbrier, head of computer programming for Event Handlers Incorporated, and your newfound mentor.

"It's fun!" you reply. "It's great to see something actually work, but I still don't have much of an idea what the other programmers are talking about when they mention 'object-oriented programming.' I think everything is an object, and objects have methods, but I'm not really clear on this whole thing at all."

"Well then," Lynn says, "let me explain about methods, classes, and objects."

Previewing the SetUpSite Program Using the EventSite Class

You will now preview the SetUpSite program that is saved on your Student Disk.

To preview the SetUpSite program on your Student Disk:

1 Start your text editor, and then open the **Chap2EventSite.java** file from the Chapter.02 folder on your Student Disk and examine the code. This file contains a class definition for a class that stores information about event sites that Event Handlers Incorporated uses to host events that it plans.

2 Go to the command line, and then type **javac Chap2EventSite.java** to compile the Chap2EventSite.java file.

3 Use your text editor to open the **Chap2SetUpSite.java** file from the Chapter.02 folder, and then examine the code. This file contains a program that assigns values to the data in an event site that Event Handlers Incorporated uses to hold events, and then displays that data on the screen. You will create a similar program in this chapter.

4 At the command line, type **javac Chap2SetUpSite.java** to compile the Chap2SetUpSite.java file.

5 Type **java Chap2SetUpSite** to execute the program. Information about an event site used by Event Handlers Incorporated will appear on the screen as shown in Figure 2-1.

Figure 2-1: Output of the Chap2SetUpSite program

Although the output shown in Figure 2-1 is modest, you have just witnessed several important programming concepts in action. The Chap2EventSite file contains a class definition that represents a real-life object: a site at which Event Handlers can hold an event. The class includes methods to assign values to and get values from data fields that pertain to event sites. The Chap2SetUpSite file creates an actual site with data representing a site number, a fee, and a manager's name. You will create similar files in this chapter.

SECTION A

objectives

In this section you will learn how to create

- Methods with no arguments
- Methods that require a single argument
- Methods that require multiple arguments
- Methods that return values

Programming Using Methods

Creating Methods with No Arguments

A **method** is a series of statements that carry out some task. Any class can contain an unlimited number of methods. Within a class, the simplest methods you can invoke don't require any arguments or return any values. For example, consider the simple First Java program's First class that you saw in Chapter 1 and that appears in Figure 2-2.

```
public class First
{
  public static void main(String[] args)
  {
    System.out.println("First Java program");
  }
}
```

Figure 2-2: The First class

Suppose you want to add three additional lines of output to this program to display your company's name and address. Of course, you can simply add three new println() statements, but you might choose instead to create a method to display the three lines.

> Although there are differences, if you have programmed using other programming languages, you can think of methods as being similar to procedures, functions, or subroutines.

There are two major reasons to create a method in this case. First, the main() method will remain short and easy to follow because main() will contain just one statement to call a method rather than three separate println() statements to perform the work of the method. More importantly, a method is easily *reusable*. After you create the name and address method, you can use it in any program that needs the company's name and address. In other words, you do the work once, and then you can use the method many times. A method must include the following:

- A declaration (or header or definition)
- An opening curly bracket
- A body
- A closing curly bracket

The method declaration contains the following:

- Optional access modifiers
- The return type for the method
- The method name
- An opening parenthesis
- An optional list of method arguments (you separate the arguments with commas if there is more than one)
- A closing parenthesis

You first learned about access modifiers in Chapter 1. The access modifier for a method can be any of the following modifiers: public, private, friendly, protected, private protected, or static. Most often, methods are given public access. Endowing a method with public access means any class can use it. Additionally, like main(), any method that can be used from anywhere within the class (that is, any class-wide method) requires the keyword modifier static. Therefore, you can write the nameAndAddress() method shown in Figure 2-3. According to its declaration, the method is public and static. It returns nothing, so its return type is void. The method receives nothing, so its parentheses are empty. Its body, consisting of three println() statements, appears within curly brackets.

 tip

You will learn about the use of each of the non-public modifiers throughout this text.

```
public static void nameAndAddress()

{

  System.out.println("Event Handlers Incorporated");

  System.out.println("8900 U.S. Hwy 14");

  System.out.println("Crystal Lake, IL 60014");

}
```

Figure 2-3: The nameAndAddress() method

You place the entire method within the program that will use it, but not within any other method. Figure 2-4 shows where you can place a method in the First program.

```
public class First
{
  public static void main(String[] args)
  {
    System.out.println("First Java program");
  }
// You can place additional methods here,
// outside the main() method
}
```

Figure 2-4: Placement of methods

If the main() method calls the nameAndAddress() method, then you simply use the nameAndAddress() method's name as a statement within the body of main(). Figure 2-5 shows the complete program.

```
public class First
{
  public static void main(String[] args)
  {
    nameAndAddress();
    System.out.println("First Java program");
  }
  public static void nameAndAddress()
  {
      System.out.println
        ("Event Handlers Incorporated");
      System.out.println("8900 U.S. Hwy 14");
      System.out.println("Crystal Lake, IL 60014");
  }
}
```

Figure 2-5: First class calling the nameAndAddress() method

The output from the program shown in Figure 2-5 appears in Figure 2-6. Because the main() method calls the nameAndAddress() method before it prints the phrase "First Java program", the name and address appear first in the output.

Figure 2-6: Output of the First program with the nameAndAddress() method

If you want to use the nameAndAddress() method in another program, one additional step is required. In the Java programming language, the new program, with its own main() method, is a different class. If you place the method named nameAndAddress() within the new class, the compiler will not recognize it unless you write it as `First.nameAndAddress();` to notify the new class that the method is located in the First class. Notice the use of the class name, followed by a dot, and then followed by the method. You already used similar syntax for the System.out.println() method.

. . . .

Two different classes each can have their own method named nameAndAddress(). Such a method in the second class would be entirely distinct from the identically named method in the first class.

. . . .

Next, you will create a new class named SetUpSite that you eventually will use to set up one EventSite object. For now, the class will contain a main() method and a statementOfPhilosophy() method for Event Handlers Incorporated.

To create the SetUpSite class:
1 Open a new document in your text editor.
2 Type the following shell program to create a SetUpSite class and an empty main() method:

```
public class SetUpSite
{
   public static void main(String[] args)
   {
   }
}
```

3   Place the cursor to the right of the opening bracket in the main() method, press the **Enter** key to start a new line, and then type **statementOfPhilosophy();** between the curly brackets of the main() method to place a call to a statementOfPhilosophy() method.

4   Type the following code for the statementOfPhilosophy() method just before the closing curly bracket for the SetUpSite class code:

```
public static void statementOfPhilosophy()
{
  System.out.println("Event Handlers Incorporated is");
  System.out.println
    ("dedicated to making your event");
  System.out.println("a most memorable one.");
}
```

5   Save the file as **SetUpSite.java** in the Chapter.02 folder on your Student Disk.

6   At the command line, compile the program by typing **javac SetUpSite.java**. If you receive any error messages, you must remedy the problems. Figure 2-7 shows the error message received when `println()` is spelled incorrectly within the SetUpSite.java file. Notice the message indicates that the file is SetUpSite.java, the line on which the error occurs is line 10, and the error is "method prinln...not found..." To help you, Java displays the offending line, and a caret appears just below and after the word that the compiler doesn't understand. If you examine the code, you see that `println()` was spelled incorrectly. To correct the error, you would return to the SetUpSite.java file, fix the mistake, save the file, and then compile it again.

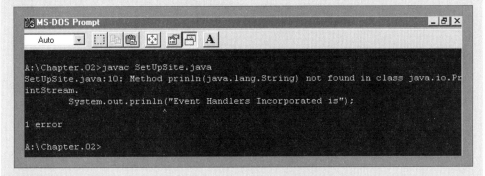

Figure 2-7: SetUpSite program with a syntax error

7   Execute the program using the command **java SetUpSite**. Your output should look like Figure 2-8.

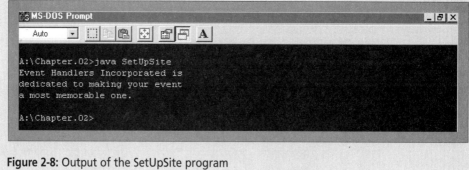

Figure 2-8: Output of the SetUpSite program

▶ **tip**

> If you want one class to call another class's method, both classes should reside in the
> same folder. If they are not saved in the same place, your compiler will issue the error
> message, "undefined variable or class name."

Next, you will see how to call the statementOfPhilosophy() method from
another class.

To call a method from another class:

1 First, open a new document in your text editor, and then enter the program
that appears in Figure 2-9.

```
public class TestStatement
{
  public static void main(String[] args)
  {
    System.out.println
    ("Calling method from another class:");
    SetUpSite.statementOfPhilosophy();
  }
}
```

Figure 2-9: TestStatement program

2 Save the file as **TestStatement.java** in the Chapter.02 folder on your Student
Disk.

help

3 Compile the program with the command **javac TestStatement.java**.

If necessary, correct any errors, save the file, and then repeat Step 3 to compile the file again.

4 Execute the program with the command **java TestStatement**. Your output should look like Figure 2-10.

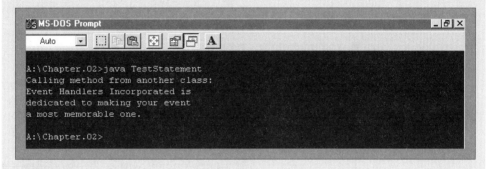

Figure 2-10: Output of the TestStatement program

Methods That Require a Single Argument

Some methods require additional information. If a method could not receive communications from you, called **arguments**, then you would have to write an infinite number of methods to cover every possible situation. For example, when you make a restaurant reservation, you do not need to employ a different method for every date of the year at every possible time of day. Rather, you can supply the date and time as information to the method, which then is carried out in the same manner, no matter what date and time are involved. If you design a method to square numeric values, it makes sense to design a square() method that you can supply with an argument that represents the value to be squared, rather than having to develop a square1() method, a square2() method, and so on.

An important principle of object-oriented programming is the notion of **implementation hiding**. When you make a request to a method, you don't know the details of how the method is executed. For example, when you make a reservation, you do not need to know how the reservation is actually made at the restaurant—perhaps it is written in a book, marked on a large chalkboard, or entered into a computerized database. The implementation details are of no concern to you as a client, and if the restaurant changes its methods from one year to the next, the *change* does not affect your use of the reservation method. With well-written object-oriented programming methods, the invoking program must know the name of the method and what type of information to send it (and what type of return to expect), but the program does not need to know how the method works. Additionally, you can substitute a new, improved method and, as long as the interface to the method does not change, you won't need to make any changes in programs invoking the method.

▶ tip

At any call, the println() method can receive any one of an infinite number of arguments. No matter what message is sent to println(), the message displays correctly.

▶ tip

Hidden implementation methods often are referred to as existing in a **black box**.

When you write the method declaration for a method that can receive an argument, you need to include the following items within the method declaration parentheses:

- The type of the argument
- A local name for the argument

For example, the declaration for a public method named predictRaise() that displays a person's salary plus a 10 percent raise could have the declaration `public void predictRaise(double moneyAmount)`. You can think of the parentheses in a method declaration as a funnel into the method—data arguments listed there are "dropping in" to the method.

The argument double moneyAmount within the parentheses indicates that the predictRaise() method will receive a figure of type double. Within the method, the figure (or salary amount) will be known as moneyAmount. Figure 2-11 shows a complete method.

```
public void predictRaise(double moneyAmount)

{

  double newAmount;

  newAmount = moneyAmount * 1.10;

  System.out.println

    ("With raise salary is " + newAmount);

}
```

Figure 2-11: The predictRaise() method

The predictRaise() method is a void method because it does not need to return any value to any class that uses it—its only function is to receive the moneyAmount value, multiply it by 1.10 (resulting in a 10 percent salary increase), and then display the result.

Within a program, you can call the predictRaise() method by using either a constant value or a variable as an argument. Thus, both `predictRaise(472.25);` and `predictRaise(mySalary);` would invoke the predictRaise() method correctly, assuming that mySalary was declared as a double value and assigned an appropriate value. You can call the predictRaise() method any number of times, with a different constant or variable argument each time. Each of these arguments becomes known as moneyAmount within the method. The identifier moneyAmount holds any double value passed into the method. Interestingly, if the value in the method call is a variable, it might possess the same identifier as moneyAmount or a different one, like mySalary. The identifier moneyAmount is simply the name the value "goes by" while it is being used within the method, no matter what name it "goes by" in the calling program.

▶ **tip**

● ●

The variable moneyAmount is a local variable to the predictRaise() method.

● ●

If a programmer changes the way in which the 10 percent raise is calculated—for example, by coding `newAmount = moneyAmount + (moneyAmount * .10);`—no program that uses the predictRaise() method will ever know the difference. The program will pass a value into predictRaise() and then a calculated result will appear on the screen.

Figure 2-12 shows a complete program that uses the predictRaise() method twice. The program's output appears in Figure 2-13.

```java
public class DemoRaise
{
   public static void main(String[] args)
   {
      double mySalary = 200.00;
      System.out.println("Demonstrating some raises");
      predictRaise(400.00);
      predictRaise(mySalary);
   }
   public static void predictRaise(double moneyAmount)
   {
      double newAmount;
      newAmount = moneyAmount * 1.10;
      System.out.println("With raise salary is " +
         newAmount);
   }
}
```

Figure 2-12: Complete program using the predictRaise() method twice

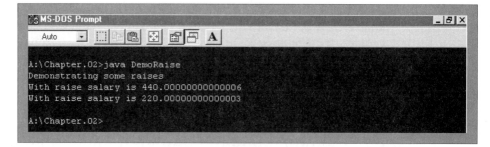

Figure 2-13: Output of the DemoRaise program

 tip

Notice the output in Figure 2-13. Floating-point arithmetic is always somewhat imprecise.

Methods That Require Multiple Arguments

A method can require more than one argument. You can pass multiple arguments to a method by listing the arguments within the call to the method and separating them with commas. For example, rather than creating a predictRaise() method that adds a 10 percent raise to every person's salary, you might prefer to create a method to which you can pass two values—the salary to be raised as well as a percentage figure by which to raise it. Figure 2-14 shows a method that uses two such arguments.

```
public static void predictRaiseGivenIncrease

  (double moneyAmount, double percentRate)

{

  double newAmount;

  newAmount = moneyAmount * (1 + percentRate);

  System.out.println("With raise salary is " +

    newAmount);

}
```

Figure 2-14: The predictRaiseGivenIncrease() method

 tip

Notice that a declaration for a method that receives two or more arguments must list the type for each argument separately, even if the arguments have the *same* type.

In the header of the predictRaiseGivenIncrease() method, the arguments in parentheses are shown on separate lines to fit in this book's margin space. You also could place the parentheses and arguments on the same line as the function header.

In Figure 2-14, two arguments (double moneyAmount and double percentRate) appear within the parentheses in the method header. The arguments are separated by a comma, and each argument requires its own named type (in this case, both are double) as well as an identifier. When values are passed to the method in a statement like `predictRaiseGivenIncrease(mySalary,promisedRate);`, the first value passed will be referenced as moneyAmount within the method, and the second value passed will be referenced as percentRate. Therefore, it is very important that arguments passed to the method be passed in the correct order. The call `predictRaiseGivenIncrease(200.00,.10);` results in output representing a 10 percent raise based on a $200 salary amount (or $220), but `predictRaiseGivenIncrease(.10,200.00);` results in output representing a 200 percent raise based on a salary of 10 cents (or $20.10).

If two method arguments are the same type—for example, two doubles—passing them to a method in the wrong order results in a logical error. If an argument expects arguments of diverse types, then passing arguments in reverse order constitutes a syntax error.

You can write a method so that it takes any number of arguments in any order. However, when you call a method, the arguments you send to a method must match, in both number and type, the arguments listed in the method declaration. Thus, a method to compute an automobile salesperson's commission amount might require arguments such as an integer value of a car sold, a double percentage commission rate, and a character code for the vehicle type. The correct method will execute only when three arguments of the correct types are sent in the correct order.

The arguments in a method call often are referred to as **actual parameters**. The variables in the method declaration that accept the values from the actual parameters are the **formal parameters**.

Methods That Return Values

The return type for a method can be any type used in the Java programming language, which includes the primitive (or scalar) types int, double, char, and so on, as well as class types (including class types you create). Of course, a method also can return nothing, in which case the return type is void.

A method's return type is known more succinctly as a method's type. For example, the declaration for the nameAndAddress() method is written `public static void nameAndAddress()`. This method is public and it returns no value, so it is type void. A method that returns `true` or `false` depending on whether or not an employee worked overtime hours might be `public boolean` overtime( ). This method is public and it returns a boolean value, so it is type boolean.

The header for a method that displays a raise amount is public static void predictRaise(double moneyAmount). If you want to create a method to return the new, calculated salary value rather than display the raised salary, the header would be public static double calculateRaise(double moneyAmount). Figure 2-15 shows this method.

```
public static double calculateRaise(double moneyAmount)
{
    double newAmount;

    newAmount = moneyAmount * 1.10;

    return newAmount;
}
```

Figure 2-15: The calculateRaise() method

Notice the return type double in the method header. Also notice the return statement that is the last statement within the method. The **return** statement causes the value stored in newAmount to be sent back to any method that calls the calculateRaise() method.

If a method returns a value, then when you call the method, you usually will want to use the returned value, although you are not required to do so. For example, when you invoke the calculateRaise() method, you might want to assign the value to a double variable named myNewSalary, as in **myNewSalary = calculateRaise(mySalary);**. The calculateRaise() method returns a double, so it is appropriate to assign the returned value to a double variable.

Alternatively, you can choose to display a method's returned value directly without storing it in any variable, as in **System.out.println("New salary is " + calculateRaise(mySalary));**. In this last statement, the call to the calculateRaise() method is made from within the println() method call. Because calculateRaise() returns a double, you can use the method call calculateRaise() in the same way that you would use any simple double value. For example, besides printing the value of calculateRaise(), you can perform math with it, assign it, and so on.

Next, you will add a method to the SetUpSite class that both receives an argument and returns a value. The purpose of the method is to take the current year and calculate how long Event Handlers Incorporated has been in business.

To add a method that receives an argument and returns a value:

1 Open the **SetUpSite.java** file in the text editor.

2 Position the cursor to the right of the opening curly bracket of the main() method of the class, and then press the **Enter** key to start a new line.

3 Type **int currentYear = 2000;** to declare a variable to hold the current year, and then press the **Enter** key.

4 Type **int age;** to declare another variable to hold the age of Event Handlers Incorporated.

5 Position the cursor at the end of the call to the statementOfPhilosophy() method in the main() method of the class, and then press the **Enter** key to start a new line. You will add a call to receive the current year and calculate how long Event Handlers Incorporated has been in business by subtracting the year of its inception, which is 1977.

6 Type **age = calculateAge(currentYear);** as a call to a calculateAge() method.

7 Press the **Enter** key, and then type **System.out.println("Serving you for " + age + " years");** to print the number of years the company has been in business. Now you will write the calculateAge() method.

8 Position the cursor after the closing bracket of the statementOfPhilosophy() method, press the **Enter** key to start a new line before the closing bracket of the program, and then enter the method shown in Figure 2-16. The method will receive an integer value. Within the calculateAge() method, the value will be known as currDate. Note that the name currDate docs not possess the same identifier as currentYear, which is the variable being passed in, although it could. Notice also that the method declaration indicates an int value will be returned.

```
public static int calculateAge(int currDate)
{
  int yrs;
  yrs = currDate - 1977;
  return yrs;
}
```

Figure 2-16: The calculateAge() method

9 Save the file, compile it, and correct any errors. Execute the program and confirm that the results are correct. See Figure 2-17.

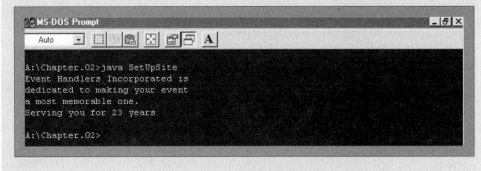

Figure 2-17: Output of the SetUpSite program with the CalculateAge() method

 # SUMMARY

- A method is a series of statements that carry out some task. Using a method makes programs easier to follow. Methods are easily reusable.

- Any class can contain any number of methods.

- Methods must include a declaration (or header or definition), an opening curly bracket, a body, and a closing curly bracket. A method declaration contains optional access modifiers, the return type for the method, the method name, an opening parenthesis, an optional list of method arguments, and a closing parenthesis.

- The access modifier for a method can be any of the modifiers `public`, `private`, `friendly`, `protected`, `private protected`, or `static`. Most often, methods are given public access.

- Any method that is a classwide method requires the keyword modifier `static`.

- You place a method within the program that will use it, but not within any other method. If you place a method call within a class that does not contain the method, you must use the class name, followed by a dot, followed by the method.

- Some methods require a message or argument.

- An important principle of object-oriented programming is the notion of implementation hiding, or concealing the details of how the method is executed.

- When you write the method declaration for a method that can receive an argument, you need to include the type of the argument, and a local name for the argument within the method declaration parentheses.

- You can call a method within a program using either a constant value or a variable as an argument.

- You can pass multiple arguments to methods by listing the arguments and separating them by commas within the call to the method.

- The arguments you send to the method must match in both number and type the parameters listed in the method declaration.

- The return type for a method (the method's type) can be any Java type, including `void`.

- You use a return statement to send a value back to a program that calls a method.

Q U E S T I O N S

1. The Java platform's term for a series of statements that carry out some task is a
   _____.
   a. procedure
   b. method
   c. subroutine
   d. function

2. A Java class _____.
   a. cannot contain methods
   b. must contain at least one method
   c. cannot contain more than eight methods
   d. can contain any number of methods

3. Methods must include all of the following except _____.
   a. a declaration
   b. a call to another method
   c. curly brackets
   d. a body

4. All method declarations contain _____.
   a. the keyword `static`
   b. one or more access modifiers
   c. arguments
   d. parentheses

5. Which of the following is not a method access modifier?
   a. `general`
   b. `private`
   c. `friendly`
   d. `protected`

6. A method named printStatistics() is void and takes no arguments. Which of the following is a correct call to printStatistics()?
   a. `printStatistics();`
   b. `void printStatistics();`
   c. `void printStatistics(void);`
   d. `void printStatistics(73.4);`

7. A public method named computeSum() is located in classA. To call the method from within classB, use the statement _____ .
   a. `computeSum(classB);`
   b. `classB(computeSum());`
   c. `classA.computeSum();`
   d. You cannot call computeSum() from within classB.

8. Which of the following method declarations is correct for a method named displayFacts() if the method receives an int argument?
   a. `public void int displayFacts()`
   b. `public void displayFacts(int)`
   c. `public void displayFacts(int data)`
   d. `public void displayFacts()`

9. The method with the declaration `public int aMethod(double d)` has a method type _____ .
   a. `int`
   b. `double`
   c. `void`
   d. You cannot determine the method type.

10. Which of the following is a correct call to a method declared as `double aMethod(char code)`?
    a. `double aMethod();`
    b. `double aMethod('V');`
    c. `aMethod(int 'M');`
    d. `aMethod('Q');`

11. A method named max() that requires two integer arguments is declared as _____ .
    a. `public void max()`
    b. `public void max(int a,b)`
    c. `public void max(int a, int b)`
    d. `public void max (a,b)`

12. A method is declared as `public void showResults(double d, int i)`. Which of the following is a correct method call?
    a. `showResults(double d, int i);`
    b. `showResults(12.2, 67);`
    c. `showResults(4, 99.7);`
    d. Two of these answers are correct.

13. The method with the declaration `public char procedure(double d)` has a method type of _____ .
    a. `public`
    b. `char`
    c. `procedure`
    d. `double`

14. The method `public boolean testValue(int response)` returns
_____ .

     a. a boolean value

     b. an integer value

     c. no value

     d. You cannot determine what is returned.

15. Which of the following could be the last legally coded line of a method declared as
`public int getVal(double sum)`?

     a. `return;`

     b. `return 77;`

     c. `return 2.3;`

     d. Any of these could be the last coded line of the method.

E X E R C I S E S

1. Name any device you use every day. Discuss how implementation hiding is demonstrated in the way this device works. Is it a benefit or a drawback to you that implementation hiding exists for methods associated with this object?

2. a. Create a class named Numbers whose main() method holds two integer variables. Assign values to the variables. Create two additional methods, sum() and difference(), that compute the sum of and difference between the values of the two variables, respectively. Each method should perform the computation and display the results. In turn, call each of the two methods from main(), passing the values of the two integer variables. Save the program as Numbers.java in the Chapter.02 folder on your Student Disk.

     b. Add a method named product() to the Numbers class. The product() method should compute the multiplication product of two integers, but not display the answer. Instead, it should return the answer to the calling main() program, which displays the answer. Save the program as Numbers.java.

3. Create a class named Eggs. Its main() method holds an integer variable named numberOfEggs to which you will assign a value. Create a method to which you pass numberOfEggs. The method displays the eggs in dozens; for example, 50 eggs is 4 full dozen (and 2 left over). Save the program as Eggs.java in the Chapter.02 folder on your Student Disk.

4. Create a class named Monogram. Its main() method holds three character variables that hold your first, middle, and last initials, respectively. Create a method to which you pass the three initials that displays the initials twice—once in the order *first, middle, last*, and a second time in traditional monogram style (*first, last, middle*). Save the program as Monogram.java in the Chapter.02 folder on your Student Disk.

5. Create a class named Exponent. Its main() method holds an integer value, and in turn passes the value to a method that squares the number and a method that cubes the number. The main() method prints the results. Create the two methods that respectively square and cube an integer that is passed to them, returning the calculated value. Save the program as Exponent.java in the Chapter.02 folder on your Student Disk.

6. Create a class named Cube that displays the result of cubing a number. Pass a number to a method that cubes a number and returns the result. The display should execute within the method that calls the cube method. Save the program as Cube.java in the Chapter.02 folder on your Student Disk.

7. Create a program that displays the result of a sales transaction. The calculation requires three numbers. The first number represents the product price. The second number is the salesperson commission. These two numbers should be added together. The third value represents a customer discount; subtract this third number from the result of the addition. Create two classes. The first class contains the method to do the calculation. The three numbers are passed to this method by a statement in the other class. The display is performed in the class that calls the calculation method. Save the program as Calculator.java in the Chapter.02 folder on your Student Disk.

8. Write a program that displays the result of dividing two numbers and displays the remainder. Do the calculation and display in the same method, which is a separate method from the main() method. Save the program as Divide.java in the Chapter.02 folder on your Student Disk.

In this section you will learn

■ Class concepts

■ How to create classes

■ About instance methods

■ How to declare objects

■ How to organize your classes

Using Classes

Classes

When you think in an object-oriented manner, everything is an object, and every object is a member of a class. You can think of any inanimate physical item as an object—your desk, your computer, and the building in which you live are all called objects in everyday conversation. You also can think of living things as objects—your houseplant, your pet fish, and your sister are objects. Events also are objects—the stock purchase you made, the mortgage closing you attended, or a graduation party that was held in your honor are all objects.

tip

· ·

In the Java programming language, a program you write to use other classes is a class itself.

· ·

Everything is an object, and every object is member of a more general class. Your desk is a member of the class that includes all desks, and your pet fish a member of the class that contains all fish. An object-oriented programmer would say that your desk is an instance of the Desk class and your fish is an instance of the Fish class. These statements represent **is-a relationships** because you can say, "My oak desk with the scratch on top *is a* Desk and my goldfish named Moby *is a* Fish." The difference between a class and an object parallels the difference between abstract and concrete. An object is an **instantiation** of a class; an object is one tangible example of a class. Your goldfish, my guppy, and the zoo's shark each constitute one instantiation of the Fish class.

The concept of a class is useful because of its reusability. Objects **inherit** attributes from classes. For example, if you are invited to a graduation party, you automatically know many things about the object (the party). You assume there will be a starting time, a number of guests, some quantity of food, and some kind of gifts. You understand what a party entails because of your previous knowledge of the Party class of which all parties are members. You don't know the number of guests or the date or the time of this particular party, but you understand that because all parties have a date and a time, then this one must too. Similarly, even though every stock market purchase is unique, each stock purchase must have a dollar amount and a number of shares. All objects have predictable attributes because they are members of certain classes.

In addition to their attributes, class objects have methods associated with them, and every object that is an instance of a class is assumed to possess the same methods. For example, for all parties, at some point you must set the date and time. You might name these methods setDate() and setTime(). Party guests need to know the date and time, and might use methods named getDate() and getTime() to find out the date and time of the party.

Your graduation party, then, might possess the identifier myGraduationParty. As a member of the Party class, myGraduationParty, like all parties, might have data members for the date and time and methods setDate() and setTime(). When you use them, the setDate() and setTime() methods require arguments, or information passed to them. For example, myGraduationParty.setDate("May 12") and myGraduationParty.setTime("6 P.M.") invoke methods that are available for myGraduationParty and send it arguments. When you use an object and its methods, think of being able to send a message to the object to direct it to accomplish some task—you can tell the party object named myGraduationParty to set the time and date you request. Even though yourAnniversaryParty also is a member of the Party class, and even though it also has setDate() and setTime() methods, you will want to send different arguments to yourAnniversaryParty than I want to send to myGraduationParty. Within any object-oriented program, you are continuously making requests to objects' methods, and often including arguments as part of those requests.

Additionally, some methods used in a program must return a message or value. If one of your party guests uses the getDate() method, it is in the hope that the method will respond to the guest with the desired information. Similarly, within object-oriented programs, methods often are called upon to return a piece of information to the source of the request. For example, a method within a Payroll class that calculates federal withholding tax might return a tax figure in dollars and cents, and a method within an Inventory class might return true or false depending on the method's determination of whether an item is at the reorder point.

There are two parts to object-oriented programming. First, you must create the classes of objects from which objects will be instantiated, and second, you must write other classes to use the objects (and their data and their methods). The same programmer does not need to accomplish these two tasks. Often, you will write programs that use classes created by others; similarly, you might create a class that others will use to instantiate objects within their own programs. You can call a program or class that instantiates objects of another prewritten class as a **class client** or **class user**.

Creating a Class

When you create a class, first you must assign a name to the class, and then you must determine what data and methods will be part of the class. Suppose you decide to create a class named Employee. One instance variable of Employee might be an employee number, and two necessary methods might be a method to set (or provide a value for) the employee number and another method to get (or retrieve) that employee number. To begin, you create a class header with three parts:

- An optional access modifier
- The keyword `class`
- Any legal identifier you choose for the name of your class

For example, a header for an Employee class is `public class Employee`. The keyword `public` is a class access modifier. You can use the following class access modifiers when defining a class: `public`, `final`, or `abstract`. If you do not specify an access modifier, access becomes `friendly`.

Public classes are accessible by all objects, which means that public classes can be **extended**, or used as a basis for any other class. The most liberal form of access is `public`. Public access means that if you develop a good Employee class, and some day you want to develop two more specific classes, SalariedEmployee and HourlyEmployee, then you will not have to start from scratch. Each new class can become an extension of the original Employee class, inheriting its data and methods. The other access modifiers (or the omission of any access modifier) impose at least some limitations on extensibility. (You use the other access modifiers only under special circumstances.) You will use the public access modifier for most of your classes.

After writing the class header `public class Employee`, you write the body of the Employee class, containing its data and methods, between a set of curly brackets. Figure 2-18 shows the shell for the Employee class.

```
public class Employee

{

   // Instance variables and methods go here

}
```

Figure 2-18: Employee class shell

You place the instance variables, or fields, for the Employee class as statements within the curly brackets. For example, you can declare an employee number that will be stored as an integer simply as `int empNum;`. However, programmers frequently include an access modifier for each of the class fields and declare the empNum as `private int empNum;`.

The allowable field modifiers are `private`, `public`, `friendly`, `protected`, `private protected`, `static`, and `final`. Most class fields are private, which provides the highest level of security. Private access means that no other classes can access a field's values, and only methods of the same class are allowed to set, get, or otherwise use private variables. Private access is sometimes called **information hiding,** and is an important component of object-oriented programs. A class's private data can be changed or manipulated only by a class's own methods, and not by methods that belong to other classes. In contrast, most class methods are not usually private. The resulting private data/public method arrangement provides a means for you to control outside access to your data—only a class's nonprivate methods can be used to access a class's private data. The situation is similar to hiring a public receptionist to sit in front of your private office controlling the messages passed in to you (perhaps deflecting trivial or hostile ones) and the messages you pass out (perhaps checking your spelling, grammar, and any legal implications). The way in which the nonprivate methods are written controls how you use the private data.

If you do not provide an access specifier for a class field, its access is `friendly`, which is more liberal access than private.

The field modifiers are the same as the method modifiers with one addition—the `final` modifier. You will learn to use the `final` modifier in Chapter 3.

The entire class so far appears in Figure 2-19. It defines a public class named Employee, with one field, which is a private integer named empNum.

```
public class Employee
{
   private int empNum;
}
```

Figure 2-19: Employee class with one data field

Next, you will create a class to store information about event sites for Event Handlers Incorporated.

To create the class:

1   Open a new document in your text editor.

2   Type the following class header and the curly brackets to surround the class body:

```
public class EventSite
{
}
```

3 Type **private int siteNumber;** between the curly brackets to insert the private data field that will hold an integer site number for each event site used by the company.

4 Save the file as **EventSite.java** in the Chapter.02 folder on your Student Disk.

5 To ensure you have not made any typographical errors, compile the class by typing **javac EventSite.java** at the command-line prompt. If necessary, correct any errors, save your work, and then compile again. Do not execute the class.

Using Instance Methods

Besides data, classes contain methods. For example, one method you need for an Employee class that contains an empNum is the method to retrieve (or return) any Employee's empNum for use by another class. A reasonable name for this method is getEmpNum() and its declaration is `public int getEmpNum()` because it will have public access, return an integer (the employee number), and possess the identifier getEmpNum(). Figure 2-20 shows the complete getEmpNum() method.

```
public int getEmpNum()

{

   return empNum;

}
```

Figure 2-20: The getEmpNum() method

The getEmpNum() method contains just one statement: the statement that accesses the value of the private empNum field.

Notice that, unlike the class methods you created in Section A of this chapter, the getEmpNum() method does not employ the `static` modifier. The keyword `static` is used for classwide methods, but not for methods that "belong" to objects. If you are creating a program with a main() method that you will execute to perform some task, then many of your methods will be static so you can call them from within main(). However, if you are creating a class from which objects will be instantiated, most methods will probably be nonstatic as you will be associating the methods with individual objects. Methods used with object instantiations are called **instance methods**.

> **tip**
>
> You can call class methods without creating an instance of the class. Instance methods require an instantiated object.

Next, you will add an instance method to the EventSite class that will retrieve the value of an event site's number.

To add an instance method to the EventSite class:

1 Open the **EventSite.java** file in your text editor.

2 Within the EventSite class's curly brackets and after the declaration of the siteNumber field, enter the following getSiteNumber() method to return the site number to any calling class:

```
public int getSiteNumber()
{
   return siteNumber;
}
```

3 Save the file.

When a class contains data fields, you want a means to assign values to the data fields. For an Employee class with an empNum field, you need a method with which to set the empNum. Figure 2-21 shows a method that sets the empNum. The method is a void method because there is no need to return any value to a calling program. The method receives an integer, locally called emp, to be assigned to empNum.

```
public static void setEmpNum(int emp)

{

   empNum = emp;

}
```

Figure 2-21: The setEmpNum() method

Next, you will add a setSiteNumber() method to the EventSite class. This method takes an integer argument and assigns it to the siteNumber of an EventSite object.

To add a method to the EventSite class:

1 Add the following method to the **EventSite.java** file after the final curly bracket for the getSiteNumber() method, but prior to the closing curly bracket for the EventSite class:

```
public void setSiteNumber(int n)
{
   siteNumber = n;
}
```

The argument *n* represents any number sent to this method.

2 Save the file, compile it, and then correct any syntax errors. (You cannot run this file as a program.)

Declaring Objects

Declaring a class does not create any actual objects. A class is just an abstract description of what an object will be like if any objects are ever actually instantiated. Just as you might understand all the characteristics of an item you intend to manufacture long before the first item rolls off the assembly line, you can create a class with fields and methods long before you instantiate any objects that are members of that class.

A two-step process creates an object that is an instance of a class. First, you supply a type and an identifier, just as when you declare any variable, and then you allocate computer memory for that object. For example, you might define an integer as `int someValue;` and you might define an Employee as `Employee someEmployee;`, where someEmployee stands for any legal identifier you choose to represent an Employee.

When you declare an integer as `int someValue;`, you notify the compiler that an integer named someValue will exist, and you reserve computer memory for it at the same time. When you declare the someEmployee instance of the Employee class, you are notifying the compiler that you will use the identifier someEmployee. However, you are not yet setting aside computer memory in which the Employee named someEmployee might be stored—that is done only for primitive type variables. To allocate the needed memory, you must use the **new operator**. After you define someEmployee with the `Employee someEmployee;` statement, the statement that actually sets aside enough memory to hold an Employee is `someEmployee = new Employee();`. You also can define and reserve memory for someEmployee in one statement, as in `Employee someEmployee = new Employee();`. In this statement, Employee is the object's type (as well as its class), and someEmployee is the name of the object. The equals sign is the assignment operator, so a value is being assigned to someEmployee. The `new` operator is allocating a new, unused portion of computer memory for someEmployee. The value that the statement is assigning to someEmployee is a memory address at which it is to be located. You do not need to be concerned with what the actual memory address is—when you refer to someEmployee, the compiler will locate it at the appropriate address for you—but someEmployee does need to know its own address.

tip Every object name is also a reference—that is, a computer memory location.

The last portion of the statement, `Employee()`, with its parentheses, looks suspiciously like a method name. In fact, it is the name of a method that constructs an Employee object. Employee() is a **constructor method**. You will write your own constructor methods later in this section, but when you don't write a constructor method for a class object, Java writes one for you, and the name of the constructor method is always the same as the name of the class whose objects it constructs.

Next, you will instantiate an EventSite object.

To instantiate an object

1   Open the **SetUpSite.java** file from the Chapter.02 folder in your text editor.

2   Place the cursor at the end of the opening curly bracket within the main() method of the SetUpSite class, press the **Enter** key to start a new line, and then type **EventSite oneSite = new EventSite();** to allocate memory for a new EventSite object named oneSite.

3   Save the file and then compile it. If necessary, correct any errors, and save and compile again.

After an object has been instantiated, its methods can be accessed using the object's identifier, a dot, and a method call. For example, if an Employee class method to change a salary is written using the code in Figure 2-22, and an Employee was declared with `Employee clerk = new Employee();`, then the clerk's salary can be changed to 350.00 with the call `clerk.changeSalary(350.00);`. The method changeSalary() is applied to the object clerk, and the argument 350.00 (a double type value) is passed to the method.

```
public void changeSalary(double newAmount)

{

   salary = newAmount;

}
```

Figure 2-22: The changeSalary() method

Within the same program, the statements `Employee secretary = new Employee();` and `secretary.changeSalary(420.00);` would apply the same changeSalary() method, but using a different argument value, to different objects that belong to the same class. Figure 2-23 shows the getEmpNum() method.

```
public int getEmpNum()

{

   return empNum;

}
```

Figure 2-23: The getEmpNum() method

Next, you will add calls to the getSiteNumber() and setSiteNumber() methods for the oneSite object member of the EventSite class.

To add the calls to the methods for the oneSite object member:

1 Open the file **SetUpSite.java** in your text editor.

2 Just below the declaration for oneSite, provide the SetUpSite() method with a variable to hold any site number returned from the getSiteNumber() method by typing **int number;**, and then pressing the **Enter** key.

3 Next, call the method setSiteNumber() to set the site number for oneSite. Type **oneSite.setSiteNumber(101);**. The number in parentheses could be any integer number.

4 After the statement that prints the age of the company, System.out.println("Serving you for " + age + " years");, call the getSiteNumber() method and assign its return value to the number variable by typing **number = oneSite.getSiteNumber();**, and then pressing the **Enter** key.

5 Add a call to the println() method to display the value stored in number by typing **System.out.println("The number of the event site is " + number);**.

6 Save the program file as **SetUpSite.java** in the Chapter.02 folder on your Student Disk.

7 Compile the program by typing **javac SetUpSite.java**. Correct any errors and compile again, if necessary.

8 Execute the program by typing **java SetUpSite**. Your output should look like Figure 2-24.

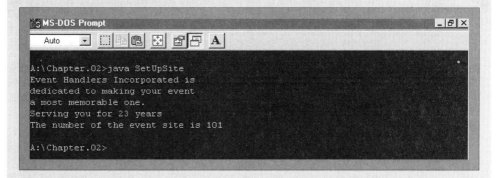

Figure 2-24: Output of the SetUpSite program

Organizing Classes

Most classes you create will have more than one data field and more than two methods. For example, in addition to requiring an employee number, an Employee needs a last name, a first name, and a salary, as well as methods to set and get those fields. Figure 2-25 shows how you could code the data fields for Employee.

```
public class Employee
{
   private int empNum;
   private String empLastName;
   private String empFirstName;
   private double empSalary;
// Methods will go here
}
```

Figure 2-25: Employee class with data fields

Although there is no requirement to do so, most programmers place data fields in some logical order at the beginning of a class. For example, the empNum is most likely used as a unique identifier for each employee (what database users often call a **primary key**), so it makes sense to list the employee number first in the class. An employee's last name and first name "go together," so it makes sense to store these two Employee components adjacently. Despite these common-sense rules, there is a lot of flexibility in how you position your data fields within any class.

> A unique identifier is one that should have no duplicates within an application. In other words, although an organization might have many employees with the last name Johnson or a salary of $400.00, there will only be one employee with employee number 128.

Because there are two String components in the current Employee class, they might be declared within the same statement, such as `private String empLastName, empFirstName;`. However, it usually is easier to identify each Employee field at a glance if the fields are listed vertically.

Even if the only methods created for the Employee class include one set method and one get method for each instance variable, eight methods are required. If you consider an Employee record for most organizations, you will realize that usually many more fields are required (such as an address, a phone number, a hire date, the number of dependents, and so on), and many more methods. Finding your way through the list can become a formidable task. For ease in locating class methods, many programmers prefer to store them in alphabetical order. If you name all methods that get values so they begin with "get" and name all methods that set values so they being with "set," alphabetical order also results in functional groupings. Figure 2-26 shows how the complete class definition for an Employee might appear.

tip

Another reasonable course of action is to pair the get and set methods for a particular field. In other words, you can choose to place the getEmpNum() and setEmpNum() methods adjacently.

```java
public class Employee
{
  private int empNum;
  private String empLastName;
  private String empFirstName;
  private double empSalary;
  public int getEmpNum()
  {
    return empNum;
  }
  public String getFirstName()
  {
    return empFirstName;
  }
  public String getLastName()
  {
    return empLastName;
  }
  public double getSalary()
  {
    return empSalary;
  }
  public void setEmpNum(int e)
  {
    empNum = e;
  }
```

Figure 2-26: Employee class with data fields and methods

```
public void setFirstName(String first)

{

    empFirstName = first;

}

public void setLastName(String last)

{

    empLastName = last;

}

public void setSalary(double sal)

{

    empSalary = sal;

}

}
```

Figure 2-26: Employee class with data fields and methods (continued)

The Employee class still is not a particularly large class, and each of its methods is very short, but it is already becoming quite difficult to manage. It certainly can support some well-placed comments, as shown in Figure 2-27.

```
// Programmer: Joyce Farrell

// Date: February 13, 2000

// Employee.java to hold employee data

public class Employee

{

    // private data members

    private int empNum;

    private String empLastName;

    private String empFirstName;
```

Figure 2-27: Employee class with data fields, methods, and comments

```
    private double empSalary;
    // getEmpNum method returns employee number
    public int getEmpNum()
    {
      return empNum;
    }
    // getFirstName method returns employee first name
    public String getFirstName()
    {
      return empFirstName;
    }
    // ... and so on
}
```

Figure 2-27: Employee class with data fields, methods, and comments (continued)

Although good program comments are crucial to creating understandable code, you will leave them out of many examples in this book to save space.

To expand the EventSite class to contain data fields and methods:

1 Open the **EventSite.java** file from the Chapter.02 folder in the text editor. Your program looks like Figure 2-28.

```
public class EventSite
{
  private int siteNumber;
  public int getSiteNumber()
  {
    return siteNumber;
  }
```

Figure 2-28: EventSite.java program

```
public void setSiteNumber(int n)

{

   siteNumber = n;

}

}
```

Figure 2-28: EventSite.java program (continued)

You will add two new data fields to the EventSite class: a double to hold a usage fee for the site, and a String to hold the site manager's last name.

2 Position the cursor at the end of the declaration of the `private int siteNumber;` variable, press the **Enter** key to start a new line, and then type **private double usageFee;** and **private String managerName;** on separate lines.

You also will enter four new methods to set and get data from each of the two new fields. To ensure that the methods are easy to locate later, you will place them in alphabetical order within the class.

3 Position the cursor after the end of the closing curly bracket of the getSiteNumber() method, press the **Enter** key to start a new line, and then enter the following getUsageFee() method.

```
public double getUsageFee()
{
   return usageFee;
}
```

4 Position the cursor at the end of the `private String managerName;` declaration, press the **Enter** key to start a new line, and then enter the following getManagerName() method:

```
public String getManagerName()
{
   return managerName;
}
```

5 Position the cursor after the closing bracket of the getSiteNumber() method, press the **Enter** key to start a new line, and then enter the following setUsageFee() method.

```
public void setUsageFee(double amt)
{
   usageFee = amt;
}
```

6 Position the cursor after the closing curly bracket of the getUsageFee() method, press the **Enter** key, and then enter the following setManagerName() method.

```
public void setManagerName(String name)
{
   managerName = name;
}
```

7 Start a line above each of the methods and add a comment describing the function of the method.

8 Save the file and compile it. If necessary, correct any errors, save the file, and then compile again.

You have created an EventSite class that contains both data and methods. However, no actual event sites exist yet. You must write a program that instantiates one or more EventSite objects to give actual values to the data fields for that object, and to manipulate the data in the fields using the class methods. Next, you will create a program to test the new expanded EventSite class.

To create the test program:

1 Open a new document in the text editor, and then enter the class that tests the new expanded EventSite class. The class should look like Figure 2-29.

```
// Programmer: <your name>
// Date: <current date>
// Program: TestExpandedClass
// Tests the expanded EventSite class
public class TestExpandedClass
{
   public static void main(String[] args)
   {
      EventSite oneSite = new EventSite();
      oneSite.setSiteNumber(101);
      oneSite.setUsageFee(32508.65);
```

Figure 2-29: The TestExpandedClass class

```
        oneSite.setManagerName("Jefferson");

        System.out.print("The number of the event site is ");

        System.out.println(oneSite.getSiteNumber());

        System.out.println("Usage fee "

           + oneSite.getUsageFee());

        System.out.println("Manager is "

           + oneSite.getManagerName());

    }

}
```

Figure 2-29: The TestExpandedClass class (continued)

> You should get into the habit of documenting your programs with your name, today's date, and a brief explanation of the program. Your instructor might ask you to insert additional information as comment text, as well.

2 Save the file as **TestExpandedClass.java** in the Chapter.02 folder on your Student Disk. Compile the program and correct any errors, if necessary.

3 Execute the class with the command-line statement **java TestExpandedClass**. Your output should look like Figure 2-30.

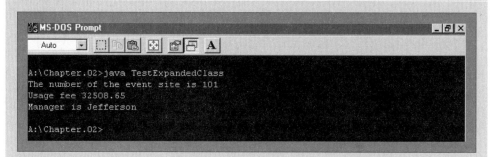

Figure 2-30: Output of the TestExpandedClass program

Using Constructors

When you create a class, such as Employee, and instantiate an object with a statement like `Employee chauffeur = new Employee();`, you are actually calling a method named Employee() that is provided by the Java compiler. A **constructor**

method is a method that establishes an object. The constructor method named Employee() establishes one Employee with the identifer chauffeur, and provides the following specific initial values to the Employee's data fields:

- Numeric fields are set to 0 (zero).
- Character fields are set to Unicode '\u0000'.
- The boolean fields are set to `false`.
- The object type fields are set to `null` (or empty).

If you do not want an Employee's fields to hold these default values, or if you want to perform additional tasks when you create an Employee, then you can write your own constructor. Any constructor method you write must have the same name as the class it constructs, and constructor methods cannot have a return type. For example, if every Employee has a starting salary of 300.00, then you could write the constructor method for the Employee class that appears in Figure 2-31. Any Employee instantiated will have a default empSal figure of 300.00.

```
Employee()

{

  empSal = 300.00;

}
```

Figure 2-31: Employee class constructor

You can write any statement in a constructor. Although you usually would have no reason to do so, you could print a message from within a constructor or perform any other task. Next, you will add a constructor to the EventSite class and demonstrate that it is called when an EventSite object is instantiated.

To add a constructor to the EventSite class:

1 Open the **EventSite.java** file in your text editor.

2 Place the cursor at the end of the line containing the last field declaration (`private String managerName;`), and then press the **Enter** key to start a new line.

3 Add the following constructor function that sets any EventSite siteNumber to 999 and any manager's name to "ZZZ" upon construction.

```
EventSite()
{
  siteNumber = 999;
  managerName = "ZZZ";
}
```

4   Save the file, compile it, and correct any errors.

5   Open a new text file and create a test class named TestConstructor using the code shown in Figure 2-32.

```
public class TestConstructor
{
  public static void main(String[] args)
  {
    EventSite oneSite = new EventSite();
    System.out.print
      ("The number of the event site is ");
    System.out.println
      (oneSite.getSiteNumber());
    System.out.print("The manager is ");
    System.out.println(oneSite.getManagerName());
  }
}
```

Figure 2-32: TestConstructor class

6   Save the file as **TestConstructor.java** in the Chapter.02 folder on your Student Disk, compile the file, and correct any syntax errors.

7   Execute the program and confirm that it declares a oneSite object of type EventSite, calls the constructor, and assigns the indicated initial values, as shown in Figure 2-33.

Figure 2-33: Output of the TestConstructor program

S U M M A R Y

- When you think in an object-oriented manner, everything is an object and every object is a member (an instance, or an instantiation) of a class. This concept is known as an is-a relationship.

- Objects inherit attributes from classes. Class objects have attributes and methods associated with them. Class instance methods that will be used with objects usually are not `static`.

- You can send messages to objects. Additionally, some methods used in a program must return a message or value.

- There are two parts to object-oriented programming: creating the classes of objects from which objects will be instantiated, and writing other classes to use the objects.

- A class header contains an optional access modifier, the keyword `class`, and any legal identifier you choose for the name of your class.

- The class access modifiers are `public`, `final`, and `abstract`; you can also choose to specify no modifier. Public classes are accessible by all objects, which is the most liberal form of access. Public classes can be extended, or used as a basis for any other class.

- The instance variables, or fields, of a class are placed as statements within the class's curly brackets.

- Allowable field modifiers include `private`, `public`, `friendly`, `protected`, `private protected`, `static`, and `final`. Most class fields are private, which provides the highest level of security.

- Information hiding is an important component of object-oriented programs; a class's private data can be changed or manipulated only by a class's own methods.

- Declaring a class does not create any actual objects; you must instantiate any objects that are members of a class.

- To create an object that is an instance of a class, you supply a type and an identifier, and then you allocate computer memory for that object using the `new` operator.

- Most programmers place data fields in some logical order at the beginning of a class. Many programmers prefer to store data fields in alphabetical order.

- A constructor method establishes an object and provides specific initial values for the object's data fields. A constructor method always has the same name as the class of which it is a member. You can write your own constructor methods. Constructor methods might not have a return type.

- By default, numeric fields are set to 0 (zero), character fields are set to Unicode '\u0000', boolean fields are set to `false`, and object type fields are set to `null`.

QUESTIONS

1. Every object is a member or instance of a more general _____.
    a. class
    b. program
    c. method
    d. syntax

2. The data components of a class often are referred to as the _____ of that class.
    a. access types
    b. instance variables
    c. methods
    d. objects

3. Class objects have both attributes and _____.
    a. fields
    b. data
    c. methods
    d. instances

4. You send messages to an object through its _____.
    a. fields
    b. methods
    c. classes
    d. data

5. You create classes, from which _____ are instantiated.
    a. fields
    b. data
    c. other classes
    d. objects

6. A program or class that instantiates objects of another prewritten class is a(n) _____.
    a. class client
    b. superclass
    c. object
    d. patron

7. A class header must contain _____.
    a. an access modifier
    b. the keyword `class`
    c. the keyword `static`
    d. the keyword `public`

8. Which of the following access modifiers can you use to define a class?

    a. `open`

    b. `static`

    c. `abstract`

    d. `concrete`

9. Most classes are created with the access modifier _____.

    a. `private`

    b. `public`

    c. `liberal`

    d. `open`

10. The body of a class is written _____.

    a. as a single statement

    b. within parentheses

    c. between curly brackets

    d. as a method call

11. Allowable field modifiers include _____.

    a. `private`

    b. `final`

    c. both of these

    d. none of these

12. Which of the following is not a field modifier?

    a. `public`

    b. `friendly`

    c. `protected`

    d. `protected public`

13. Most class fields are _____.

    a. private

    b. public

    c. static

    d. final

14. The concept of allowing a class's private data to be changed only by a class's own methods is known as _____.

    a. structured logic

    b. object orientation

    c. information hiding

    d. data masking

15. At the time you declare a class, you _____.

    a. declare one object of the class

    b. instantiate one object of the class

    c. declare multiple objects of the class

    d. instantiate no actual objects

16. When you declare a variable as in **double salary;**, you _____ .
    a. also must explicitly allocate memory for it
    b. need not explicitly allocate memory for it
    c. must explicitly allocate memory for it only if it is stored in a class
    d. can declare it to use no memory

17. When you declare an object that is an instance of a class, you _____ .
    a. also must explicitly allocate memory for it
    b. need not explicitly allocate memory for it
    c. must explicitly allocate memory for it only if it is stored in a class
    d. can declare it to use no memory

18. To allocate memory you must use the _____ operator.
    a. **alloc**
    b. **malloc**
    c. **create**
    d. **new**

19. You can allocate memory for an object _____ .
    a. with an assignment statement
    b. in the same statement as the object declaration
    c. either of these
    d. none of these

20. If an object someThing has a method someMethod(), then you can call the method using the statement _____ .
    a. **someThing/someMethod();**
    b. **someThing.someMethod();**
    c. **someMethod/someThing();**
    d. **someMethod.someThing();**

21. If a class is named Student(), then the class constructor name is _____ .
    a. any legal Java identifier
    b. any legal Java identifier that begins with *S*
    c. StudentConstructor
    d. Student

22. If you use the default constructor, _____ .
    a. numeric fields are set to 0 (zero)
    b. character fields are set to blank
    c. boolean fields are set to true
    d. object type fields are set to 0 (zero)

23. A constructor can contain _____ .
    a. assignment statements
    b. println() statements
    c. either of these
    d. none of these

E X E R C I S E S

1. a. Create a class named Pizza. Data fields include a String for toppings (such as "pepperoni"), an integer for diameter in inches (such as 12), and a double for price (such as 13.99). Include methods to get and set values for each of these fields. Save the class as Pizza.java in the Chapter.02 folder on your Student Disk.

    b. Create a class named TestPizza that instantiates one Pizza object and demonstrates the use of the Pizza set and get methods. Save this class as TestPizza.java in the Chapter.02 folder of your Student Disk.

2. a. Create a class named Student. A Student has fields for an ID number, number of credit hours earned, and number of points earned. (For example, many schools compute grade point averages based on a scale of 4, so a three credit hour class in which a student earns an A is worth 12 points.) Include methods to assign values to all fields. A Student also has a field for grade point average. Include a method to compute the grade point average field by dividing points by credit hours earned. Write methods to display the values in each Student field. Save this class as Student.java in the Chapter.02 folder on your Student Disk.

    b. Write a class named ShowStudent that instantiates a Student object from the class you created. Compute the Student grade point average, and then display all the values associated with the Student. Save the program as ShowStudent.java in the Chapter.02 folder on your Student Disk.

    c. Create a constructor method for the Student class you created. The constructor should initialize each Student's ID number to 9999 and his or her grade point average to 4.0. Write a program that demonstrates that the constructor works by instantiating an object and displaying the initial values.

3. a. Create a class named Circle with fields named radius, area, and diameter. Include a constructor that sets the radius to 1. Also include methods named setRadius(), getRadius(), computeDiameter(), which computes a circle's diameter, and computeArea(), which computes a circle's area. (The diameter of a circle is twice its radius, and the area is 3.14 multiplied by the square of the radius.) Save the class as Circle.java in the Chapter.02 folder of your Student Disk.

    b. Create a class named TestCircle whose main() method declares three Circle objects. Using the setRadius() method, assign one Circle a small radius value and assign another a larger radius value. Do not assign a value to the radius of the third circle; instead, retain the value assigned at construction. Call computeDiameter() and computeArea() for each circle and display the results. Save the program as TestCircle.java in the Chapter.02 folder on your Student Disk.

4. a. Create a class named Checkup with fields that hold a patient number, two blood pressure figures (systolic and diastolic), and two cholesterol figures (LDL and HDL). Include methods to get and set each of the fields. Include a method named computeRatio() that divides LDL cholesterol by HDL cholesterol and displays the result. Include an additional method named ExplainRatio() that explains that LDL is known as "good cholesterol" and that a ratio of 3.5 or lower is considered optimum. Save the class as Checkup.java in the Chapter.02 folder of your Student Disk.

b. Create a class named TestCheckup whose main() method declares four Checkup objects. Provide values for each field for each patient. Then display the values. Blood pressure numbers are usually displayed with a slash between the systolic and diastolic values. (Typical numbers are values like 110/78 or 130/90.) With the cholesterol figures, display the explanation of the cholesterol ratio calculation. (Typical numbers are values like 100 and 40 or 180 and 70.) Save the program as TestCheckup.java in the Chapter.02 folder on your Student Disk.

5. Write a program that displays employee IDs and first and last names of employees. Use two classes. The first class contains the employee data and separate methods to set the IDs and names. The other class creates objects for the employees and uses the objects to call the set methods. Create several employees and display their data. Save the program as Employee.java in the Chapter.02 folder on your Student Disk.

6. Write a program that displays an invoice of several items. It should contain the item name, quantity, price, and total cost on each line for the quantity and item cost. Use two classes. The first class contains the item data and methods to get and set the item name, quantity and price. The other class creates objects for the items and uses the objects to call the set and get methods. Save the program as Invoice.java in the Chapter.02 folder on your Student Disk.

7. Write a program that schedules several meetings for a meeting room. It should contain the day of the week, starting time, and ending time for each meeting. Use two classes. The first class contains the meeting data and methods to get and set the day of the week and times. The other class creates objects for the meetings and uses the objects to call the set and get methods. Save the program as RoomSchedule.java in the Chapter.02 folder on your Student Disk.

8. Each of the following files saved in the Chapter.02 folder on your Student Disk has syntax and/or logical errors. In each case, determine and fix the problem. After you correct the errors, save each file using the same filename preceded with *Fix*. For example, DebugTwo1.java will become FixDebugTwo1.java.
   a. DebugTwo1.java
   b. DebugTwo2.java
   c. DebugTwo3.java
   d. DebugTwo4.java

Advanced Object Concepts

case ▶ Lynn Greenbrier, your mentor at Event Handlers Incorporated, pops her head into your cubicle on Monday morning. "How's the programming going?" she asks.

"I'm getting the hang of using objects," you tell her, "but I want to create lots of objects and it seems like I am going to need so many methods for the classes that I create that it's going to be very hard to keep track of them." You pause a moment and add, "And all these set methods are driving me crazy—I wish an object could just start with values."

"Anything else bothering you?" Lynn asks.

"Well," you reply, "I don't mean to complain, but shouldn't some objects and methods that are used by all kinds of programmers already be created for me? I can't be the first person who ever thought about taking a square root of a number or calculating a billing date for 10 days after service."

"You are in luck!" Lynn smiles. "Java's creators have already thought about these things. Let me tell you about some of the more advanced things you can do with your classes."

In this section you will learn

- About blocks and scope
- How to overload a method
- About the concept of ambiguity
- How to send an argument to a constructor
- How to overload a constructor

Class Features

Blocks and Scope

Within any class or method, the code between a pair of curly brackets is called a **block**. For example, the program shown in Figure 3-1 contains two blocks. The first block, or **outside block**, begins immediately after the method declaration and ends at the end of the method. The second block, or **inside block**, is contained within the second set of curly brackets and contains three statements: the declaration of anotherNumber and two println() statements. The inside block is **nested** within the outside block.

 tip

Although you can create as many blocks as you need within any program, it is not wise to do so without a reason, and it is considered to be poor programming style if you do.

```
public static void methodWithTwoBlocks()
{
   int aNumber = 22;
   // aNumber comes into existence
   System.out.println("Number is " + aNumber);
   {
      int anotherNumber = 99;
      // anotherNumber comes into existence
      System.out.println("aNumber is " + aNumber);
      System.out.println("anotherNumber is " +
         anotherNumber);
   } // End of block - anotherNumber ceases to exist
   System.out.println("aNumber is " + aNumber);
} // End of outer block - aNumber ceases to exist
```

Figure 3-1: The methodWithTwoBlocks() method

tip

•••

A block can exist entirely within another block, or entirely outside and separate from another block, but blocks can never overlap.

•••

If you declare a variable in one program that you write, you cannot use that variable in another program. Similarly, when you declare a variable within a block, you cannot reference that variable outside the block. The portion of a program within which you can reference a variable is the variable's **scope**. A variable comes into existence, and **comes into scope**, when you declare it. A variable ceases to exist, and **goes out of scope**, at the end of the block in which it is declared.

In the methodWithTwoBlocks() method shown in Figure 3-1, the variable aNumber exists from the point of its declaration until the end of the method. This means aNumber exists both in the outer block and within the inner block and can be used anywhere in the method. The variable anotherNumber comes into existence within the inner block, and anotherNumber ceases to exist when the inner block ends, and cannot be used beyond its block.

Figure 3-2 shows some invalid statements. The first assignment `aNumber = 75;` is invalid because aNumber has not been declared yet. Similarly, Invalid statement 2, `anotherNumber = 489;`, is invalid because it has not been declared yet. Invalid statement 3 is also invalid because anotherNumber still has not been declared. After you declare anotherNumber, you can use it for the remainder of the block, but Invalid statement 4 is outside the block—anotherNumber has gone out of scope. The last statement in Figure 3-2, `aNumber = 29;`, will not work because it falls outside the block in which aNumber was declared; it actually falls outside the methodWithTwoBlocks() method.

```
public static void methodWithTwoBlocks()

{

  aNumber = 75; // Invalid statement 1

  int aNumber = 22;

  System.out.println("aNumber is " + aNumber);

  anotherNumber = 489;   // Invalid statement 2

  {

    anotherNumber = 165; // Invalid statement 3

    int anotherNumber = 99;

    System.out.println("aNumber is " + aNumber);
```

Figure 3-2: The methodWithTwoBlocks() method with some invalid statements

```
    System.out.println("anotherNumber is " +
      anotherNumber);
  }

    System.out.println("aNumber is " + aNumber);

    System.out.println("anotherNumber is " +
      anotherNumber); // Invalid statement 4
}
aNumber = 29; // Invalid statement 5
```

Figure 3-2: The methodWithTwoBlocks() method with some invalid statements (continued)

 tip

There is no requirement that you vertically align the opening and closing brackets for a block, but your programs are much easier to read if you do.

Within a method, you can declare a variable with the same name multiple times, as long as each declaration is in its own, nonoverlapping block. For example, the two declarations of variables named someVar in Figure 3-3 are valid because each variable is contained within its own block. The first instance of someVar has gone out of scope before the second instance comes into scope.

```
public static twoDeclarations()
{
  { // Begin first block
    int someVar = 7;
    System.out.println(someVar);
  } // End first block
  { // Begin second block
    int someVar = 845;
    System.out.println(someVar);
  } // End second block
}
```

Figure 3-3: The twoDeclarations() method

You cannot declare the same variable name more than once within nested blocks. For example, in Figure 3-4, the second declaration of aValue causes an error because you cannot declare the same variable twice within the outer block of the method. By the same reasoning, the third declaration of aValue is also invalid, even though it appears within a new block. The block that contains the third declaration is entirely within the outside block, so the first declaration of aValue has not gone out of scope.

```
public static methodWithRedeclarations()

{

  int aValue = 35;

  System.out.println(aValue);

  int aValue = 99;   // Invalid - second declaration

  {

    int anotherValue = 58; // Valid

    int aValue = 99; // Invalid - third declaration

    // This block is inside the outer block

  }

}
```

Figure 3-4: Invalid methodWithRedeclarations()

If you declare a variable within a class, and use the same variable name within a method of the class, then the variable used inside the method takes precedence, or **overrides**, the first variable. For example, consider a class that holds Employee information including two integer fields, aNum and aDept, as shown in Figure 3-5.

```
public class Employee

{

  private int aNum = 44;

  private int aDept = 55;

  public void empMethod()

  {

    int aNum = 88;

    // aNum overrides the class variable aNum
```

Figure 3-5: Employee class with an overriding variable

```
      System.out.println("aNum is " + aNum);

      System.out.println("aDept is " + aDept);

   }

   public void anotherEmpMethod()

   {

      System.out.println("aNum is " + aNum);

      System.out.println("aDept is " + aDept);

   }

}
```

Figure 3-5: Employee class with an overriding variable (continued)

Figure 3-5 shows an Employee class with two integers and two void methods. If a program instantiates an Employee object with a statement such as `Employee adminAssistant = new Employee();`, then either empMethod() or anotherEmpMethod() can be called using the adminAssistant object and the dot operator.

When the method call is `adminAssistant.empMethod();`, the output will indicate that aNum is 88 and aDept is 55. The empMethod() will use the local aNum valued at 88, but use the class aDept valued at 55. When the method call is `adminAssistant.anotherEmpMethod();`, the output will show that aNum is 44 and aDept is 55; in both cases, the class variables are used because they have not been overridden within anotherEmpMethod(). When you write programs, it is best to avoid confusing situations that arise when you give the same name to a class variable and a method variable, but if you do use the same name, you need to be aware that the method variable will override the class variable.

Next, you will create a method with several blocks to demonstrate block scope.

To demonstrate block scope:

1 Start your text editor, and then open a new document, if necessary.

2 Type the header for a class named DemoBlock as **public class DemoBlock**. On the next three lines, type the opening curly bracket (**{**), the main() method header as **public static void main(String[] args)**, and main()'s opening curly bracket (**{**).

3 On a new line that is indented one column, declare an integer by typing **int x = 1111;**.

4 On new, indented lines, type the following two println() statements:

```
System.out.println("Demonstrating block scope");
System.out.println("In first block x is " + x);
```

5 Begin a new block by typing an opening curly bracket ({) on the next line. Within the new block, declare another integer by typing `int y = 2222;`. Within this new block, type the following two statements to display the values of *x* and *y*:

```
System.out.println("In second block x is " + x);
System.out.println("In second block y is " + y);
```

6 End the block by typing a closing curly bracket (}). On the next line, begin a new block with an opening curly bracket. Within this new block, declare a new integer with the same name as the integer declared in the previous block by typing `int y = 3333;`.

7 Enter two println() statements, a method call, and two more println() statements, as follows:

```
System.out.println("In third block x is " + x);
System.out.println("In third block y is " + y);
demoMethod();
System.out.println("After method x is " + x);
System.out.println("After method block y is " + y);
```

8 Close this block by typing a closing curly bracket.

9 Type `System.out.println("At the end x is " + x);`, and then type a closing curly bracket. This last statement in the program displays the value of *x*.

10 Finally, enter the following demoMethod() that creates its own *x* and *y*, assigns different values, and then displays them:

```
public static void demoMethod()
{
  int x = 8888, y = 9999;
  System.out.println("In demoMethod x is " + x);
  System.out.println("In demoMethod block y is "
    + y);
}
```

11 Type the final closing curly bracket, and then save the file as **DemoBlock.java** in the Chapter.03 folder on your Student Disk. At the command prompt, compile the file by typing the command `javac DemoBlock.java`. If necessary, correct any errors and compile again.

12 Run the program by typing the command `java DemoBlock`. Your output should look like Figure 3-6.

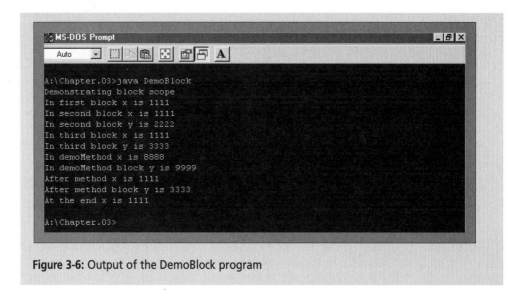

Figure 3-6: Output of the DemoBlock program

It is important to understand the impact that blocks have on your variables. Once you understand the scope of variables, you can locate the source of many errors within your programs more easily.

To gain a more complete understanding of blocks and scope:

1 Change the values of *x* and *y* in the program, and try to predict the exact output before resaving, recompiling, and rerunning the program.

Overloading

Overloading involves using one term to indicate diverse meanings. When you use the English language, you overload words all the time. When you say "open the door," "open your eyes," and "open a computer file," you are talking about three very different actions using very different methods and producing very different results. However, anyone who speaks English fluently has no trouble understanding your meaning because the verb *open* is understood in the context of the noun that follows it.

When you overload a Java method, you write multiple methods with a shared name. The compiler understands your meaning based on the arguments you use with the method. For example, suppose you create a class method to apply a simple interest rate to a bank balance. The method receives two double arguments—the balance and the interest rate—and displays the multiplied result. Figure 3-7 shows the method.

```
public static void simpleInterest(double bal, double rate)

{

  double interest;

  interest = bal * rate;

  System.out.println("Interest on " + bal + " at " +

    rate + " interest rate is " + interest);

}
```

Figure 3-7: The simpleInterest() method with two double arguments

The simpleInterest() method can receive integer arguments even though it is defined as needing double arguments because integers will be promoted or cast automatically to doubles, as you learned in Chapter 1.

When a program calls the simpleInterest() method and passes double values, as in `simpleInterest(1000.00, 0.04)`, the simple interest will be calculated correctly as four percent of 1000.00. Assume, however, that the interest rate passed to the simpleInterest() method comes from inconsistent user input. Some users who want to indicate an interest rate of four percent might type .04, and others might type 4 assuming that they are typing four percent. When the simpleInterest() method is called with the arguments 10000.00 and .04, the interest is calculated correctly as 40.00. When the method is called using 1000.00 and 4, the interest is calculated incorrectly as 4000.00.

Beginning programmers often confuse overloading with overriding. You will learn to override methods in Chapter 6.

A solution to this problem is to overload the simpleInterest() method. **Overloading** involves writing multiple methods with the same name, but with different arguments. For example, in addition to the simpleInterest() method shown in Figure 3-7, you could add the method shown in Figure 3-8.

```
public static void simpleInterest(double bal, int rate)

  // Notice rate type
```

Figure 3-8: The simpleInterest() method with a double and an integer argument

```
{
  double interest, rateAsPercent;
  rateAsPercent = rate/100.0;
    // Converts whole number rate to decimal equivalent
  interest = bal * rateAsPercent;
  System.out.println("Interest on " + bal + " at " +
    rate + " interest rate is " + interest);
}
```

Figure 3-8: The simpleInterest() method with a double and an integer argument (continued)

tip

Note the rateAsPercent figure is calculated by dividing by 100.0, and not by 100. If two integers are divided, the result is a truncated integer; dividing by a double 100.0 causes the result to be a double. Alternatively, you could use a cast.

If the method simpleInterest() is called using two double arguments, as in `simpleInterest(1000.00, .04)`, the first simpleInterest() method shown in Figure 3-7 will execute. However, if an integer is used as the second parameter in the call to simpleInterest(), as in `simpleInterest(1000.00, 4)`, then the method shown in Figure 3-8 will execute and the whole number rate figure will be divided by 100.0 correctly before it is used to determine the interest earned.

Of course, you could use methods with different names to solve the dilemma of producing an accurate simple interest figure—for example, simpleInterestRateUsingDouble() and simpleInterestRateUsingInt(). Using this approach would require that you place a decision within your program to determine which of the two methods to call, but it is more convenient to use one method name and then let the compiler determine which method to use. Also, it is easier to remember one reasonable name for tasks that are functionally identical except for argument types.

tip

You will learn about placing a decision within your program in Chapter 4.

Next, you will overload methods to display event dates for Event Handlers Incorporated. The methods will take one, two, or three integer arguments. If there is one argument, it is the month, and the event is scheduled for the first of the given month in the year 2001. If there are two arguments, they are the month and the day in the year 2000. Three arguments represent the month, day, and year.

tip

In addition to creating your own class to store dates, you can use a built-in Java class to handle dates. You will learn about this class in Section B.

To overload an overloadDate() method to take one, two, or three arguments:

1 Open a new file in your text editor.

2 Create the following DemoOverload class, with three integer variables and three calls to an overloadDate() method:

```
public class DemoOverload
{
  public static void main(String[] args)
  {
    int month = 6, day = 24, year = 2003;
    overloadDate(month);
    overloadDate(month,day);
    overloadDate(month,day,year);
  }
```

3 Create the following overloadDate() method that requires one argument:

```
public static void overloadDate(int mm)
{
  System.out.println("Event date " + mm +
    "/1/2001");
}
```

4 Create the following overloadDate() method that requires two arguments:

```
public static void overloadDate(int mm, int dd)
{
  System.out.println("Event date " + mm + "/" +
    dd + "/2001");
}
```

5 Create the following overloadDate() method that requires three arguments:

```
public static void overloadDate(int mm, int dd, int yy)
{
  System.out.println("Event date " + mm + "/" +
    dd + "/" + yy);
}
```

6 Type the closing curly bracket for the DemoOverload class.

7 Save the file as **DemoOverload.java** in the Chapter.03 folder on your Student Disk.

8 Compile the program, correct any errors, recompile if necessary, and then execute the program. Figure 3-9 shows the output. Notice that whether you call the overloadDate() method using one, two, or three arguments, the date prints correctly because you have successfully overloaded the overloadDate() method.

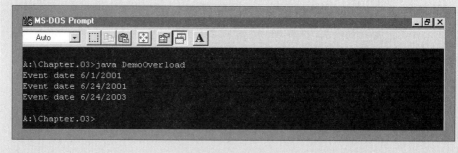

Figure 3-9: Output of the DemoOverload program

Ambiguity

When you overload a method, you run the risk of creating an **ambiguous** situation—one in which the compiler cannot determine which method to use. For example, consider the simple method shown in Figure 3-10.

```
void simpMeth(double d)
{
   System.out.println("Method receives double parameter");
}
```

Figure 3-10: The simpMeth() method with a double argument

If you declare doubleValue as a double variable, and intValue as an int variable, then either method call (`simpMeth(doubleValue);` or `simpMeth(intValue);`) will result in the output "Method receives double parameter". When you call the method with the double argument, the method works as expected. When you call the method with the integer argument, then the integer is cast as (or promoted to) a double, and the method works as well.

Note that if the method with the declaration `void simpMeth(double d)` **did not exist (but the declaration** `void simpMeth(int i)` **did exist), then the method call** `simpMeth(doubleValue);` **would fail. Although an integer can be promoted to a double, a double cannot become an integer. This makes sense if you consider the potential loss of information when a double value is reduced to an integer.**

If you add a second overloaded simpMeth() method within a program that takes an integer parameter (as shown in Figure 3-11), then the output changes when you call `simpMeth(intValue);`. Instead of promoting an integer argument to a double, the compiler recognizes a more exact match for the method call that uses the integer argument, so it calls the version of the method that produces the output "Method receives integer parameter".

```
void simpMeth(int i)

{

   System.out.println("Method receives integer parameter");

}
```

Figure 3-11: The simpMeth() method with an integer argument

A more complicated and potentially ambiguous situation arises when the compiler cannot make a determination as to which of several versions of a method to use. Consider the following overloaded simpleInterest() method declarations:

```
public static void simpleInterest(double bal, double rate)
public static void simpleInterest(double bal, int rate)
   // Notice rate type
```

A call to simpleInterest() with two double arguments executes the first version of the method, and a call to simpleInterest() with a double and an integer argument executes the second version of the method. With each of these calls, the compiler can find an exact match for the arguments you are sending. However, if you call simpleInterest() using two integer arguments, as in simpleInterest(300,6);, an ambiguous situation arises because there is no exact match for the method call. Because two integers can be promoted to two doubles (thus matching the first version of the overloaded method), or just one integer can be promoted to a double (thus matching the second version), the compiler does not know which version of the simpleInterest() method to use and the program will not execute. You could argue that *int, int* is "closer" to *double, int* than it is to *double, double*, but the compiler does not presume to make such decisions for you.

tip

An overloaded method is not ambiguous on its own—it only becomes ambiguous if you create an ambiguous situation. A program with potentially ambiguous methods will run problem-free if you do not make any ambiguous method calls.

It is important to note that you can overload methods correctly by providing different argument lists for methods with the same name. Methods with identical names that have identical argument lists but different return types are not overloaded—they are illegal. For example, int aMethod(int x) and void aMethod(int x) cannot coexist within a program. The compiler determines which of several versions of a method to call based on argument lists. When the method call aMethod(17); is made, the compiler will not know which method to execute because both methods take an integer argument.

Sending Arguments to Constructors

In Chapter 2, you learned that Java automatically provides a constructor method when you create a class. You also learned that you can write your own constructor method, and that you often do so when you want to ensure that fields within classes are initialized to some appropriate default value. Additionally, you can write constructor methods that receive arguments. Such arguments often are used for initialization purposes when the values that you want to assign to objects upon creation might vary.

For example, consider the Employee class with four data fields shown in Figure 3-12. Its constructor method assigns 999 to each potentially instantiated Employee's empNum. Any time an Employee object is created using a statement such as `Employee partTimeWorker = new Employee();`, even if no other data-assigning methods are ever used, you are ensured that the partTimeWorker Employee, like all Employees, will have an initial empNum of 999.

```
public class Employee

{

  private int empNum;

  private double empSalary;

  // Constructor method

  Employee()

  {

    empNum = 999;

  }

  // Other methods go here

}
```

Figure 3-12: Employee class

You can use a setEmpNum() method to assign values to individual Employee objects after construction, but a constructor method assigns the values at the time of creation.

Alternatively, you might choose to create Employees with initial empNums that differ for each Employee. To accomplish this within a constructor, you need to pass an employee number to the constructor. Figure 3-13 shows an Employee constructor that receives an argument. With this constructor, an argument is passed in using a statement such as `Employee partTimeWorker = new Employee(881);`. When the constructor executes, the integer within the method call is passed to Employee() and assigned to the empNum.

```
Employee(int num)

{

  empNum = num;

}
```

Figure 3-13: Employee constructor method with an argument

To demonstrate a constructor with an argument, you will use a new commented version of the EventSite class you created in Chapter 2.

To alter a constructor:

1 Open a new file in your text editor, and then enter the EventSite class shown in Figure 3-14. This file is similar to the EventSite.java text file you created in Chapter 2, but comments have been added for clarity. Save the file as **EventSite.java** in the Chapter.03 folder on your Student Disk.

```
public class EventSite

{

  private int siteNumber;

  private double usageFee;

  private String managerName;

  // Constructor

  EventSite()

  {

    siteNumber = 999;

    managerName = "ZZZ";

  }

  // getManagerName() gets managerName

  public String getManagerName()

  {

    return managerName;

  }
```

Figure 3-14: EventSite.java class

```
// getSiteNumber() gets the siteNumber

public int getSiteNumber()

{

  return siteNumber;

}

// getUsageFee() gets the usageFee

public double getUsageFee()

{

  return usageFee;

}

// setManagerName() assigns a name to the manager

public void setManagerName(String name)

{

  managerName = name;

}

// setSiteNumber() assigns a site number

public void setSiteNumber(int n)

{

  siteNumber = n;

}

// setUsageFee() assigns a value to the usage fee

public void setUsageFee(double amt)

{

  usageFee = amt;

}

}
```

Figure 3-14: EventSite.java class (continued)

2 Modify the existing constructor by typing the following code so that the constructor takes an argument for the site number and then assigns the argument value to the siteNumber field:

```
EventSite(int siteNum)
{
  siteNumber = siteNum;
  managerName = "ZZZ";
}
```

3 Save the file and then compile and correct any errors.

4 Open a new text file to create a short program to demonstrate the constructor at work by typing the following code:

```
public class DemoConstruct
{
  public static void main(String[] args)
  {
    EventSite aSite = new EventSite(678);
    System.out.println("Site number is " +
      aSite.getSiteNumber());
  }
}
```

5 Save this file as **DemoConstruct.java** in the Chapter.03 folder, and then compile and test the program. The site number (678) should be assigned to the aSite object.

Overloading Constructors

If you create a class from which you instantiate objects, Java automatically provides you with a constructor. Unfortunately, if you create your own constructor, the automatically created constructor no longer exists. Therefore, once you create a constructor that takes an argument, you no longer have the option of using the automatic constructor that requires no arguments.

Fortunately, as with any other method, you can overload constructors. Overloading constructors provides you with a way to create objects with or without initial arguments, as needed. For example, in addition to using the constructor method provided shown in Figure 3-14, you can create the second constructor method for the Employee class shown in Figure 3-15. When both constructors reside within the Employee class, you have the option of creating an Employee object either with or without an initial empNum value. When you create an Employee object with `Employee aWorker = new Employee();`, the constructor with no arguments is called and the Employee object receives an initial empNum value of 999. When you create an Employee object with `Employee anotherWorker = new Employee(7677);`, the constructor that requires an integer is used, and the anotherWorker Employee receives an initial empNum of 7677.

```
Employee()

{

  empNum = 999;

}
```

Figure 3-15: Employee constructor method with no argument

Similarly, you could create constructors that require two, three, or more arguments. You can use the arguments to initialize field values, but you also can use arguments for any other purpose. For example, you could use the presence or absence of an argument simply to determine which of two possible constructors to call, yet not make use of the argument within the constructor method. As long as the constructor argument lists differ, there is no ambiguity in which constructor method to call.

Next, you will overload the EventSite constructor to take either no arguments, in which case the site number is 999, or an argument that is the site number.

To overload the EventSite constructor:

1 In your text editor, open the **EventSite.java** text file from the Chapter.03 folder on your Student Disk.

2 Position the cursor at the end of the comment // Constructor, type **s** to make the word *Constructor* plural, and then press the **Enter** key to start a new line.

3 Above the existing constructor that requires an argument, add the new overloaded constructor that requires no argument by typing the following:

```
EventSite()
{
  siteNumber = 999;
  managerName = "ZZZ";
}
```

4 Save the file, compile, and correct any errors.

5 In your text editor, open the **DemoConstruct.java** text file from the Chapter.03 folder on your Student Disk.

6 Position the cursor at the end of the statement EventSite aSite = new EventSite(678);, and then press the **Enter** key to start a new line.

7 Create a new EventSite with no constructor argument by typing **EventSite anotherSite = new EventSite();**.

8 Position the cursor after the println() statement that displays the site number of aSite, `System.out.println("Site number is " + aSite.getSiteNumber());`, and then press the **Enter** key to start a new line. Then type the following statement to print the site number of anotherSite:

```
System.out.println("Another site number is " +
    anotherSite.getSiteNumber());
```

9 Save, compile, and test the program. The two site numbers should print as 678 and 999.

10 Close your text editor.

S U M M A R Y

- A block is the code between a pair of curly brackets. You can nest blocks within other blocks.

- A variable's scope is the portion of a program within which you can reference it. A variable comes into existence, and comes into scope, when you declare it, and it ceases to exist, and goes out of scope, at the end of the block in which it is declared.

- Within a method, you can declare a variable with the same name multiple times as long as each declaration is in its own, nonoverlapping block. Within nested blocks, you cannot declare the same variable name more than once.

- If you declare a variable within a class and use the same variable name within a method of the class, then the variable used inside the method takes precedence, or overrides, the first variable.

- Overloading involves writing multiple methods with the same name but different argument lists. Methods that have identical argument lists but different return types are not overloaded; they are illegal.

- Constructor methods can receive arguments and be overloaded. If you explicitly create a constructor for a class, the automatically created constructor no longer exists.

Q U E S T I O N S

1. The code between a pair of curly brackets in a method is a _____.
   a. function
   b. block
   c. brick
   d. sector

2   When a block exists within another block, the blocks are _____ .
a. structured
b. nested
c. sheltered
d. illegal

3.   The portion of a program within which you can reference a variable is the variable's

_____ .

a. range
b. space
c. domain
d. scope

4.   A variable ceases to exist at the end of the _____ in which it is declared.
a. statement
b. block
c. class
d. program

5.   You can declare a variable with the same name multiple times _____ .
a. within a statement
b. within a block
c. within a method
d. never

6.   You can declare two variables with the same name as long as _____ .
a. they appear within the same block
b. they are assigned different values
c. they are of different types
d. their scopes do not overlap

7.   If you declare a variable within a class and declare and use the same variable name within a method of the class, _____ .
a. the variable used inside the method takes precedence
b. the class variable takes precedence
c. they become the same variable with the same memory address
d. an error will occur

8.   A method variable will _____ a class variable with the same name.
a. acquiesce to
b. destroy
c. override
d. alter

9.   Using a single method name to execute diverse tasks is known as _____ .
a. overriding
b. overexecuting
c. overloading
d. overcompensating

10. Overloaded methods must have the same _____ .
   a. name
   b. number of arguments
   c. argument names
   d. type of argument

11. Overloaded methods cannot have the same _____ .
   a. name
   b. number of arguments
   c. number and type of arguments
   d. return type

12. A situation in which the compiler cannot determine which method to use is said to be _____ .
   a. dubious
   b. suspicious
   c. unreconciled
   d. ambiguous

13. If a method is written to receive a double argument, and you pass an integer to the method, then the method will _____ .
   a. work correctly; the integer will be promoted to a double
   b. work correctly; the integer will remain an integer
   c. execute; but any output will be incorrect
   d. not work; an error message will be issued

14. Methods with the same name that have identical argument lists but different return types are _____ .
   a. legal
   b. overloaded
   c. unstructured
   d. illegal

15. A constructor _____ arguments.
   a. can receive
   b. cannot receive
   c. must receive
   d. can receive a maximum of 10

16. A constructor _____ overloaded.
   a. can be
   b. cannot be
   c. must be
   d. is always automatically

17. If you do not create a constructor for a class, _____ .
   a. you cannot instantiate objects
   b. Java automatically creates one
   c. the class will not compile
   d. the class will simply exist without a constructor

18. If you create one constructor method for a class, and the constructor requires a
double argument, you _____ when you instantiate a member of the class.

    a. must provide an argument

    b. must not provide an argument

    c. can provide any number of arguments

    d. can provide one or no arguments as needed

E X E R C I S E S

1.   a. Create a class named Commission that includes three variables: a double sales figure,
a double commission rate, and an integer commission rate. Create two overloaded
methods named computeCommission(). The first method takes two double arguments representing sales and rate, multiplies them, and then displays the results. The
second method takes two arguments: a double sales figure and an integer commission
rate. This method must divide the commission rate figure by 100.0 before multiplying by the sales figure and displaying the commission. Supply appropriate values for
the variables and write a main() method that tests each overloaded method. Save the
program as Commission.java in the Chapter.03 folder on your Student Disk, and
then compile and test the program.

    b. Add a third overloaded method to the Commission program you created in
Exercise 1a. The third overloaded method takes a single argument representing
sales. When this method is called, the commission rate is assumed to be 7.5 percent
and the results are displayed. To test this method, add an appropriate call in the
Commission program's main() method. Save the program, compile, and test it.

2. Create a class named Pay that includes five double variables that hold hours worked,
rate of pay per hour, withholding rate, gross pay, and net pay. Create three overloaded computeNetPay() methods. Gross pay is computed as hours worked multiplied
by pay per hour. When computeNetPay() receives values for hours, pay rate, and
withholding rate, it computes the gross pay and reduces it by the appropriate withholding amount to produce the net pay. When computeNetPay() receives two arguments, the withholding rate is assumed to be 15 percent. When computeNetPay()
receives one argument, the withholding is assumed to be 15 percent and the hourly
rate is assumed to be 4.65. Write a main() method that tests all three overloaded
methods. Save the program as Pay.java in the Chapter.03 folder on your Student Disk.

3.   a. Create a class named Household that includes data fields for the number of occupants and the annual income, as well as methods named setOccupants(), setIncome(),
getOccupants(), and getIncome() that set and return those values, respectively.
Additionally, create a constructor that requires no arguments and automatically sets
the occupants field to 1 and the income field to 0. Save this file as Household.java in
the Chapter.03 folder on your Student Disk. Create a program named TestHousehold
that demonstrates that each of the methods works correctly. Save the file as
TestHousehold.java in the Chapter.03 folder on your Student Disk.

    b. Create an additional overloaded constructor for the Household class you created in
Exercise 3a. This constructor receives an integer argument and assigns the value to
the occupants field. Add any needed statements to TestHousehold to ensure that
the overloaded constructor works correctly, save it, and then test it.

c. Create a third overloaded constructor for the Household class you created in Exercises 3a and 3b. This constructor receives two arguments, the values of which are assigned to the occupants and income fields, respectively. Alter the TestHousehold program to demonstrate that each version of the constructor works properly. Save the program and then compile and test it.

4. Create a class named Box that includes integer data fields for length, width, and height. Create three constructors that require one, two, and three arguments, respectively. When one argument is used, assign it to length, assign zeros to height and width, and print "Line created". When two arguments are used, assign them to length and width, assign zero to height, and print "Rectangle created". When three arguments are used, assign them to the three variables and print "Box created". Save this file as Box.java in the Chapter.03 folder of your Student Disk. Create a program named TestBox that demonstrates that each of the methods works correctly. Save the test file as TestBox.java in the Chapter.03 folder on your Student Disk.

5. What is the result when you compile and run the following code? Why?

```
class Scope
{
  int scopeInt = 1;
  void scopeDisplay()
  {
    int scopeInt = 10;
    System.out.println("scopeInt = " + scopeInt);
  }
  public static void main(String[] args)
  {
    Scope scopeExercise = new Scope();
    scopeExercise.scopeDisplay();
  }
}
```

6. a. What is the result when you compile and run the following code? Why?

```
class Overload
{
  public static void main(String[] args)
  {
    Overload overloadExercise = new Overload();
    overloadExercise.methodOv();
    overloadExercise.methodOv(6.1, 3);
  }
  void methodOv()
  {
    System.out.println("no arguments");
  }
  void methodOv(double dblArg, int intArg)
  {
    System.out.println("dblArg = " + dblArg +
      "intArg = " + intArg);
  }
}
```

b. What happens when you compile and run the program shown in Exercise 6a if you replace the line `overloadExercise.methodOv(6.1, 3);` with `overloadExercise.methodOv(6, 3);`, and why?

c. What happens if you change the program shown in Exercise 6a as follows, and why?

```
class Overload
{
  public static void main(String[] args)
  {
    Overload overloadExercise = new Overload();
    overloadExercise.methodOv(6.1, 3.2);
  }
  void methodOv(double dblArg, float fltArg)
  {
    System.out.println("dblArg = " + dblArg +
      "fltArg = " + fltArg);
  }
  void methodOv(float fltArg, double dblArg)
  {
    System.out.println("dblArg = " + dblArg +
      "fltArg = " + fltArg);
  }
}
```

d. If the program shown in Exercise 6c results in a compile error, how would you fix the program so it compiles and runs successfully?

SECTION B
objectives

In this section you will learn:

- About the `this` reference
- How to use constants
- How to use prewritten classes and methods that are automatically imported
- How to use prewritten methods that you import

Using Methods

The `this` Reference

When you start creating classes from which objects you will instantiate, the classes can become large very quickly. Besides data fields, each class can have many methods, including several overloaded versions. If you instantiate many objects of a class, the computer memory requirements can become substantial. Fortunately, it is not necessary to store a separate copy of each variable and method for each instantiation of a class.

Usually, you want each instantiation of a class to have its own data fields. If an Employee class contains fields for employee number, name, and salary, every individual Employee object will need its own unique number, name, and salary values. However, when you create a method for the Employee class, any Employee object can use the same method. Whether the method performs a calculation, sets a field value, or constructs an object, the instructions are the same for each instantiated object. Therefore, you store just one copy of a method that all instantiated objects use.

When you use an object method, you use the object name, a dot, and the method name—for example, `aWorker.getEmpNum();`. When you refer to the aWorker.getEmpNum() method, you are referring to the general, shared Employee class getEmpNum() method; aWorker has access to the method because aWorker is a member of the Employee class. However, within the getEmpNum() method, when you access the empNum *field,* you are referring to aWorker's private, individual copy of the empNum field. Because many Employees might exist, but just one copy of the method exists no matter how many Employees there are, when you call `aWorker.getEmpNum();`, the compiler needs to determine *whose* copy of empNum should be returned by the single getEmpNum() method. The compiler accesses the correct object's field because you implicitly pass to the getEmpNum method a reference to aWorker. This reference is called the **this** reference. For example, the two getEmpNum() methods shown in Figure 3-16 perform identically. The first method simply uses the `this` reference without you being aware of it; the second method uses the `this` reference explicitly.

The keyword `this` **is a reserved word in Java.**

••

When you pass a reference, you pass a memory address.

••

```
public void getEmpNum()

{

   return empNum;

}

public void getEmpNum()

{

   return this.empNum;

}
```

Figure 3-16: The getEmpNum() methods with implicit and explicit this references

Usually, you do not want or need to refer to the this reference within the methods you write, but the this reference is always there, working behind the scenes, so the data field for the correct object can be accessed.

••

Recall that methods associated with individual objects are instance methods.

••

In Chapter 2, you learned that most methods you create within a class are nonstatic. Nonstatic methods are methods that you associate with individual objects. You also created static methods. For example, the main() method in a program and the methods main() calls without an object reference are static. These methods do not have a this reference because they have no object associated with them; they are **class methods**.

You can also create class variables. **Class variables** are variables that are shared by every instantiation of a class. For example, you might have a company ID number that is the same for all Employee objects. You can add a static class variable to the class definition, as shown in Figure 3-17. The figure also shows a simple method to display the employee number along with the employee's COMPANY_ID.

```
public class Employee
{
  static private int COMPANY_ID = 12345;
  private int empNum;
  private double empSalary;
  Employee(int num)
  // Constructor requiring employee number
  {
    empNum = num;
  }
  public void showCompanyID()
  {
    System.out.println("Worker " + empNum
      + " has company ID " + COMPANY_ID);
  }
  // Other class methods can go here
}
```

Figure 3-17: Employee class with a static ID number field

No matter how many Employee objects are eventually instantiated, each will refer to the single COMPANY_ID field. For example, if two Employees are created with Employee firstWorker = new Employee(444); and Employee secondWorker = new Employee(777);, when you write the statement firstWorker.showCompanyID(), its output is Worker 444 has COMPANY_ID 12345, and when you write secondWorker.showCompanyID();, the statement's output is Worker 777 has COMPANY_ID 12345. The different workers have individual IDs, but the same company ID.

Additionally, if you change the value of COMPANY_ID in the Employee class, the value changes for all class instantiations. Therefore, besides values such as a company ID, good candidates for static class variables are fields such as a legal minimum wage or a maximum number of hours that an employee is allowed to work in a single week. When such values change for one employee, they change uniformly for all employees.

Working with Constants

In Chapter 1, you learned to create literal constants within a program. A literal constant is a fixed value, such as the literal string "First Java program". A literal constant also can be a number, such as 7 or 5.68, or a character such as *R*. After a program is compiled, these constants are reduced to binary machine language, and they will never change. Variables, on the other hand, *do* change. When you declare int empNum;, you expect that the value stored in empNum will be different at different times or for different employees.

Sometimes, however, a variable or data field should be **constant**; that is, it should not be changed during the execution of a program. The concept of a *constant variable* is somewhat of an oxymoron. For example, the value for a company ID is fixed, so you do not want any methods to alter the company ID value while a program is running. To prevent alteration, insert the keyword final in the company ID declaration so the name COMPANY_ID becomes a **symbolic constant**, which indicates that when you compile any program that uses an object that contains the COMPANY_ID, the field has a final, unalterable value. By convention, constant fields are written using all uppercase letters. The compiler does not require using uppercase identifiers for constants, but using uppercase identifiers helps you distinguish symbolic constants from variables. For readability, you can insert underscores between words in symbolic constants.

Mathematical constants are good candidates for receiving final **status. For example, when PI is defined as** static final double PI = 3.14159;, **it appropriately becomes a constant that should never take on any other value. A fixed sales tax rate** static final double SALES_TAX = 0.075; **remains fixed for every use within a program.**

You can use the keyword final **with methods or classes. When used in this manner,** final **indicates limitations placed on inheritance. You will learn more about inheritance as you become more proficient at object-oriented programming.**

You cannot change the value of a symbolic constant after declaring it; any attempt to do so will result in a compiler error. You must initialize a constant with a value, which makes sense when you consider that a constant cannot be changed later. If a constant does not receive a value upon creation, it can never receive a value at all. Figure 3-18 shows a typical declaration of a constant.

```
public class Employee
{
   static final private int COMPANY_ID = 12345;
   // Rest of class goes here
```

Figure 3-18: Employee class with the symbolic constant COMPANY_ID

A constant always has the same value within a program, so you probably are wondering why you cannot use the actual literal value. For example, why not code `12345` when you need the company ID rather than going to the trouble of creating the COMPANY_ID symbolic constant? There are at least three good reasons to use the symbolic constant rather than the literal one:

- The number 12345 is more easily recognized as the company ID if it is associated with an identifier like COMPANY_ID.
- If the company ID changes, you would change the value of COMPANY_ID at one location within your program—where the constant is defined—rather than searching for every use of 12345 to change it to a different number.
- Even if you are willing to search for every instance of 12345 in a program to change it to a new company ID value, you might inadvertently change the value 12345 that is being used differently for something else, like an employee's employee number or salary.

Next, you will create a class variable to hold the location of the company headquarters for Event Handlers Incorporated. The location of the company headquarters for Event Handlers is an ideal candidate for a class variable. Because the location of the headquarters is the same for every event no matter where the actual event is held, the value for the headquarters should be stored just once, but every EventSite object should have access to the information.

To create a class variable for the EventSite class:

1. In your text editor, open the **EventSite.java** text file from the Chapter.03 folder on your Student Disk. This file defines the EventSite class.

2. Position the cursor after the opening bracket of the class, and then press the **Enter** key to start a new line.

3. Type the class variable `static final public String HEADQUARTERS = "Crystal Lake, IL";`.

> A static variable can be either `public` or `private`. If the variable is `private`, then you must write a method in your program to access it.

4. Save the file and compile.

5. Start a new file in your text editor, and then create the demonstration program named DemoClassVar shown in Figure 3-19. This program shows the headquarters is the same for all EventSites.

```java
public class DemoClassVar
{
  public static void main(String[] args)
  {
    EventSite oneSite = new EventSite();
    EventSite anotherSite = new EventSite();
    oneSite.setSiteNumber(101);
    anotherSite.setSiteNumber(202);
    System.out.print("The number of one site is ");
    System.out.println(oneSite.getSiteNumber());
    System.out.print("Headquarters located at ");
    System.out.println(oneSite.HEADQUARTERS);
    System.out.print("The number of another site is ");
    System.out.println(anotherSite.getSiteNumber());
    System.out.print("Headquarters located at ");
    System.out.println(anotherSite.HEADQUARTERS);
  }
}
```

Figure 3-19: DemoClassVar program

6 Save the file as **DemoClassVar.java** in the Chapter.03 folder. Compile and test the program. Figure 3-20 shows the program's output.

```
A:\Chapter.03>java DemoClassVar
The number of one site is 101
Headquarters located at Crystal Lake, IL
The number of another site is 202
Headquarters located at Crystal Lake, IL

A:\Chapter.03>
```

Figure 3-20: Output of the DemoClassVar program

Using Automatically Imported, Prewritten Constants and Methods

There are many times when you need to create classes from which you will instantiate objects. You can create an Employee class with fields appropriate for describing employees and their functions, and an Inventory class with fields appropriate for whatever type of item it is that you manufacture. There are, however, many classes that a wide variety of programmers need. Rather than having each Java programmer "reinvent the wheel," the creators of Java created nearly 500 classes for you to use in your programs.

You already used several of the prewritten classes without being aware of it. System, Character, Boolean, Byte, Short, Integer, Long, Float, and Double are actually classes from which you can create objects. These classes are stored in a **package**, which is simply a folder that provides a convenient grouping for classes, which is sometimes called a **library of classes**. There are many Java packages containing classes that are available only if you explicitly name them within your program, but the group of classes that contains the previously listed classes is used so frequently that it is available automatically to every program you write. The package that is implicitly imported into every Java program is named java.lang. The classes it contains are the **fundamental classes**, or basic classes, as opposed to the **optional classes** that must be explicitly named.

▶ tip

You will begin to import optional classes explicitly later in this chapter.

The class java.lang.Math contains constants and methods that you can use to perform common mathematical functions. A commonly used constant is PI. Within the Math class, the declaration for PI is `public final static double PI = 3.14159265358979323846;`. Notice that PI is:

- `public`, so any program can access it directly
- `final`, so it cannot be changed
- `static`, so only one copy exists
- `double`, so it holds a large floating-point value

▶ tip

In geometry, PI is an approximation of the value of the ratio of the circumference of a circle to its diameter.

All of the constants and methods in the Math class are `static`, which means they are class variables and class methods.

▶ tip

Another useful constant is E, which represents the base of natural logarithms. Its definition is `public final static double E = 2.7182818284590452354;`.

You can use the value of PI within any program you write by referencing the full package path in which PI is defined—for example `areaOfCircle = java.lang.Math.PI * radius * radius;`. However, the Math class is imported automatically into your programs, so if you simply reference `Math.PI`, Java will recognize this code as a shortcut to the full package path. Therefore, the preferred (and simpler) statement is `areaOfCircle = Math.PI * radius * radius;`.

In addition to constants, there are many useful methods available within the Math class. For example, the Math.max() method returns the larger of two values, and the method Math.abs() returns the absolute value of a number. The statement `largerValue = Math.max(32, 75);` results in largerValue assuming the value 75, and the statement `posVal = Math.abs(-245);` results in posVal assuming the value 245. Figure 3-21 lists some common Math class methods.

Method	Meaning
abs(x)	Absolute value of x
acos(x)	Arccosine of x
asin(x)	Arcsine of x
atan(x)	Arctangent of x
atan2(x,y)	Theta component of the polar coordinate (r,theta) that corresponds to the Cartesian coordinate x,y
ceil(x)	Smallest integral value not less than x (ceiling)
cos(x)	Cosine of x
exp(x)	Exponent, where e is the base of the natural logarithms
floor(x)	Largest integral value not greater than x
log(x)	Natural logarithm of x
max(x,y)	Larger of x and y
min(x,y)	Smaller of x and y
pow(x,y)	x raised to the y power
random()	Random double number between 0.0 and 1.0
rint(x)	Closest integer to x (x is a double, and the return value is expressed as a double)
round(x)	Closest integer to x (where x is a float or double, and the return value is an integer or long)

Figure 3-21: Common Math class methods (continues)

Method	Meaning
sin(x)	Sine of x
sqrt(x)	Square root of x
tan(x)	Tangent of x

Figure 3-21: Common Math class methods (continued)

••

Because all constants and methods in the Math class are classwide, there is no need to create an instance. You cannot instantiate objects of type Math because the constructor for the Math class is private and your programs cannot access the constructor. If you want to prohibit someone from creating an instance of a class you create, you can use the same technique.

••

Unless you are a mathematician, you won't use many of these Math class methods, and it is unwise to do so unless you understand their purposes. For example, because it is illegal to take the square root of a negative number, the method call `imaginaryNumber = Math.sqrt(-12);` causes a compiler error and does not execute.

Next, you will use the Math class to perform some basic calculations.

To write a program that uses some Math class methods:

1 Open a new file in your text editor. Type the DemoMath class header **public class DemoMath**. On a new line, type the opening curly bracket for the class, and then press the **Enter** key.

2 Type the main() method header **public static void main(String[] args)**, press the **Enter** key, and then type the opening curly bracket for the main() method.

3 Create a double variable named val by typing **double val = 26.9;**, and then press the **Enter** key.

4 Type the following statement that displays the value on the screen: **System.out.println("The value is " + val);**.

5 On separate lines, type the following statements to demonstrate the Math class methods:

```
System.out.print("Absolute value of val is ");
System.out.println(Math.abs(val));
System.out.print("Absolute value of -val is ");
System.out.println(Math.abs(-val));
```

```
System.out.print("The square root of val is ");
System.out.println(Math.sqrt(val));
System.out.print("Val rounded is ");
System.out.println(Math.round(val));
```

▶ **tip**

> The expression **-val** means "negative val". The minus sign (-) used in this manner is a unary or single-argument operator. You will learn more about unary operators in Chapter 4.

6   Add closing curly brackets for the main() method and for the class.

7   Save the program as **DemoMath.java** in the Chapter.03 folder on your Student Disk, compile the program, run it, and then compare your results to Figure 3-22.

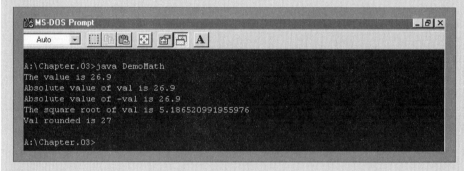

Figure 3-22: Output of the DemoMath program

8   Add additional statements that demonstrate any of the other Math methods that you might use in your programs. Save, compile, and test the program again.

Using Prewritten Imported Methods

Java contains hundreds of classes, only a few of which—such as java.lang—are included automatically in the programs you write. To use any of the other prewritten classes, you must use one of three methods:

- Use the entire path with the class name
- Import the class
- Import the package of which the class you are using is a part

For example, the java.util class package contains useful methods that deal with dates and times. Within this package, a class named Date is defined. You can instantiate an object of type Date from this class by using the full class path, as in `java.util.Date myAnniversary = new java.util.Date();`. Alternatively, you can shorten the declaration of myAnniversary to `Date myAnniversary = new Date();` by including `import java.util.Date;` as the first line in your program. An import statement allows you to abbreviate the lengthy class names by notifying the Java program that when you use *Date*, you mean the java.util.Date class. You must place any import statement you use before any executing statement in your program. That is, you can have a blank line or a comment line—but nothing else—prior to an import statement.

Notice that the import statement ends with a semicolon.

Date is not a reserved word; it is a class you are importing. If you do not want to import the java utility's Date class, you are free to write your own Date class.

An alternative to importing a class is to import an entire package of classes. You can use the asterisk (*) as a **wildcard symbol** to represent all the classes in a package. Therefore, the import statement `import java.util.*;` imports the Date class and any other java.util classes as well. There is no disadvantage to importing the extra classes, and you will most commonly see the wildcard method in professionally written Java programs.

You cannot use the Java language wildcard exactly like a DOS or UNIX wildcard because you cannot import all the Java classes with `import java.*;`. **The wildcard works only with specific packages such as** `import java.util.*;` **or** `import java.lang.*;`.

The import statement does not move the entire imported class or package into your program as its name implies. Rather, it simply notifies the program that you will be using the data and method names that are part of the imported class or package.

The Date class has several constructors. For example, if you construct a Date object with five integer arguments, they become the year, month, day, hour, and minutes. A Date object constructed with three integer arguments assumes the arguments to be the year, month, and day, and the time is set to midnight. The constructor that takes no argument assigns the current moment to a Date object. The current moment is the number of milliseconds that have elapsed since midnight, January 1, 1970. Therefore, the statement `Date myAnniversary = new Date();` assigns a value that is a very large 12- or 13-digit number to the myAnniversary variable. You can retrieve this number with a method named getTime(). The statement `System.out.println("Milliseconds since 1/1/70 are " + myAnniversary.getTime();` results in the output `Milliseconds since 1/1/70 are 1003122000000` when the program is run at midnight on October 15, 2001.

tip

••

If you set the hours in a Date object, a 24-hour clock is assumed—for example, 13 is 1 P.M.

••

Although it is interesting, the number of milliseconds elapsed since 1970 is not a useful piece of information for most people. Fortunately, the Date class contains a variety of other useful methods such as setMonth(), getMonth(), setDay(), getDay(), setYear(), and getYear(), which supply more useful information. The program shown in Figure 3-23 shows the values of two dates being set and retrieved.

```java
import java.util.*;
public class DemoDate
{
  public static void main(String[] args)
  {
    Date toDay = new Date();
    Date birthDay = new Date(82,6,14);
    System.out.println(toDay);
    System.out.print("Current month is ");
    System.out.println(toDay.getMonth());
    System.out.print("Current day is ");
    System.out.println(toDay.getDate());
    System.out.print("Current year is ");
    System.out.println(toDay.getYear());
    System.out.print("Birth month is ");
    System.out.println( birthDay.getMonth());
    System.out.print("Birth day is ");
    System.out.println(birthDay.getDate());
    System.out.print("Birth year is ");
    System.out.println(birthDay.getYear());
  }
}
```

Figure 3-23: DemoDate program

You can perform arithmetic using dates. For example, if toDay is declared to hold today's date with `Date toDay = new Date();`, then you can use the following code to find out when a bank certificate that matures in 180 days will fall due by adding 180 to the day part of the Date object:

```
toDay.setDate(toDay.getDate() + 180);
System.out.println("In 180 days it will be " + toDay);
```

tip

The compiler will interpret an incorrect date, such as March 32, as being April 1. This makes many calculations with dates easier. For example, if you bill a customer on August 30 and allow 10 days for payment, you can add 10 to the billing day, and the compiler will understand August 40 to be September 9.

tip

For information about time, including how leap years and leap seconds are calculated, go to the U.S. Naval Observatory Web site at http://tycho.usno.navy.mil.

Any year that you use with these Date class methods is a value that is 1900 less than the actual year. For example, 82 means 1982 and 105 means 2005. The month is a value from 0 through 11; January is 0, February is 1, and so on. This is a minor annoyance that makes date calculations easier; you must be aware of it when analyzing the meaning of a date.

Next, you will use the Date class by declaring some Date variables and keeping track of the length of time it takes for the program to run.

To write a program that uses the Date class:

1 Open a new file in your text editor.

2 For the first line in the file, type **import java.util.*;**, and then press the **Enter** key and indent the line two spaces.

3 Begin a DemoDate class with the header **public class DemoDate**. Press the **Enter** key, type the opening curly bracket for the class, and then press the **Enter** key again.

4 On the new line, indent two more spaces and then type the following main() class header: **public static void main(String[] args)**. On a new line, enter the opening curly bracket for the main() method, and then press the **Enter** key.

5 Declare a variable named startTime and assign it the current time by typing **Date startTime = new Date();**.

6 Declare another variable to hold the day your Java programming class began—for example, **Date classStart = new Date(100,7,25);** (where 100,7,25 in this example is August 25, 2000). Don't forget that the current year is 1900 less than the actual year and that the months are numbered 0 through 11.

7 Display the current date and the class start date by typing the following:

```
System.out.println("The current date is " + startTime);
System.out.println("The class started on " + classStart);
```

8 Save the file as **DemoDate.java** in the Chapter.03 folder on your Student Disk.

Now enter a statement to print the time it takes to run this program. You will create a new endTime object that will hold the current date and time of its creation. Depending on the speed of the computer processor you are using, this time should be a few hundred milliseconds later than it was when the program started. The calculation involves using the getTime() method for the endTime and startTime objects and displaying the difference between the two values.

To use the getTime() method:

1 Press the **Enter** key and then type the following code to include the getTime() method:

```
Date endTime = new Date();
System.out.print("Time elapsed is ");
System.out.print(endTime.getTime() -
  startTime.getTime());
System.out.println(" milliseconds");
```

2 Add the closing curly bracket for the main() method as well as the closing curly bracket for the program.

3 Save the program and then compile and test the program.

help

When you compile the DemoDate.java program, you might receive the following error from the compiler: DemoDate.java uses or overrides a deprecated API. Recompile with "-deprecation" for details. 1 warning. This warning indicates that your program compiled successfully. A **deprecated API** simply indicates that your program uses something that has been improved in subsequent versions of Java.

4 Add some extra println() statements to the program and save, compile, and run the program again. Does the program take longer to execute?

 # S U M M A R Y

- You store just one copy of a method for use with each object. You store separate copies of data fields for each object.

- The compiler accesses the correct object's data fields because you implicitly pass a `this` reference to class methods. Static methods do not have a `this` reference because they have no object associated with them. Static methods also are called class methods.

- Static class variables are those variables that are shared by every instantiation of a class.

- After a program is compiled, literal constants never change.

- The values stored in symbolic constants never change. You create a symbolic constant by inserting the keyword `final` before a variable name. By convention, constant fields are written using all uppercase letters. A constant must be initialized with a value.

- Java contains nearly 500 prewritten classes.

- Classes are stored in a package, which is simply a folder that provides a convenient grouping for classes.

- The package that is implicitly imported into every Java program is named java.lang. The classes it contains are the fundamental classes, as opposed to the optional classes that must be explicitly named.

- The class java.lang.Math contains constants and methods that can be used to perform common mathematical functions. All of the constants and methods in the Math class are static, which means that they are class variables and class methods. Common useful Math class methods include those used for finding an absolute value, taking a square root, and rounding.

- To use a prewritten class other than java.lang, you must use the entire path with the class name, import the class, or import the package that contains the class.

- An import statement allows you to abbreviate the lengthy class names by notifying the Java program that when you use class names you are referring to those within the imported class. Any import statement you use must be placed before any executing statement in your program.

- An alternative to importing a class is to import an entire package of classes. To do so, you can use the asterisk (*) as a wildcard symbol to represent all the classes in a package.

- The Date class has several constructors: one that takes no argument and assigns the current moment to a Date object, and others that take the date, or the date and time.

- The current moment is the number of milliseconds that have elapsed since midnight, January 1, 1970. You can retrieve this number with a method named getTime().

- The Date class contains a variety of other useful methods such as setMonth(), getMonth(), setDay(), getDay(), setYear(), and getYear(), which supply more useful information.

- You can perform arithmetic using Date class objects.

Q U E S T I O N S

1. Usually, you want each instantiation of a class to have its own copy of _____ .
   a. the data fields
   b. the class methods
   c. both of these
   d. none of these

2. If you create a class and instantiate two objects, you usually store _____ for use with the objects.
   a. one copy of each method
   b. two copies of the same method
   c. two different methods
   d. data only, not methods,

3. When you create multiple class objects and use a class method, the compiler accesses the correct object's data because you _____ .
   a. explicitly pass the object
   b. explicitly pass a copy of the object
   c. explicitly pass a reference to the object
   d. implicitly pass a reference to the object

4. The this reference _____ .
   a. can be used implicitly
   b. must be used implicitly
   c. must not be used implicitly
   d. must not be used

5. The this reference specifies which _____ you are referencing.
   a. method
   b. object
   c. class
   d. program

6. Methods that you associate with individual objects are _____ .
   a. `private`
   b. `public`
   c. `static`
   d. `nonstatic`

7. Static methods are also called _____ methods.
   a. `this`
   b. `private`
   c. `class`
   d. `nonreferenced`

8. Static methods do not have a _____ .
   a. return type
   b. argument list
   c. header
   d. `this` reference

9. Variables that are shared by every instantiation of a class are _____ .
   a. class variables
   b. `private` variables
   c. `public` variables
   d. illegal

10. The word closest in meaning to *static* as used by the Java programming language is _____ .
   a. *hidden*
   b. *difficult*
   c. *single*
   d. *multiple*

11. If you change the value of a static variable in a class, it is changed for _____ .
   a. only new objects instantiated after the change
   b. only objects already in existence before the change
   c. all objects of the class
   d. no objects of the class

12. The keyword `final` in a variable declaration indicates _____ .
   a. the end of the program
   b. a static field
   c. a symbolic constant
   d. that no more variables will be declared in the program

13. A symbolic constant _____ .
   a. must be initialized
   b. cannot be changed during program execution
   c. both of these
   d. none of these

14. Java classes are stored in a folder or _____ .
   a. packet
   b. package
   c. bundle
   d. gaggle

15. The classes in java.lang _____ into every program you write.
   a. are implicitly imported
   b. are implicitly copied
   c. must be explicitly imported
   d. must not be explicitly imported

16. Which of the following statements determines the square root of `number` and assigns it to the variable `s`?
   a. `s = sqrt(number);`
   b. `s = Math.sqrt(number);`
   c. `number = sqrt(s);`
   d. `number = Math.sqrt(s);`

17. To use any of the prewritten classes besides those in the java.lang package, you must _____ .
   a. use the entire path with the class name
   b. import the class
   c. import the package of which the class you are using is a part
   d. use any of these methods

18. The wildcard symbol used with the import statement is the _____ .
   a. ampersand
   b. plus sign
   c. exclamation point
   d. asterisk

19. The date constructed with `Date oneDay = new Date(103,1,2);` is _____ .
   a. January 1, 2003
   b. January 2, 2003
   c. February 1, 2003
   d. February 2, 2003

20. The date stored in a Date object is stored in _____ .
   a. milliseconds
   b. seconds
   c. minutes
   d. years

E X E R C I S E S

1. Create a class named Shirt with data fields for collar size and sleeve length. Include a constructor method that takes arguments for each field. Also include a String class variable named material and initialize it to "cotton". Write a program named TestShirt to instantiate three Shirt objects with different collar sizes and sleeve lengths, and then display all the data, including material, for each shirt. Save both the Shirt.java and TestShirt.java programs in the Chapter.03 folder of your Student Disk.

2. Create a class named CheckingAccount with data fields for an account number and a balance. Include a constructor method that takes arguments for each field. Include a double class variable that holds a value for the minimum balance required before a monthly fee is applied to the account, and set the minimum balance to 200.00. Write a program named TestAccount in which you instantiate two CheckingAccount objects and display the account number, balance, and minimum balance without fee for both accounts. Save each file in the Chapter.03 folder on your Student Disk.

3. Write a Java program to determine the answers for each of the following:
   a. The square root of 30
   b. The sine and cosine of 100
   c. The value of the floor, ceiling, and round of 44.7
   d. The larger and the smaller of the character *K* and the integer 70

4. Write a program to calculate how many milliseconds it is from today until the first day of summer (assume that this date is next June 21).

5. Write a program to calculate how many days it is from today until the end of the current year.

6. What is the result when you compile and run the following code, and why?

```java
public class MathEx6
{
  public static void main(String[] args)
  {
    System.out.println(Math.round(1.49));
    System.out.println(Math.round(1.50));
    System.out.println(Math.round(-1.49));
    System.out.println(Math.round(-1.50));
  }
}
```

7. What is the result when you compile and run the following code, and why?

```
public class MathEx7
{
  public static void main(String[] args)
  {
    System.out.println(Math.ceil(1.49));
    System.out.println(Math.ceil(1.50));
    System.out.println(Math.ceil(-1.49));
    System.out.println(Math.ceil(-1.50));
  }
}
```

8. What is the result when you compile and run the following code, and why?

```
public class MathEx8
{
  public static void main(String[] args)
  {
    System.out.println(Math.floor(1.49));
    System.out.println(Math.floor(1.50));
    System.out.println(Math.floor(-1.49));
    System.out.println(Math.floor(-1.50));
  }
}
```

9. Modify the Employee class shown in Figure 3-17 by changing the class name to EmployeeWithDate. Then change the showCompanyID() method so it shows the current date in addition to the employee number and company ID. Save the file as EmployeeWithDate.java in the Chapter.03 folder on your Student Disk. Then write a program that creates and displays two or more EmployeeWithDate objects. Save this new program as UseEmployeeWithDate.java in the Chapter.03 folder on your Student Disk.

10. Each of the following files in the Chapter.03 folder on your Student Disk has syntax and/or logical errors. In each case, determine the problem and fix the program. After you correct the errors, save each file using the same filename preceded with *Fix*—for example, save DebugThree1.java as FixDebugThree1.java.
    a. DebugThree1.java
    b. DebugThree2.java
    c. DebugThree3.java
    d. DebugThree4.java

CHAPTER 4

Input, Selection, and Repetition

case ▶ "Why are you frowning?" asks Lynn Greenbrier, your mentor at Event Handlers Incorporated.

"It's fun writing programs," you tell her, "but I don't think my programs can do much yet. When I use programs written by other people, I'm allowed to respond to questions and make choices. In addition, other people's programs keep running for a while—the programs I write finish as soon as they start."

"You're disappointed because the programs you've written so far simply carry out a sequence of steps," Lynn says. "You need to make your programs interactive by accepting user input. Then you need to learn about the two powerful structures—decision making and looping."

Previewing the ChooseManager Program Using the Event Class

To preview the ChooseManager program using the Event class:

1 In your text editor, open the **Chap4Event.java** file from the Chapter.04 folder on your Student Disk and examine the code. This file contains a class definition for a class that stores information about events that Event Handlers Incorporated will handle. You will create a similar class file in this chapter.

2 At the command line, compile the Chap4Event.java file using the command `javac Chap4Event.java`.

3 Open the **Chap4ChooseManager.java** file from the Chapter.04 folder on your Student Disk and examine the code. This file contains a program that will demonstrate prompting the user for input and creating objects based on the input.

4 At the command line, compile the Chap4ChooseManager.java file using the command `javac Chap4ChooseManager.java`.

5 Execute the program by typing the command `java Chap4ChooseManager`. At the prompt to enter C, P, or N, ignore the directions and enter an *invalid* letter. Do this as many times as you like—the program will prompt you again until you enter a valid letter. Then enter C, P, or N to see the name of the manager and the minimum charge assigned to your event. You will create a similar program in this chapter.

In this section you will learn:

- How to accept keyboard input
- About the decision structure
- How to use an `if` statement
- How to use an `if...else` statement
- How to use compound statements in an `if` or `if...else` structure
- How to nest `if` statements

Input and Decision Making

Simple Keyboard Input

In Chapters 1 through 3 of this text, you wrote programs that created objects, performed mathematical calculations, and produced output. A shortcoming of these programs is that you must know the values with which you want to work at the time you write the program. It would be far more useful to provide a program with values at **run time**, that is, while the program is executing. A program that accepts values at run time is **interactive** because it exchanges communications, or interacts with the user. Providing values during the execution of a program requires input, and the simplest form of input to use is keyboard entry from the program's user.

You already have used the System class and its out object and println() method to produce output. A similar object is in. The in object has access to a method named read() that retrieves data from the keyboard. Figure 4-1 shows a program that accepts simple user input.

```
public class DemoInput
{
  public static void main(String[] args)  throws Exception
  {
    char userInput;
    System.out.println("Please enter a character ");
    userInput = (char)System.in.read();
    System.out.println("You entered " + userInput);
  }
}
```

Figure 4-1: DemoInput program

The DemoInput class shown in Figure 4-1 has just one method—a main() method. At the end of the line containing the main() method header is the phrase `throws Exception`. The main() methods you have written that use `System.out.println();` have not required this phrase, but programs you write using `System.in.read();` do. An **exception** is an error situation. Because errors should be infrequent, they are the "exception to the rule." When a program user provides input, all sorts of error situations can arise. For example, the keyboard might be disconnected or the user might enter the wrong type of data. As you become a better Java programmer, you will learn to handle these exceptional situations by writing code to take appropriate action, such as issuing detailed messages that explain the problem to the user. For now, however, you can let the compiler handle the problem by **throwing the exception,** or passing the error to the operating system. The code `throws Exception` after the main() header accomplishes this; a program that reads keyboard input will not compile without this phrase.

You write `Exception` with an uppercase *E* because it is a class name. Classes, by convention, begin with uppercase letters.

In Figure 4-1, a character named userInput is declared inside the main() method of the DemoInput program. The string "Please enter a character " prints on the screen. A message requesting user input commonly is called a **prompt** because it prompts or coaches the user to enter an appropriate response.

You are not required to supply a prompt every time there is user input, but you almost always will want to do so. Unless you supply a prompt, your user will see a blank screen and have little idea of how to proceed.

The statement userInput = `(char)System.in.read();` in the DemoInput program accomplishes three separate tasks:

■ The method call `System.in.read();` gets the input from the keyboard. The read() method accepts a byte and returns an integer.
■ The cast `(char)` converts the returned integer into a character.
■ The assignment userInput = assigns the converted character to the variable userInput.

At first, it might not seem to make sense that `System.in.read();` returns an integer value. However, there are two reasons that Java's creators chose to have `System.in.read();` behave in this way:

■ To the computer, all values are actually integers because computers store input (as well as everything else) as a series of 0s and 1s. The character *A*, for example, is stored in Unicode as 0000 0000 0100 0001, which also can be expressed as '\u0041' or decimal 65.

■ The System.in.read() method needs to return a value to indicate that no input is available. For example, when you use System.in.read() to read records from a disk file, at some point the compiler reaches the end of the file and no more input is available. Java's creators decided that the System.in.read() method should return the value -1 when the compiler reaches the end of a file. To accomplish this, the read() method must have a return type of int.

See Section B of Chapter 1 for more information about Unicode.

The final statement in the DemoInput program shown in Figure 4-1, `System.out.println("You entered " + userInput);`, **echoes**, or repeats, the userInput character. When you write interactive programs, it is often a good idea to echo the input so the user can visually confirm that the correct data was input.

When you run the DemoInput program, the prompt appears on the screen. The program will not proceed any further until you type a character and press the Enter key. The read() method accepts precisely one byte of input. Therefore, you cannot enter a floating-point number or a string of characters.

Next, you will write a simple program that accepts three bytes of user input and echoes them.

To write a program that accepts and echoes user input:

1 Start your text editor and then open a new text file.

2 Type the following class header for a UsersInitials class: **public class UsersInitials**. Press the **Enter** key, type the opening curly bracket for the class, and then press the **Enter** key again.

3 Type the following header for the main() method: **public static void main(String[] args) throws Exception**. Press the **Enter** key, type the opening curly bracket for the main() method, and then press the **Enter** key again.

4 Type the following declarations for three character variables: **char firstInit, middleInit, lastInit;**.

5 On new lines, prompt the user for three initials by typing the following:

```
System.out.println("Please enter your three initials.");
System.out.println
  ("Do not use periods between initials.");
System.out.println("Press Enter when you're done.");
```

The instruction "Do not use periods between initials." is important because you will write the program to accept only three characters from the keyboard. If a user enters *A.B.C.*, then six characters were entered—three letters and three periods. The first letter would become firstInit, the first period would become secondInit, and the second letter would become thirdInit. There would be no room to store the second period, the third letter, or the last period.

tip

6 On new lines, type the following code to read each of the three initials into the appropriate variables:

```
firstInit = (char)System.in.read();
middleInit = (char)System.in.read();
lastInit = (char)System.in.read();
```

7 On a new line, type the following code to write the statements that will echo the three initials to the screen:

```
System.out.println("Your initials are " + firstInit +
    middleInit + lastInit);
```

8 On new lines, type the two closing curly brackets that respectively close the main() method and the UsersInitials class.

9 Save the file as **UsersInitials.java** in the Chapter.04 folder on your Student Disk, and then compile and run the program. When you are prompted for three initials, enter any three characters and confirm that they are echoed to the screen correctly. Your output should look like Figure 4-2.

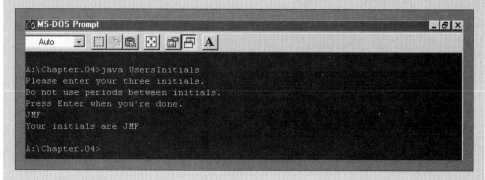

Figure 4-2: Output of the UsersInitials program

The UsersInitials program works correctly as long as the user follows directions and enters three initials and presses the Enter key only *once* after typing all three initials. However, just as the user cannot type periods between initials, a problem also arises if the user presses the Enter key after typing each initial, as you will see next.

To demonstrate that the user should not press the Enter key after typing each initial:

1 Run the UsersInitials program again at the command prompt. When you see the prompt to enter your initials, type an initial and then press the **Enter** key. The program will terminate before you can type the second initial. The output will display only one initial, as shown in Figure 4-3.

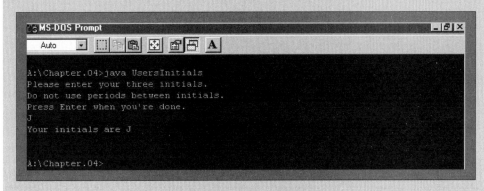

```
A:\Chapter.04>java UsersInitials
Please enter your three initials.
Do not use periods between initials.
Press Enter when you're done.
J
Your initials are J

A:\Chapter.04>
```

Figure 4-3: Output of the UsersInitials program after the user presses the Enter key between initials

The problem occurs because when you use read() to accept a character from the keyboard, every key you press—including the Enter key—is accepted, one at a time. When you type your first initial, it is correctly stored in the firstInit variable. When you press the Enter key after entering the first initial, the value for the Enter key is stored in two bytes—the middleInit and the lastInit variables. When all three variables display on the screen, you see the first initial and the cursor on a new line below the initial. The cursor advances a line because the middleInit and lastInit together hold the Enter key value.

 tip

The values for the two bytes occupied by the Enter key are '\u000D' and '\u000A', or decimal 13 and 10. When you store the Enter key, you do not need to be concerned with these values any more than you need be concerned that the letter *E* is stored as '\u0046'. It is important to know, however, that every character is stored using a code.

Currently, you can deal with this input problem by being very specific in your instructions to the user and insisting that the user type all three initials before pressing the Enter key. Alternatively, you can ask the user for one initial at a time, and take care of the Enter key yourself. You can absorb the extra Enter key after each initial by reading it in with two read() method calls, and then not storing the bytes anywhere, as you will see next.

▶ tip

Depending on the version of JDK you are using, you might require only one extra read()
statement to absorb the Enter key. For now, use one or two read() statements so all
programs work correctly with your compiler. After you learn to loop, you will learn a
more elegant, compiler-independent method to eliminate the Enter key problem.

To eliminate the Enter key problem in the UsersInitials program:

1 In the UsersInitials.java text file, delete the following three lines of code that
prompt the user for initials:

```
System.out.println("Please enter your three initials.");
System.out.println
  ("Do not use periods between initials.");
System.out.println("Press Enter when you're done.");
```

2 Replace the deleted lines with the following single statement:
`System.out.print("Enter your first initial and press
Enter. ");`.

3 Position the cursor at the end of the read() statement that reads the firstInit
variable, and then press the **Enter** key to start a new line. Then type the following statements to read in the two Enter key bytes without storing them:
`System.in.read(); System.in.read();`.

4 Press the **Enter** key, and then type the following prompt for the second initial
on the new line: `System.out.print("Enter your second initial
and press Enter. ");`.

5 Position the cursor at the end of the statement that reads the middleInit
variable, and then press the **Enter** key to start a new line. Then type the following statements to read the Enter key pressed after the second initial, and
to prompt for the third initial:

```
System.in.read(); System.in.read();
System.out.print
  ("Enter your third initial and press Enter. ");
```

▶ tip

You might choose to place a final `System.in.read(); System.in.read();` statement
after the statement that reads the third initial in order to discard its Enter key. Because
the program doesn't accept any more input after reading the third initial, these extra
read() statements will not affect program execution. However, if you add extra read()
statements to absorb the last Enter, the Enter key following the third initial already will
be discarded if you decide to add additional input steps to this program later.

6 Save, compile, and run the program. Respond to each prompt by typing
your initial and then pressing the **Enter** key. Your output should display
your three initials correctly.

Drawing Flowcharts

When computer programmers write programs, they seldom simply sit down at a keyboard and begin typing. Programmers must plan the complex portions of programs using paper and pencil tools. Programmers often use pseudocode or flowcharts to help them plan a program's logic. Using **pseudocode** requires you to write down the steps required to accomplish a given task. You write pseudocode in English; you concentrate on the logic required, and not the syntax used in any programming language. As a matter of fact, a task you pseudocode does not have to be a computerized task. If you have ever written a list of things you must accomplish during a day (1. Wash car, 2. Study for test, 3. Buy birthday gift for Mom), then you have written pseudocode. A **flowchart** is similar to pseudocode, but you write the steps you need in diagram form, as a series of shapes connected by arrows.

Some programmers use a wide variety of shapes to represent different tasks in their flowcharts, but you can draw simple flowcharts that express very complex situations using just rectangles and diamonds. You use a rectangle to represent any unconditional step, and a diamond to represent any decision. For example, Figure 4-4 shows a flowchart of a day's tasks.

Figure 4-4: Flowchart of a day's tasks

Sometimes your days don't consist of a series of unconditional tasks—some of the tasks may or may not occur based on decisions you make. Flowchart creators place decisions within diamond shapes and draw paths to alternative courses of action emanating from sides of the diamonds. Figure 4-5 shows a flowchart of a day's tasks in which some of the tasks are based on decisions.

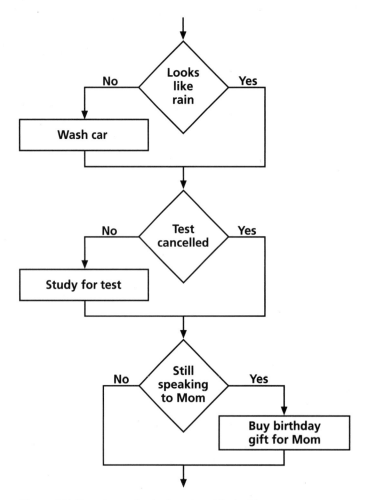

Figure 4-5: Flowchart of a day's tasks with decisions

Making Decisions with the `if` Structure

You already can write a program that produces different output based on input; for example, a user who types *JFK* into the UsersInitials program receives different output than a user who types *FDR*. Additionally, after you learn to write programs that can accept input, you gain a powerful new capability—you are able to alter the events that occur within a program based on user input. Now you can make decisions.

Making a **decision** involves choosing between two alternative courses of action based on some value within a program. For example, the program that produces your paycheck can make decisions about the proper amount to withhold for taxes, the program that guides a missile can alter its course, and a program that monitors your blood pressure during surgery can determine when to sound an alarm. Making decisions is what makes computer programs seem "smart."

The value upon which a decision is made is always a boolean value, which is always one of two values—true or false. Figure 4-6 shows the logic of the decision structure.

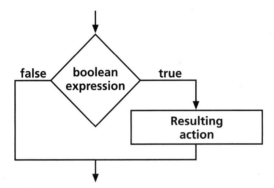

Figure 4-6: Decision structure

One statement you can use to make a decision is the **if statement**. For example, you can store a value in an integer variable named someVariable, and then print the value of someVariable when the user wants to see it. As you can see in Figure 4-7, you can prompt the user to enter *Y* or *N* (for "Yes" or "No") and store the response in a character variable.

```
char userResponse;

int someVariable = 512;

System.out.println

    ("Do you want to see the value of someVariable?");

System.out.println("Enter Y for yes or N for no");

char userResponse = (char)System.in.read();
```

Figure 4-7: Storing a user's response

You can use the entered character as part of a boolean expression that will be evaluated as true or false. Figure 4-8 shows the six comparison operators that result in boolean values, as you learned in Chapter 1.

Operator	Description	true Example	false Example
<	Less than	3 < 8	8 < 3
>	Greater than	4 > 2	2 > 4
==	Equal to	7 == 7	3 == 9
<=	Less than or equal to	5 <= 5	8 <= 6
>=	Greater than or equal to	7 >= 3	1 >= 2
!=	Not equal to	5 != 6	3 != 3

Figure 4-8: Comparison operators

The double equals sign (==) is used to determine equality; the following is the `if` statement that makes the decision to print:

```
if(userResponse == 'Y')
  System.out.println
    ("The value of someVariable is " + someVariable);
```

tip

Remember that you reference character values using single quotation marks.

If the userResponse variable holds the value 'Y', then the boolean value of the expression `userResponse == 'Y'` is `true` and the subsequent println() statement will execute. If the value of the expression `userResponse == 'Y'` is `false`, then the println() statement will not execute. The `userResponse == 'Y'` expression will be `false` if userResponse holds anything other than 'Y', including 'y', 'N', 'n', 'A', or any other value.

The boolean expression `(userResponse == 'Y')` must appear within parentheses. You are not required to leave a space between the keyword `if` and the opening parentheses, but if you do, the statement is easier to read and is less likely to be confused with a method call. There is no semicolon at the end of the first line of the `if` statement `if(userResponse == 'Y')` because the statement does not end there. The statement ends after the println() call, so that is where you type the semicolon. You also could type the same statement on one line and execute it in the same manner. However, the two-line format is more conventional and easier to read, so you usually will type `if` and the boolean expression on one line, press the Enter key, and then indent a few spaces before coding the action that will occur if the boolean expression evaluates as `true`. Be careful, though—when you use the two-line format, do not type a semicolon at the end of the first line, as in the following example:

```
if(userResponse == 'Y');
// Notice the incorrect semicolon here
   System.out.println("The value of someVariable is "
     + someVariable);
```

When this `if` expression is evaluated, the statement ends if it evaluates as `true`. Whether the expression evaluates as `true` or `false`, execution continues with the next independent statement that prints someVariable. In this case, the `if` statement accomplishes nothing.

Another very common programming error occurs when a programmer uses a single equals sign rather than the double equals sign when attempting to determine equivalency. The expression `userResponse = 'Y'` does not compare userResponse to 'Y'. Instead, it attempts to assign the value 'Y' to the userResponse variable. When the expression is part of an `if` statement, this assignment is illegal. The confusion arises in part because the single equals sign is used within boolean expressions in `if` statements in many other programming languages such as COBOL, Pascal, and BASIC. Adding to the confusion, Java programmers use the word *equals* when speaking of equivalencies. For example, you might say, "If userResponse equals 'Y'..." rather than "If userResponse is equivalent to 'Y'..."

An alternative to using a boolean expression, such as `userResponse == 'Y'`, is to store the boolean expression's value in a boolean variable. For example, if userSaidYes is a boolean variable, then `userSaidYes = (userResponse == 'Y');` compares userResponse to 'Y' and stores `true` or `false` in userSaidYes. Then you can write the `if` as `if(userSaidYes)`... This adds an extra step to the program, but makes the `if` statement more similar to an English statement.

The `if...else` Structure

Consider the following statement:

```
if(userResponse == 'Y')
   System.out.println("The value of someVariable is "
     + someVariable);
```

Such a statement is sometimes called a **single-alternative if** because you only perform an action based on one alternative, which is the case when userResponse is 'Y'. Often, you require two options for the next course of action, or a **dual-alternative if**. For example, if the user does not respond 'Y' to a prompt, you might want to print a message that at least acknowledges that the response was received. The **if...else statement** provides the mechanism to perform one action when a boolean expression evaluates as `true` and performs a different action when a boolean expression evaluates as `false`. Figure 4-9 shows the logic for the `if...else` structure. Figure 4-10 shows an example `if...else` structure coded in Java. In Figure 4-10, the value of someVariable is printed when userResponse is equivalent to 'Y'. When userResponse is any other value, the program prints the message "Too bad.".

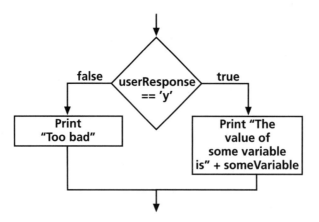

Figure 4-9: The if...else structure

```
if(userResponse == 'Y')

  System.out.println("The value of someVariable is "

    + someVariable);

else

  System.out.println("Too bad.");
```

Figure 4-10: Dual-alternative if

When you execute the code shown in Figure 4-10, only one of the println() statements will execute; the one that executes depends upon the evaluation of (userResponse == 'Y'). Each println() statement is a complete statement, so each statement ends with a semicolon.

Next, start writing a program for Event Handlers Incorporated that determines which of several employees will be assigned to manage a client's scheduled event. To begin, you will prompt the user to answer a question about the event type, and then the program will display the name of the manager who handles such events. There are two event types: corporate events are handled by Dustin Britt, and private events are handled by Carmen Lindsey.

To write a program that chooses between two managers:

1 Open a new text file, and then enter the following code to choose a manager:

```
public class ChooseManager
{
    public static void main(String[] args) throws Exception
    {
```

2 On a new line, declare a variable that will hold the type of event by typing `char eventType;`.

3 On a new line, type the following three-line prompt that explains what is expected of the user:

```
System.out.println
    ("Enter type of event you are scheduling");
System.out.println("C for a corporate event");
System.out.println("P for a private event");
```

4 On a new line, type the following statement that reads in the type of event: `eventType = (char)System.in.read();`.

5 On a new line, type the following print() statement that explains the output: `System.out.print("The manager for this event will be ");`.

6 Code the following `if...else` structure to determine which of two managers will be assigned to the event.

```
if(eventType == 'C')
    System.out.println("Dustin Britt");
else
    System.out.println("Carmen Lindsey");
```

7 Type the two closing curly brackets to end the main() method and the ChooseManager class.

8 Save the program as **ChooseManager.java** in the Chapter.04 folder on your Student Disk, and then compile and run the program. Confirm that the program selects the correct manager when you choose *C* for a corporate event or *P* for a private event.

Compound Statements

Often there is more than one action to take following the evaluation of a boolean expression within an `if` statement. For example, you might want to print several separate lines of output or perform several mathematical calculations. To execute more than one statement that depends on the evaluation of a boolean expression, you use a pair of curly brackets to place the dependent statements within a block.

For example, the program segment shown in Figure 4-11 determines whether an employee has worked more than 40 hours in a single week, and if so, the program computes regular and overtime salary and prints the results.

```
if(hoursWorked > 40)

{

  regularPay = 40 * rate;

  overTimePay = (hours - 40) * 1.5 * rate;

    // Time and a half for hours over 40

  System.out.println("Regular pay is " + regularPay);

  System.out.println("Overtime pay is " + overTimePay);

} // The if structure ends here
```

Figure 4-11: An `if` statement with multiple dependent statements

tip

••

When you create a block, you do not have to place multiple statements within it. It is perfectly legal to block a single statement.

••

If you compare Figures 4-11 and 4-12, you will see that in Figure 4-11, the regularPay calculation, the overTimePay calculation, and the println() statement are executed only when hours > 40 is true. In Figure 4-12, the curly brackets are omitted. Within this program, when hours > 40 is true, regularPay is calculated and the `if` expression ends. The next three statements that compute overTimePay and print the results always execute every time the program runs, no matter what value is stored in hours. These last three statements are *not* dependent on the `if` statement; they are independent, stand-alone statements. The indentation might be deceiving; it looks as though four statements depend on the `if` statement, but it is not indentation that causes statements following an `if` statement to be dependent. Rather, curly brackets are required if the four statements must be treated as a block.

```
if(hoursWorked > 40)

  regularPay = 40 * rate;  // The if structure ends here

  overTimePay = (hours - 40) * 1.5 * rate;

  System.out.println("Regular pay is " + regularPay);

  System.out.println("Overtime pay is " + overTimePay);
```

Figure 4-12: An `if` statement with a single dependent statement

The code shown in Figure 4-12 might not compile if regularPay was not assigned a value—the compiler will recognize that you are attempting to print the value of regularPay without calculating it. However, if you have assigned a value to regularPay, you can compile the program but the output still will not be what you intended. Within the code segment shown in Figure 4-12, if hoursWorked is greater than 40, then the program properly calculates both regular and overtime pay. Because `hoursWorked > 40` is `true`, the `regularPay` calculation is made. The overTimePay calculation and the println() statements will execute as well because they are just statements that always execute and do not depend on the `if` statement.

However, in Figure 4-12, if the hoursWorked value is 40 or less—30, for example—then the regularPay calculation will not execute (it executes only `if(hours > 40)`), but the next three independent statements will execute. The variable regularPay will hold whatever value you have previously assigned to it—0.0, for example—and the program will calculate the value of overTimePay as a negative number (because 30 - 40 results in -10). Therefore, the output will be incorrect.

Just as you can block statements to depend on an `if`, you also can block statements to depend on an `else`. Figure 4-13 shows an `if` structure with two dependent statements and an `else` with two dependent statements. The program executes the final two println() statements without regard to the hoursWorked variable's value; the println() statements are not part of the `if` structure.

```
if(hoursWorked > 40)

{

  regularPay = 40 * rate;

  overTimePay = (hours - 40) * 1.5 * rate;

  // Time and a half for hours over 40

}

else

{

  regularPay = hours * rate;

  overTimePay = 0.0;

}

System.out.println("Regular pay is " + regularPay);

System.out.println("Overtime pay is " + overTimePay);
```

Figure 4-13: An `if...else` statement with multiple dependent statements

Next, you will create an Event class. Each Event object includes two data fields: the type of event and the base price Event Handlers charges per hour for the event type. The Event class also contains a constructor method and get methods for the two fields. Later, you will construct different objects based on `if` statements.

To create the Event class:

1 Open a new text file, and then type the following class header for a class named Event: **public class Event**. Press the **Enter** key, and then type the opening curly bracket for the class on the new line.

2 On a new line, type the following declarations for two data fields to hold the type of event and the minimum hourly rate that Event Handlers charges:

```
private char eventType;
private double eventMinRate;
```

3 On a new line, type the following constructor for the Event class. The constructor will require two arguments with which you will fill the two data fields.

```
public Event(char event, double rate)
{
   eventType = event;
   eventMinRate = rate;
}
```

4 On new lines, type the following two get methods that return the field values:

```
public char getEventType()
{
   return eventType;
}
public double getEventMinRate()
{
   return eventMinRate;
}
```

5 Type the closing curly bracket for the class.

6 Save the file as **Event.java** in the Chapter.04 folder on your Student Disk, and then compile the file and correct any errors.

Now that you have created an Event class, you can modify the ChooseManager program to perform multiple tasks based on user input. Not only will you display a message to indicate which manager is assigned to the event, but you also will instantiate a unique Event object, with different minimum rates to charge based on the type of event.

To modify the ChooseManager program:

1   Open the **ChooseManager.java** text file from the Chapter.04 folder. You will declare two constants to hold the corporate hourly rate and the private hourly rate. If these hourly rates change in the future, they will be easy to locate at the top of the file, where you can change their values.

2   Position the cursor just after the opening curly bracket for the ChooseManager class, press the **Enter** key to start a new line, and then type the following two constants:

```
static final double CORP_RATE = 75.99;
static final double PRI_RATE = 47.99;
```

Within the main() method of the ChooseManager class, you will define an Event object named anEvent. You do not want to construct the Event object until you discover whether it will be a corporate or private event; you simply want to declare it now.

3   Position the cursor to the right of the statement that declares the eventType character variable, press the **Enter** key to start a new line, and then type the event declaration as **Event anEvent;**.

4   Next, type the following lines to modify the `if...else` structure that currently prints a manager's name so that the `if` and `else` are each controlling a block of two statements. The first statement in each block still prints the manager's name. The second statement constructs an appropriate Event object.

```
if(eventType == 'C')
{
  System.out.println("Dustin Britt");
  anEvent = new Event(eventType, CORP_RATE);
}
else
{
  System.out.println("Carmen Lindsey");
  anEvent = new Event(eventType, PRI_RATE);
}
```

5   To confirm that the event was constructed properly, type the following two println() statements immediately after the closing bracket for the `if...else` structure:

```
System.out.println("Event type is " +
  anEvent.getEventType());
System.out.println("Minimum rate charged is $" +
  anEvent.getEventMinRate());
```

6   Save the program. Compile and run the program several times with different input at the prompt. Confirm that the output shows that the event has the correct manager, type, and rate based on how you respond to the prompt (with C or P).

Nested `if` and Nested `if...else`

Within an `if` or an `else` statement, you can code as many dependent statements as you need, including other `if` and `else` statements. Just as spoons are nested inside each other in a drawer, such statements with an `if` inside another `if` commonly are called **nested `if` statements**. Nested `if` statements are particularly useful when two conditions must be met before some action is taken.

For example, suppose you want to pay a $50 bonus to a salesperson only if the salesperson sells more than three items that total more than $1,000 in value during a specified time. Figure 4-14 shows the logic for this situation. Figure 4-15 shows the code to solve the problem.

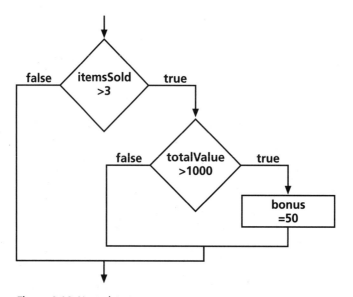

Figure 4-14: Nested `if` structure

```
if(itemsSold > 3)

  if(totalValue > 1000)

    bonus = 50;
```

Figure 4-15: Nested `if` statements

Notice there are no semicolons in the code shown in Figure 4-15 until after the `bonus = 50;` statement. The expression `itemsSold > 3` is evaluated. If this expression is `true`, then the program evaluates the second boolean expression (`totalValue > 1000`). If that expression is also `true`, then the bonus assignment executes and the `if` structure ends.

S U M M A R Y

- An interactive program accepts values at run time.

- The System.in.read() method accepts input from the keyboard.

- An exception is an error situation. You can let the compiler handle the problem by throwing the exception, or you can pass the error to the operating system.

- A message that requests user input commonly is called a prompt.

- The method System.in.read() accepts a byte from the keyboard and returns an integer value.

- When you write interactive programs, it often is a good idea to echo the input so the user can confirm visually that the data entered is correct.

- Every key typed at the keyboard must be accounted for—even the Enter key.

- Making a decision involves choosing between two alternative courses of action based on some value within a program.

- You can use the `if` statement to make a decision based on a boolean expression that evaluates as `true` or `false`. If the boolean expression enclosed in parentheses within an `if` statement is `true`, then the subsequent statement or block will execute.

- An `if` statement ends with a semicolon.

- A single-alternative `if` performs an action based on one alternative; a dual-alternative `if`, or `if...else`, provides the mechanism for performing one action when a boolean expression evaluates as `true`. When a boolean expression evaluates as `false`, a different action occurs.

- To execute more than one statement that depends on the evaluation of a boolean expression, you use a pair of curly brackets to place the dependent statements within a block.

- Within an `if` or an `else` statement, you can code as many dependent statements as you need, including other `if` and `else` statements. Nested `if` statements are particularly useful when two conditions must be met before some action occurs.

Q U E S T I O N S

1. A program that accepts values at run time is _____.
   a. compiled
   b. interactive
   c. reciprocal
   d. object-oriented

2. The in object is a member of the _____ class.
   a. Read
   b. IO
   c. System
   d. IN

3. An error situation is an _____.
   a. exclusion
   b. anomaly
   c. exemption
   d. exception

4. A program that uses System.in.read() requires the phrase _____ after the method hea
   that contains the read() method.
   a. `import io`
   b. `throws Exception`
   c. `include System`
   d. `in.read() included`

5. A message that requests user input commonly is called a _____.
   a. coach
   b. prompt
   c. hint
   d. port

6. The read() method's return type is _____.
   a. integer
   b. character
   c. double
   d. byte

7. The process of repeating input characters is called a(n) _____.
   a. prompt
   b. rehash
   c. echo
   d. iteration

8. When you use read() to accept characters from the keyboard, _____.
   a. only alphabetic letters are accepted
   b. only letters and numbers are accepted
   c. only printable characters are accepted
   d. any character, including an Enter, can be accepted

9. A decision is based on a(n) —————— value.
   a. boolean
   b. absolute
   c. definitive
   d. convoluted

10. The value of (4 > 7) is —————— .
    a. 4
    b. 7
    c. `true`
    d. `false`

11. The value of 3 != 13 is —————— .
    a. 3
    b. 13
    c. `true`
    d. `false`

12. Assuming the variable q has been assigned the value 3, which of the following statements prints XXX?
    a. `if(q != 3) System.out.println("XXX");`
    b. `if(q=3) System.out.println("XXX");`
    c. Both of these statements print XXX.
    d. Neither of these statements prints XXX.

13. Assuming the variable q has been assigned the value 3, which of the following statements prints XXX?
    a. `if(q > 0) System.out.println("XXX");`
    b. `if(q > 7); System.out.println("XXX");`
    c. Both of these statements print XXX.
    d. Neither of these statements prints XXX.

14. Assuming the variable r has been assigned the value 8, which of the following statements prints ZZZ?
    a. `if(r > 1) System.out.println("YYY");`
       `else System.out.println("ZZZ");`
    b. `if(r < 1) System.out.println("YYY");`
       `else System.out.println("ZZZ");`
    c. `if(r != 1) System.out.println("YYY");`
       `else System.out.println("ZZZ");`
    d. All of these statements print ZZZ.

15. What is the output of the following code segment?

```
s = 20;
if(s > 30)
   System.out.println("AAA");
   System.out.println("BBB");
```

    a. AAA
    b. BBB
    c. AAA BBB
    d. Nothing

16. What is the output of the following code segment?

```
t = 10;
if(t > 7)
{
  System.out.println("AAA");
  System.out.println("BBB");
}
```

a. **AAA**

b. **BBB**

c. **AAA BBB**

d. Nothing

17. When you code an `if` statement within another `if` statement, as in `if(a > b) if(c > d) x = 0;`, then the `if` statements are _____.

a. notched

b. nestled

c. nested

d. sheltered

18. When you code an `if` statement within another `if` statement, as in `if(a > b) if(c > d) x = 0;`, then _____.

a. both `a > b` and `c > d` must be `true` for *x* to be set to 0

b. either `a > b` or `c > d` must be `true` for *x* to be set to 0

c. both `a > b` and `c > d` must be `false` for *x* to be set to 0

d. under no conditions will *x* be set to 0

E X E R C I S E S

In the following exercises, save each program that you create in the Chapter.04 folder on your Student Disk.

1. a. Write a program that prompts the user for a four-character password, accepts four characters, and then echoes the characters to the screen. The class name is Password.

b. Write a program that prompts the user for a four-character password, accepts four characters, and then echoes the characters to the screen. Test the first character. If it is *B*, issue a message that the password is valid; otherwise issue a message that the password is not valid. The class name is Password2.

c. Write a program that prompts the user for a four-character password, accepts four characters, and then echoes the characters to the screen. Test all four characters. If the characters spell *B O L T*, then issue a message that the password is valid; otherwise issue a message that the password is not valid. The class name is Password3.

2. a. Write a program for a furniture company. Ask the user to choose *P* for pine, *O* for oak, or *M* for mahogany. Show the price of a table manufactured with the chosen wood. Pine tables cost $100, oak tables cost $225, and mahogany tables cost $310. The class name is Furniture.

b. Add a prompt to the program you wrote in Exercise 2a to ask the user to specify a large (*L*) or a small (*S*) table. Add $35 to the price of any large table. The class name is FurnitureSizes.

3. Write a program for a college's admissions office. Create variables to store a student's numeric high school grade point average (for example, 3.2) and an admission test score. Print the message "Accept" if the student has any of the following:

- A grade point average of 3.0 or above and an admission test score of at least 60
- A grade point average below 3.0 and an admission test score of at least 80

If the student does not meet either of the qualification criteria, print "Reject". The class name is Admission.

4. Write a program that stores an hourly pay rate and hours worked. Compute gross pay (hours times rate), withholding tax, and net pay (gross pay minus withholding tax). Withholding tax is computed as a percentage of gross pay based on the following:

Gross Pay	Withholding Percentage
Up to and including 300.00	10
300.01 and up	12

The class name is Payroll.

5. a. Write a program that stores two integers and allows the user to enter a character. If the character is *A*, add the two integers. If it is *S*, subtract the second integer from the first; if it is *M*, multiply the integers. Display the results of the arithmetic. The class name is Calculate.

b. Modify the Calculate program so the user also can enter a *D* for divide. If the second number is zero, then display an error message; otherwise divide the first number by the second and display the results. Name the modified class Calculate2.

6. a. Write a program for a lawn mowing service. The lawn mowing season lasts 20 weeks. The weekly fee for mowing a lot under 400 square feet is $25. The fee for a lot 400 square feet or more but under 600 square feet is $35 per week. The fee for a lot 600 square feet or over is $50 per week. Store the values in the length and width variables and then print the weekly mowing fee, as well as the seasonal fee. The class name is Lawn.

b. To the Lawn program created in 6a, add a prompt that asks the user whether the customer wants to pay A) once, B) twice, or C) 20 times per year. If the user enters *A* for once, the fee for the season is simply the seasonal total. If the customer requests two payments, each payment is half the seasonal fee plus a $5 service charge. If the user requests 20 separate payments, add a $3 service charge per week. Print the payment amount. The class name is Lawn2.

7. a. Write a program named Balance.java that compares your checking account balance with your savings account balance (two doubles). Assign values to both variables and compare them, and then display either "Checking is higher" or "Checking is not higher".

b. Change the Balance.java program so that it compares your checking account balance and your savings account balance to less than zero. If both statements are `true`, then display the message "Both accounts in the red". If the first balance is less than the second balance, and the first balance is greater than or equal to zero, then display the message "Both accounts in the black".

8. Modify the following Employee class so that the constructor requires the user to enter the employee number from the keyboard. The employee number should be three digits. When you are finished, compile the class as Employee.java. Write a program named InteractiveEmployee that instantiates an Employee object and uses the showCompanyID() method. Compile and test this program.

```java
public class Employee
{
   static private int COMPANY_ID = 12345;
   private int empNum;
   private double empSalary;
   Employee(int num)
   // Constructor requiring employee number
   {
      empNum = num;
   }
   public void showCompanyID()
   {
      System.out.println("Worker " + empNum
         + " has company ID " + COMPANY_ID;
   }
}
```

SECTION B

objectives

In this section you will learn:

- **How to use AND and OR operators**
- **How to use the `switch` statement**
- **How to use the conditional operator**
- **How to use the NOT operator**
- **More about operator precedence**

Special Operators, the `switch` Statement, and Precedence

AND and OR Operators

For an alternative to nested `if` statements, you can use the **AND operator** within a boolean expression to determine whether two expressions are both `true`. The AND operator is written as two ampersands (&&). For example, the code shown in Figure 4-16 works exactly the same as the code shown in Figure 4-15. The itemsSold variable is tested, and if it is greater than 3, then the totalValue is tested. If totalValue is greater than 1000, then the bonus is set to 50.

```
if(itemsSold > 3 && totalValue > 1000)
  bonus = 50;
```

Figure 4-16: Using the AND operator

You are never required to use the AND operator because using nested `if` statements always achieves the same result, but using the AND operator often makes your code more concise, less error-prone, and easier to understand.

It is important to note that when you use the AND operator, you must include a complete boolean expression on each side of the && operator. If you want to set a bonus to $400 if a saleAmount is both over 1000 and under 5000, the correct statement is `if(saleAmount > 1000 && saleAmount < 5000) bonus = 400;`. Even though the saleAmount variable is used on both sides of the AND expression, the statement `if(saleAmount > 1000 && < 5000)...` is incorrect and will not compile.

With the AND operator, both boolean expressions must be `true` before the action in the statement can occur. You can use the **OR operator,** which is written as ||, when you want some action to occur even if only one of two conditions is `true`. For example, if you want to give a bonus of $200 if a salesperson satisfies at least one of two conditions—selling more than 100 items or selling any number of items that total more than $3000 in value—then you can write the code using either one of the ways shown in Figure 4-17. Figure 4-18 shows the program logic.

tip

A common use of the OR operator is to decide to take action whether a character variable is uppercase or lowercase, as in `if(selection == 'A' || selection == 'a')` ... The subsequent action occurs whether the selection variable holds an uppercase or lowercase A.

```
// Using two ifs
if(itemsSold > 100)
   bonus = 200;
else if(totalValue > 3000)
   bonus = 200;
// Using the OR operator
if(itemsSold > 100 || totalValue > 3000)
   bonus = 200;
```

Figure 4-17: OR code using two `if` statements and the OR operator

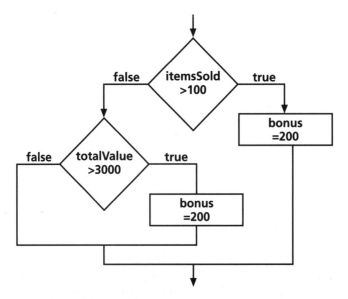

Figure 4-18: Diagram of OR logic

Sometimes situations arise in which there are more than two possible courses of action to take. Consider a situation in which salespeople can receive one of three possible commission rates based on their sales. For example, a sale totaling $1001 or more earns the salesperson an eight percent commission, a sale totaling $500 to $1000 earns six percent of the sale amount, and any sale totaling $499 or less earns five percent. Using three separate `if` statements to test single boolean expressions results in some incorrect commissions. Examine the code shown in Figure 4-19.

```
if(saleAmount > 1000)

   commRate = .08;

if(saleAmount > 500)

   commRate = .06;

if(saleAmount <= 500)

   commRate = .05;

System.out.println("Commission rate is " + commRate);
```

Figure 4-19: Incorrect assignment of three commissions

tip

> As long as you are dealing with whole dollar amounts, the expression `if(saleAmount > 1000)` can be expressed just as well as `if(saleAmount >= 1001)`. Additionally, `if(1000 < saleAmount)` and `if(1001 <= saleAmount)` have the same meaning. Use whichever has clearest meaning for you.

Using the code shown in Figure 4-19, if a saleAmount is $5000, the first `if` statement executes. The boolean expression `saleAmount > 1000` evaluates as `true` and .08 is correctly assigned to commRate. However, when a saleAmount is $5000, the next `if` expression (`saleAmount > 500`) also evaluates as `true`, so the commRate, which was .08, is incorrectly reset to .06.

A partial solution to this problem is to use an `else` following the `if(saleAmount >= 1000)` expression, as shown in Figure 4-20.

```
if(saleAmount > 1000)

   commRate = .08;

else if(saleAmount > 500)   // Notice the else

   commRate = .06;

if(saleAmount <= 500)

   commRate = .05;

System.out.println("Commission rate is " + commRate);
```

Figure 4-20: Inefficient assignment of three commissions

▶ tip

••

You can place and indent the if following an else, but a program with many nested if...else combinations soon grows very long and "deep," and with indentations, later statements in the nest would move farther and farther to the right on the page. For easier-to-read code, Java programmers commonly place each else and its subsequent if on the same line.

••

With the new code in Figure 4-20, when the saleAmount is $5000, the expression saleAmount > 1000 is true and the commRate becomes .08. When the commRate is not greater than $1000, the else statement executes and correctly sets the commRate to .06.

The code shown in Figure 4-20 works correctly, but it is somewhat inefficient. When the saleAmount is any amount over $500, either the first if sets commRate to .08 for amounts over $500, or its else sets commRate to .06 for amounts over $500. The boolean value tested in the next statement, if(saleAmount <= 500), is always false. Rather than unconditionally asking if(saleAmount <= 500), it's easier to use an else. If the saleAmount is not over 1000 and it is also not over 500, it must, by default, be less than or equal to 500. Figure 4-21 shows this improved logic and Figure 4-22 shows its code.

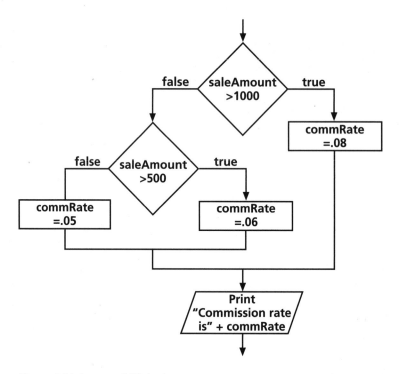

Figure 4-21: Improved OR logic

tip

```
if(saleAmount >= 1000)

  commRate = .08;

else if(saleAmount > 500)

  commRate = .06;

else commRate = .05;

System.out.println("Commission rate is " + commRate);
```

Figure 4-22: Correct assignment of three commissions

Currently, the ChooseManager program identifies an event as a corporate event and assigns an appropriate manager and rate when the user enters *C* at the event-type prompt. When the user enters any other character, the event is considered to be private. Next you will improve the ChooseManager program so that if the user does not enter either *C* or *P*, an Event object with an "invalid" X-type is instantiated.

To improve the ChooseManager program:

1 If necessary, start your text editor and open the **ChooseManager.java** file from the Chapter.04 folder on your Student Disk.

2 Change the ChooseManager.java text file as follows to change the `if...else` structure that tests the eventType so that it becomes a nested `if...else` with three possibilities. When the user inputs anything other than C or P, display an error message and create an Event object with a code 'X' for the eventType and a rate of 0.0 for the minEventRate:

 tip

```
if(eventType == 'C')
{
  System.out.println("Dustin Britt");
  anEvent = new Event(eventType, CORP_RATE);
}
```

```
    else if(eventType == 'P')
    {
      System.out.println("Carmen Lindsey");
      anEvent = new Event(eventType, PRI_RATE);
    }
    else
    {
      System.out.println("Invalid entry!");
      anEvent = new Event('X',0.0);
    }
```

3 Save the program, compile it, and then run the program several times to confirm that user responses of *C* or *P* result in valid Event objects, and that other responses result in an error message and an event of type *X*.

The switch Statement

By nesting a series of if and else statements, you can choose from any number of alternatives. For example, suppose you want to print a student's class year based on a stored number. Figure 4-23 shows the program.

```
if(year == 1)

  System.out.println("Freshman");

else if(year == 2)

  System.out.println("Sophomore");

else if(year == 3)

  System.out.println("Junior");

else if(year == 4)

  System.out.println("Senior");

else System.out.println("Invalid year");
```

Figure 4-23: Multiple alternatives

An alternative to the series of nested if statements is to use the **switch statement**. The switch statement is useful when you need to test a single variable against a series of exact integer or character values. The switch structure uses four new keywords:

- The keyword switch starts the structure and is followed immediately by a test expression enclosed in parentheses.
- The keyword case is followed by one of the possible values for the test expression and a colon.

- The keyword `break` optionally terminates a `switch` structure at the end of each `case`.
- The keyword `default` optionally is used prior to any action that should occur if the test variable does not match any `case`.

tip

You are not required to list the case values in ascending order as shown here. It is most efficient to list the most common case first, instead of the case with the lowest value.

For example, Figure 4-24 shows the `case` structure used to print the four school years.

```
switch(year)

{

  case 1:

    System.out.println("Freshman");

    break;

  case 2:

    System.out.println("Sophomore");

    break;

  case 3:

    System.out.println("Junior");

    break;

  case 4:

    System.out.println("Senior");

    break;

  default:

    System.out.println("Invalid year");

}
```

Figure 4-24: Sample case structure

The `switch` structure shown in Figure 4-24 begins by evaluating the year variable shown in the `switch` statement. If the year is equal to the first `case` value, which is 1, then the statement that prints "Freshman" will execute. The `break` statement bypasses the rest of the `switch` structure, and execution continues with any statement after the closing curly bracket of the `switch` structure.

If the year variable is not equivalent to the first `case` value of 1, then the next `case` value is compared, and so on. If the year variable does not contain the same value as any of the `case` statements, then the `default` statement or statements execute.

You can leave out the `break` statements in a `switch` structure. However, when you omit the `break`, if the program finds a match for the test variable, then all the statements within the `switch` statement from that point forward will execute. For example, if you omit each `break` statement in the code shown in Figure 4-24, when year is 3, the first two cases will be bypassed, but "Junior", "Senior", and "Invalid year" all will print. You should omit the `break` statements intentionally if you want all subsequent cases to execute once the test variable is matched.

You are never required to use a `switch` structure; you can always achieve the same results with nested `if` statements. The `switch` structure is simply a convenience that you can use when there are several alternative courses of action depending on a single integer or character variable. Additionally, it makes sense to use `switch` only when there are a reasonable number of specific matching values to be tested. For example, if every sale amount from 1 to 500 requires a five percent commission, it is not reasonable to test every possible dollar amount using the following code:

```
switch(saleAmount)
{
  case 1:
    commRate = .05;
    break;
  case 2:
    commRate = .05;
    break;
  case 3:
    commRate = .05;
    break;
  // ...and so on for several hundred more cases
```

With 500 different dollar values resulting in the same commission, one test— `if(saleAmount <= 500)`—is far more reasonable than listing 500 separate cases.

Next, you will modify the ChooseManager program to account for a new type of event. Besides corporate and private, there will be special rates for non-profit organizations. The entered code for non-profit events will be *N*, and Robin Armanetti will be the manager assigned to these events. You will convert your nested `if` statements to a `switch` structure.

To convert the ChooseManager decision-making process to a `switch` structure:

1 In the **ChooseManager.java** file, position the cursor at the end of the statement that declares the constant for PRI_RATE, press the **Enter** key to start a new line, and then type the following constant for NON_PROF_RATE:
`static final double NON_PROF_RATE = 40.99;`.

2 To the list of current prompts, add the following prompt to tell the user to enter *N* for non-profit organization events:

```
System.out.println("N for non-profit event");
```

3 Delete the if...else statements that presently are used to determine whether the user entered *C* or *P*, and then replace them with the following switch structure:

```
switch(eventType)
{
  case 'C':
    System.out.println("Dustin Britt");
    anEvent = new Event(eventType, CORP_RATE);
    break;
  case 'P':
    System.out.println("Carmen Lindsey");
    anEvent = new Event(eventType, PRI_RATE);
    break;
  case 'N':
    System.out.println("Robin Armanetti");
    anEvent = new Event(eventType, NON_PROF_RATE);
    break;
  default:
    System.out.println("Invalid entry!");
    anEvent = new Event('X',0.0);
}
```

Remember from Chapter 1 that characters are actually stored as integers. That is why they are allowed as the case variables in a switch statement.

4 Save, compile, and test the program. Make sure the correct output appears when you enter *C*, *P*, *N*, or some other value as keyboard input.

The Conditional Operator

Java provides one more way to make decisions. The **conditional operator** requires three expressions separated with a question mark and a colon, and it is used as an abbreviated version of the if...else structure. As with the switch structure, you never are required to use the conditional operator; it is simply a convenient shortcut. The syntax of the conditional operator is testExpression ? true Result : false Result;.

The first expression, testExpression, is a boolean expression that is evaluated as true or false. If it is true, then the entire conditional expression takes on the value of the expression following the question mark (trueResult). If the value of the testExpression is `false`, then the entire expression takes on the value of falseResult. For example, `biggerNum = (a > b) ? a : b;` evaluates the expression `a > b`. If a is greater than b, then the entire conditional expression takes the value of a, which then is assigned to biggerNum. If a is not greater than b, then the expression assumes the value of b, and b is assigned to biggerNum.

The NOT Operator

You use the **NOT operator**, which is written as the exclamation point (!), to negate the result of any boolean expression. Any expression that evaluates as `true` becomes `false` when preceded by the NOT operator, and any `false` expression preceded by the NOT operator becomes `true`.

For example, suppose a monthly car insurance premium is $200 if the driver is age 25 or younger, and $125 if the driver is age 26 or older. Each of the following `if` statements (which have been placed on single lines for convenience) correctly assigns the premium values:

```
if(age <= 25)   premium = 200;    else premium = 125;
if(!(age <= 25)) premium = 125;    else premium = 200;
if(age >= 26) premium = 125;    else premium = 200;
if(!(age >= 26)) premium = 200;    else premium = 125;
```

The statements with the NOT operator are somewhat harder to read, particularly because they require the double set of parentheses, but the result of the decision-making process is the same in each case. Using the NOT operator is clearer when the value of a boolean variable is tested. For example, a variable initialized as `boolean oldEnough = (age >= 25);` can become part of the relatively easy-to-read expression `if(!oldEnough)...`

Precedence

You learned in Chapter 1 that operations have higher and lower precedences. For example, within an arithmetic expression, multiplication and division are always performed prior to addition or subtraction. Figure 4-25 shows the precedence of the operators you have used.

Precedence	Operator(s)	Symbol(s)
Highest	Multiplication, division	* / %
	Addition, subtraction	+ -
	Relational	> < >= <=

Figure 4-25: Operator precedence for operators used so far (continues)

Precedence	Operator(s)	Symbol(s)
	Equality	== !=
	Logical AND	&&
	Logical OR	‖
	Conditional	?:
Lowest	Assignment	=

Figure 4-25: Operator precedence for operators used so far (continued)

In general, the order of precedence agrees with common algebraic usage. For example, in any mathematical expression such as x = a + b, the arithmetic is done first and the assignment is done last, as you would expect. The relationship of && and ‖ might not be as obvious. Consider the program segment shown in Figure 4-26 and try to predict its output.

```
int tickets = 4;

int age = 40;

char gender = 'F';

if(tickets > 3 || age < 25 && gender == 'M')

   System.out.println("Do not insure");

if((tickets > 3 || age < 25) && gender == 'M')

   System.out.println("Bad risk");
```

Figure 4-26: Demonstrating && and ‖ precedence

With the first if statement, the && takes precedence over the ‖, so age < 25 && gender == 'M' is evaluated first. The value is false because age is not less than 25 and gender is not 'M'. So the expression is reduced to "tickets > 3 or false." Because the value of the tickets variable is greater than 3, the entire expression is true, and "Do not insure" is printed.

tip

Even though the && is evaluated first in the expression age < 25 && gender == 'M' ‖ tickets > 3, **there is no harm in adding extra parentheses as in** (age < 25 && gender == 'M') ‖ tickets > 3. **The outcome is the same, but the intent is clearer to someone reading your code.**

In the second if statement shown in Figure 4-26, parentheses have been added so the ‖ is evaluated first. The expression tickets > 3 || age < 25 is true because tickets is greater than 3. So the expression evolves to "true && gender == 'M'." Because gender is not 'M', the value of the entire expression is false, and the "bad risk" statement does not print. The following are two important lessons:

- The order in which you use operators makes a difference.
- You can always use parentheses to change precedence or make your intentions clearer.

S U M M A R Y

- You can use the AND operator (&&) within a boolean expression to determine whether two expressions are both true.

- You can use the OR operator (||) when you want to carry out some action even if only one of two conditions is true.

- By nesting a series of if and else statements, you can choose from any number of alternatives.

- You use the switch statement to test a single variable against a series of exact integer or character values.

- The conditional operator requires three expressions, a question mark, and a colon, and it is used as an abbreviated version of the if...else statement.

- You use the NOT operator (!) to negate the result of any boolean expression.

- Operator precedence makes a difference. You can always use parentheses to change precedence or make your intentions clearer.

Q U E S T I O N S

1. The operator that combines two conditions into a single boolean value that is true when both of the conditions are true is _____ .
    a. $$
    b. !!
    c. ||
    d. &&

2. The operator that combines two conditions into a single boolean value that is true when at least one of the conditions is true is _____ .
    a. $$
    b. !!
    c. ||
    d. &&

3. Assuming a variable k has been initialized to 12, which of the following statements sets m to 0?

   a. `if(k > 3 && k > 6) m = 0;`
   b. `if(k < 3 && k < 20) m = 0;`
   c. `if(k > 3 && k < 0) m = 0;`
   d. All of these statements set m to 0.

4. Assuming a variable n has been initialized to 2, which of the following statements sets p to 0?

   a. `if(n > 3 && n > 6) p = 0;`
   b. `if(n > 0 && n > 1) p = 0;`
   c. `if(n < 7 && n == 2) p = 0;`
   d. All of these statements set p to 0.

5. Assuming a variable f has been initialized to 5, which of the following statements sets g to 0?

   a. `if(f > 6 || f == 5) g = 0;`
   b. `if(f < 3 || f > 4) g = 0;`
   c. `if(f >= 0 || f < 2) g = 0;`
   d. All of these statements set g to 0.

6. If you write a program that prompts a user for a response, and you want to accept the letter *A* whether it is uppercase or lowercase, the correct `if` statement is

   _____ .

   a. `if(ans =='A' || ans == 'a')`
      `System.out.println("Good response");`
   b. `if(ans == 'A' && ans == 'a')`
      `System.out.println("Good response");`
   c. Both of these statements will work properly.
   d. Neither of these statements will work properly.

7. If you write a program that prompts a user for a response, and the response should be between 1 and 4 inclusive, then the proper `if` statement is _____ .

   a. `if(ans >= '1' || ans <= '4')`
      `System.out.println("Good response");`
   b. `if(ans >= '1' && ans <= '4')`
      `System.out.println("Good response");`
   c. Both of these statements will work properly.
   d. Neither of these statements will work properly.

8. The `switch` statement tests a variable against _____ .
   a. a single boolean value
   b. several possible boolean values
   c. several possible integer or character values
   d. several possible values of any type

9. Within a `switch` structure, each possible test value is immediately followed by a(n)

   _____ .

   a. opening curly bracket
   b. colon
   c. semicolon
   d. comma

10. You can use the ——————— statement to terminate a case in a `switch` structure.
  a. `switch`
  b. `end`
  c. `case`
  d. `break`

11. The `default` case ——————— within a `switch` structure.
  a. must appear
  b. must not appear
  c. can be placed last
  d. can be placed anywhere

12. You ——————— use a `break` statement after each case in a `switch` structure.
  a. must
  b. can, and usually do,
  c. must not
  d. can, but usually do not,

13. The conditional operator requires ———————.
  a. two ampersands
  b. two pipes
  c. a question mark and a colon
  d. an exclamation point and an asterisk

14. Assuming a variable w has been assigned the value 15, then the statement
  `w == 15 ? x = 2 : x = 0;` assigns ———————.
  a. 15 to w
  b. 2 to x
  c. 0 to x
  d. nothing

15. Assuming a variable y has been assigned the value 6, then the value of `!(y < 7)` is
  ———————.
  a. 6
  b. 7
  c. `true`
  d. `false`

16. Assuming the variable z has been assigned the value 0, then the value of the expression `!(z == 0)` is ———————.
  a. 0
  b. `true`
  c. `false`
  d. illegal

17. Assuming a = 5 and b = 9, then the value of a > 0 && b < 10 || b > 1 is
_____.

   a. 5
   b. 9
   c. true
   d. false

18. Assuming a = 5 and b = 9, then the value of a > 0 || b < 10 && b > 1 is
_____.

   a. 5
   b. 9
   c. true
   d. false

19. Assuming c = 4 and d = 14, then which of the following statements is true?
   a. c > 7 && d < 5 || d > 20
   b. c > 0 && d < 5 || d > 50
   c. c > 1 && d < 6 || d > 0
   d. c < 0 && d > 0 || d < 0

E X E R C I S E S

In the following exercises, save each program that you create in the Chapter.04 folder on your Student Disk.

1. Write a program that asks a user to input an initial. Display the full name of an employee who matches the initial: *A* is Armando, *B* is Bruno, and *Z* is Zachary. All other entries should cause a "No such employee" message to display. The class name is PickEmployee.

2. Write a program that asks the user to type a vowel from the keyboard. If the character entered is not a vowel, display an error message. The class name is GetVowel.

3. Write a program that stores an IQ score. If the score is a number less than 0 or greater than 200, issue an error message; otherwise, issue an "above average", "average", or "below average" message for scores over, at, or under 100, respectively. The class name is IQ.

4. Write a program for a college's admissions office. Create variables that store a numeric high school grade point average (for example, 3.2) and an admission test score. Print the message "Accept" if the student has any of the following:

   ■ A grade point average of 3.6 or above and an admission test score of at least 60
   ■ A grade point average of 3.0 or above and an admission test score of at least 70
   ■ A grade point average of 2.6 or above and an admission test score of at least 80
   ■ A grade point average of 2.0 or above and an admission test score of at least 90

If the student does not meet any of the qualifications, print "Reject". The class name is Admissions2.

5. Write a program that stores an employee's hourly pay rate and hours worked. Compute gross pay (hours times rate), withholding tax, and net pay (gross pay minus withholding tax). Withholding tax is computed as a percentage of gross pay based on the following:

Gross Pay	Withholding Percentage
0 to 300.00	10
300.01 to 400.00	12
400.01 to 500.00	15
500.01 and over	20

The class name is Payroll2.

6. Write a program that recommends a pet for a user based on the user's lifestyle. Prompt the user to enter whether he or she lives in an apartment, house, or dormitory (A, H, or D) and the number of hours the user is home during the average day. The user will select an hour category from a menu: A) 18 or more; B) 10 to 17; C) 8 to 9; D) 6 to 7; or E) 0 to 5. Print your recommendation based on the following:

Residence	Hours Home	Recommendation
House	18 or more	Pot bellied pig
House	8 through 17	Dog
House	Less than 8	Snake
Apartment	10 or more	Cat
Apartment	Fewer than 10	Hamster
Dormitory	6 or more	Fish
Dormitory	Fewer than 6	Ant farm

The class name is PetAdvice.

7. Write a program named Siblings.java that declares two ints named myNumberOfSiblings and yourNumberOfSiblings. Display an appropriate message to indicate whether your friend has more, fewer, or the same number of siblings as you. Display the number of siblings whether the `if` statement is `true` or not.

8. Write a program named Credits.java that compares the number of college credits you have earned with the number of college credits earned by a classmate or friend. Display an appropriate message to indicate whether your classmate has earned more, fewer, or the same number of credits as you. Display the number of college credits whether the `if` statement is `true` or not.

9. Write a program named Store.java that displays a menu of three items in a store, with a price for each item. Include characters a, b, and c so the user can select a menu item. Prompt the user to choose an item using the character that corresponds to the item. After the user makes the first selection, show a prompt to ask if another selection will be made. The user should respond Y or N to this prompt (for yes or no). If the user types N, display the cost of the item. If the user types Y, allow the user to select another item and then display the total cost of the two items. Use the `switch` statement to check the menu selection.

SECTION C
objectives

In this section you will learn:
- About the loop structure
- How to use a while loop
- How to use shortcut arithmetic operators
- How to use a for loop
- How and when to use a do...while loop
- About nested loops

Looping and Shortcut Arithmetic

The while Loop

Making decisions is what makes programs seem smart; looping is what makes programs powerful. A **loop** is a structure that allows repeated execution of a block of statements. Within a looping structure, a boolean expression is evaluated. If it is `true`, then a block of statements, called the **loop body**, executes and then the boolean expression is evaluated again. As long as the expression is `true`, the statements in the loop body continue to execute. When the boolean evaluation is `false`, the loop ends. Figure 4-27 shows a diagram of the logic of a loop.

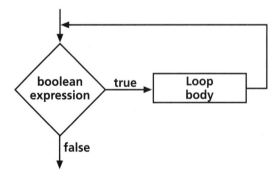

Figure 4-27: Logic of a loop

One execution of any loop is called an iteration.

You can use a **while loop** to execute a body of statements continuously while some condition continues to be `true`. A `while` loop consists of the keyword while followed by a boolean expression within parentheses, followed by the body of the loop, which can be a single statement or a block of statements surrounded by curly brackets.

For example, the code shown in Figure 4-28 causes the message "Hello" to display (theoretically) forever because there is no code to end the loop. Such a loop that never ends is called an **infinite loop**.

 tip

....

An infinite loop may not actually execute infinitely. Eventually the computer memory will be exhausted (literally and figuratively!) and execution will stop. Depending on your system, however, this could take some time.

....

```
while (4 > 2)

    System.out.println("Hello");
```

Figure 4-28: An infinite loop

In Figure 4-28, the expression 4 > 2 evaluates to true. You obviously never need to make such an evaluation, but if you do so in this while loop, the body of the loop is entered and "Hello" displays. Next, the expression is evaluated again. The expression 4 > 2 is still true, so the body is entered again. "Hello" displays repeatedly; the loop never finishes because 4 > 2 is never false.

It is always a bad idea to write an infinite loop. However, even experienced programmers write them by accident. So, before you start writing any loops at all, it is good to know how to break out of an infinite loop in case you accidentally find yourself in the midst of one. If you think your program is in a loop, you can press and hold down the Ctrl key and then press the C key or the Break key, which is located on the Pause key.

To prevent a while loop from executing infinitely, three separate actions should occur:

- Some variable, the **loop control variable**, is initialized.
- The loop control variable is tested in the while statement.
- The body of the while statement must take some action that alters the value of the loop control variable.

For example, the code in Figure 4-29 shows a variable named loopCount being set to a value of 1. The while loop tests loopCount, and if it is less than 3, then the loop body is executed. The loop body shown in Figure 4-29 consists of two statements made into a block by their surrounding curly brackets. The first statement prints "Hello", and then the second statement adds one to loopCount. The next time loopCount is evaluated, it is 2. It is still less than 3, so the loop body executes again. "Hello" prints a second time and loopCount becomes 3. Now when the expression loopCount < 3 is evaluated, it is false, so the loop ends. Program execution would continue with any subsequent statements.

> **tip**
>
> To an algebra student, a statement like `loopCount = loopCount + 1` looks wrong—a value can never be one more than itself. In programming, however, `loopCount = loopCount + 1;` takes the value of loopCount, adds one to it, and then assigns the new value back into loopCount.

```
loopCount = 1;

while (loopCount < 3)

{

   System.out.println("Hello");

   loopCount = loopCount + 1;

}
```

Figure 4-29: A simple loop that executes twice

Notice that if the curly brackets are omitted from the code shown in Figure 4-29, the `while` loop ends at the end of the "Hello" statement. Adding one to the loopCount is no longer part of the loop, so an infinite situation is created.

Also notice that if a semicolon mistakenly is placed at the end of the partial statement `while (loopCount < 3);`, the loop is also infinite. This loop has an **empty body**, or a body with no statements in it, so the boolean expression is evaluated, and because it is `true`, the loop body is entered. Because the loop body is empty, no action is taken, and the boolean expression is evaluated again. It is still `true` (nothing has changed), so the empty body is entered and the infinite loop continues.

It is very common to alter the value of a loop control variable by adding one to it, or **incrementing** the variable. However, not all loops are controlled by adding one. The loop shown in Figure 4-30 prints "Hello" twice, just as the loop in Figure 4-29 does, but its loop is controlled by subtracting 1 from a loop control variable, or **decrementing** it.

```
loopCount = 10;

while (loopCount > 8)

{

   System.out.println("Hello");

   loopCount = loopCount - 1;

}
```

Figure 4-30: Another simple loop that executes twice

In the program segment shown in Figure 4-30, the variable loopCount begins with a value of 10. The loopCount is greater than 8, so the loop body prints "Hello" and decrements loopCount so it becomes 9. The boolean expression in the `while` loop is tested again. Because 9 is more than 8, "Hello" prints and loopCount becomes 8. Now loopCount is not greater than 8, so the loop ends.

The possibilities are endless. Figure 4-31 shows the loopCount being increased by 5, and the results are still the same—the loop prints "Hello" twice. You should not use such unusual methods because they simply make a program confusing. The clearest and best method is to start loopCount at 0 or 1, and continue while it is less than 2 or 3, incrementing by one each time through the loop.

```
loopCount = 30;

while (loopCount < 40)

{

  System.out.println("Hello");

  loopCount = loopCount + 5;

}
```

Figure 4-31: A third simple loop that executes twice

Within a loop, you are not required to alter the loop control variable by adding to it or subtracting from it. To write a loop that depends upon arithmetic, you need to know as you are writing your program how many times you want a loop to execute. Often, the value of a loop control variable is not altered by arithmetic, but instead is altered by user input. For example, perhaps you want to continue performing some task while the user indicates a desire to continue. In that case, you do not know as you are writing the program whether the loop will be executed two times, 200 times, or no times at all.

Unlike a loop that you program to execute a fixed number of times, a loop that is controlled by the user is a type of indefinite loop because you are not sure how many times it will eventually loop.

Consider a simple program in which you display a bank balance and ask the user whether he or she wants to see what the balance will be after one year of interest has accumulated. Each time the user indicates a desire to continue, an increased balance appears. When the user finally indicates a desire to exit, the program ends. The program appears in Figure 4-32.

```
public class LoopingBankBal
{
  public static void main(String[] args)  throws Exception
  {
    double bankBal = 1000;
    double intRate = 0.04;
    char response;
    System.out.println
      ("Do you want to see your balance? Y or N");
    response = (char)System.in.read();
    System.in.read(); System.in.read();
    // Absorbs Enter key
    while (response == 'Y')
    {
      System.out.println("Bank balance is " + bankBal);
      bankBal = bankBal + bankBal * intRate;
      System.out.println
        ("Do you want to see next year's balance? Y or N");
      response = (char)System.in.read();
      System.in.read(); System.in.read();
        // Absorbs Enter key
    }
    System.out.println("Have a nice day!");
  }
}
```

Figure 4-32: LoopingBankBal program

tip

The program shown in Figure 4-32 continues to display bank balances while the response is *Y*. It could also be written to display while the response is not *N*, as in `while (response != 'N')`... A value that a user must supply to stop a loop is called a **sentinel value**.

The program shown in Figure 4-32 contains three variables: a bank balance, an interest rate, and a response. The program asks the user, "Do you want to see your balance?" and reads the response. Recall that the second and third read() statements are required to accept the Enter key that is typed after the Y or N entry. The loop in the program begins with `while (response == 'Y')`. If the user types any response other than Y, then the loop body never executes; instead, the next statement to execute is the "Have a nice day!" statement at the bottom of the program. However, if the user enters Y, then all five statements within the loop body will execute. The current balance will display, and then the program increases the balance by the interest rate value. The program then prompts the user to type Y or N, and two characters are entered—the response and the Enter key. The loop ends with a closing curly bracket, and program control returns to the top of the loop, where the boolean expression in the `while` loop is tested again. If the user typed Y, then the loop is entered and the increased bankBal value that was calculated is finally displayed.

Next, you will improve the ChooseManager program so the user cannot make an invalid choice for the type of event.

To improve the ChooseManager program:

1 If necessary, start your text editor and then open the **ChooseManager.java** text file from the Chapter.04 folder on your Student Disk.

2 Position the cursor to the right of the statement that reads in the character for the event type, press the **Enter** key to start a new line, and then type the beginning of the `while` loop that will continue to execute while the user's entry is not one of the three allowed event types:

```
while (eventType != 'C' && eventType != 'P'
   && eventType != 'N')
```

3 On a new line, type the opening curly bracket for the `while` loop, press the **Enter** key, and then type the two statements that will absorb the Enter key remaining from the user's data entry:

```
System.in.read(); System.in.read();
```

4 On a new line, display the following message so the user knows the data entry was invalid:

```
System.out.println("Entry must be C or P or N!");
```

5 On another new line, read in the eventType value again by typing:

```
eventType = (char)System.in.read();
```

6 On a new line, type the closing curly bracket for the `while` loop. After making it through the `while` loop you just added, the program is guaranteed that the eventType is C, P, or N, so you can make the non-profit event the default case.

7 Change the statement `case 'N':` to **`default:`,** and then delete the three lines that represent the current default case: the existing `default` keyword and the two statements that follow it.

8 Save, compile, and test the program. No matter how many invalid entries you make, the program will continue to prompt you until you enter C, P, or N.

Shortcut Arithmetic Operators

It is common to increase the value of a variable in a program. As you saw in the last section, many loops are controlled by continuously adding one to some variable, or **counting**, as in `count = count + 1;`. Similarly, in the looping bank balance program, the program increased a bank balance by an interest amount with the statement `bankBal = bankBal + bankBal * intRate;`. In other words, the bank balance became its old value plus a new interest amount using a process known as **accumulating**.

Because increasing a variable is so common, Java provides you with several shortcuts for counting and accumulating. The statement `count += 1;` is identical in meaning to `count = count + 1;`. The `+=` adds and assigns in one operation. Similarly, `bankBal += bankBal * intRate;` increases a bankBal by a calculated interest amount.

When you want to increase a variable's value by exactly one, you can use two other shortcut operators—the **prefix ++** and the **postfix ++**. To use a prefix ++, you type two plus signs before the variable name. The statement `someValue = 6;` followed by `++someValue;` results in someValue holding 7, or one more than it held before you applied the ++. To use a postfix ++, you type two plus signs just after a variable name. The statements `anotherValue = 56; anotherValue++;` result in anotherValue containing 57.

 tip

> You can use the prefix ++ and postfix ++ with variables, but not with constants. An expression such as `++84;` is illegal because an 84 must always remain as 84. However, you can create a variable as `int val = 84;` and then write `++val;` or `val++;` to increase the variable's value.

The prefix and postfix increment operators are **unary** operators because you use them with one value. Most arithmetic operators, like those used for addition and multiplication, are **binary** operators that operate on two values.

When you simply want to increase a variable's value by one, there is no difference between using the prefix and postfix increment operators. Each operator results in increasing the variable by one. However, these operators function differently. When you use the prefix ++, the result is calculated and stored, and then the variable is used. For example, if `b = 4;`, then `c = ++b;` results in both b and c holding the value 5. When you use the postfix ++, the variable is used and then the result is calculated and stored. For example, if `b = 4;` and then `c = b++;`, 4 will be assigned to c, and then after the assignment, b is increased and takes the value 5. In other words, if b = 4, then the value of b++ is also 4, but after the statement is completed, the value of b will be 5. If d = 8 and e = 8, both ++d == 9 and e++ == 8 are true expressions.

To demonstrate the effect of the prefix and postfix increment operators:

1 Open a new text file and begin a demonstration class named DemoIncrement by typing:

```
public class DemoIncrement
{
  public static void main(String[] args) throws Exception
  {
```

2 On a new line, add a variable v and assign it a value of 4. Then declare a variable named plusPlusV and assign it a value of ++v by typing:

```
int v = 4;
int plusPlusV = ++v;
```

3 The last statement, int plusPlusV = ++v;, will increase v to 5, so reset v to 4 before declaring a vPlusPlus variable to which you assign v++ by typing:

```
v = 4;
int vPlusPlus = v++;
```

4 Add the following statements to print the three values:

```
System.out.println("v is " + v);
System.out.println("++v is " + plusPlusV);
System.out.println("v++ is " + vPlusPlus);
```

5 Add the closing curly bracket for the main() method and the closing curly bracket for the DemoIncrement class.

6 Save the file as **DemoIncrement.java** in the Chapter.04 folder on your Student Disk. Compile and execute the program. Your output should look like Figure 4-33. Make sure you understand why the values display as they do.

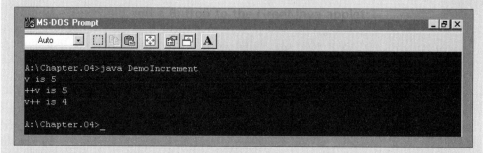

Figure 4-33: Output of the DemoIncrement program

To illustrate how comparisons are made, add a few more variables to the DemoIncrement program.

7 Position the cursor to the right of the last println() statement, and then press the **Enter** key to start a new line.

8 Add three new integer variables and two new boolean variables: The first boolean variable compares ++w to y; the second boolean variable compares x++ to y:

```
int w = 17, x = 17, y = 18;
boolean compare1 = (++w == y);
boolean compare2 = (x++ == y);
```

9 Add the following statements to display the values stored in the compare variables:

```
System.out.println("First compare is " + compare1);
System.out.println("Second compare is " + compare2);
```

10 Save, run, and compile the program. Make sure you understand why compare1's value is `true` and compare2's value is `false`.

Besides using the shortcut operator +=, you can use -=, *=, and /=. Each of these operators is used to perform the operation and assign the result in one step. For example, `balanceDue -= payment;` subtracts payment from balanceDue and assigns the result to balanceDue.

Besides using the prefix and postfix increment operators, you can use a prefix or postfix **decrement operator** (--) that reduces a variable's value by one. For example, if s and t are each assigned the value 34, then --s has the value 33 and t-- has the value 34, but t becomes 33.

The for Loop

You can use a `while` loop when you need to perform a task some predetermined number of times. A loop that executes a specific number of times is a **definite loop** or a **counted loop**. To write a definite loop, you initialize a loop control variable, and while the loop control variable does not pass a limit, you continue to execute the body of the `while` statement. To avoid an infinite loop, you must include in the body of the `while` loop a statement that alters the loop control variable. For example, the program segment shown in Figure 4-34 prints the series of integers 1 through 10. The variable val starts the loop holding a value of 1, and while the value remains under 11, the val continues to print and be incremented.

```
int val = 1;

while (val < 11)

{

  System.out.println(val);

  ++val;

}
```

Figure 4-34: Printing the integers 1 through 10 with a `while` loop

Because you need similar definite loops so frequently when you write programs, Java provides you with a shorthand notation that you can use to create a loop. When you use a **for loop**, you can indicate the starting value for the loop control variable, the test condition that controls loop entry, and the expression that alters the loop control variable all in one convenient place.

You begin a `for` loop with the keyword `for` followed by a set of parentheses. Within the parentheses there are three sections separated by exactly two semicolons. The three sections are usually used for the following:

- Initializing the loop control variable
- Testing the loop control variable
- Updating the loop control variable

The body of the `for` statement follows the parentheses. As with an `if` statement or a `while` loop, you can use a single statement as the body of a `for` loop, or you can use a block of statements enclosed in curly brackets. The `for` statement shown in Figure 4-35 produces the same output as the `while` statement shown in Figure 4-34—it prints the integers 1 through 10.

```
for(int val = 1; val < 11; ++val)

{

  System.out.println(val);

}
```

Figure 4-35: Printing the integers 1 through 10 with a `for` loop

tip

You did not have to declare the variable val within the `for` statement. If you declared val earlier in the program block, then the `for` statement would be `for(val = 1; val < 11; ++val)`. In other words, the `for` statement does not need to declare a variable; it can simply give a starting value to a previously declared variable.

Within the parentheses of the **for** statement shown in Figure 4-35, the first section prior to the first semicolon declares a variable named val and initializes it to 1. The program will execute this statement once, no matter how many times the body of the **for** loop executes.

After the initialization expression executes, program control passes to the middle, or test section, of the **for** statement. If the boolean expression found there evaluates to **true**, then the body of the **for** loop is entered. In the program segment shown in Figure 4-35, val is set to 1, so when **val < 11** is tested, it evaluates to **true**. The loop body prints the val.

After the loop body executes, the final one-third of the **for** loop executes, and val is increased to 2. Following the third section, program control returns to the second section, where val is compared to 11 a second time. Because val is still less than 11, the body executes: val (now 2) prints, and then the third, altering portion of the **for** loop executes again. The variable val increases to 3, and the **for** loop continues.

Eventually, when val is *not* less than 11 (after 1 through 10 have printed), the **for** loop ends, and the program continues with any statements that follow the **for** loop.

Although the three sections of the **for** loop are most commonly used for initializing, testing, and incrementing, you can also perform the following tasks:

- You can initialize more than one variable by placing commas between the separate statements, as in **for(g = 0, h = 1; g < 6; ++g)**.
- You can perform more than one test, as in **for(g = 0; g < 3 && h > 1; ++g)**.
- You can decrement or perform some other task, as in **for(g = 5; g >= 1; --g)**.
- You can even leave one or more portions of the **for** loop empty, although the two semicolons are still required as placeholders.

Usually you should use the **for** loop for its intended purpose, which is a shorthand way of programming a definite loop.

Occasionally, you will encounter a **for** loop that contains no body, such as **for(x = 0; x < 100000; ++x);**. This kind of loop exists simply to take time—for instance, when a brief pause is desired during the execution of a program.

tip

Java also contains a built-in method to pause program execution. The sleep() method is part of the Thread class in the java.lang package.

The do...while Loop

With all the loops you have written so far, the loop body might execute many times, but it is also possible that the loop will not execute at all. For example, recall the bank balance program that displays compound interest, part of which is shown in Figure 4-36.

```
System.out.println("Do you want to see your balance? Y or N");

response = (char)System.in.read();

System.in.read();   // Absorbs Enter key

while (response == 'Y')

{

  System.out.println("Bank balance is " + bankBal);

  bankBal = bankBal + bankBal * intRate;

  System.out.println

    ("Do you want to see next year's balance? Y or N");

  response = (char)System.in.read();

  System.in.read();   // Absorbs Enter key

}
```

Figure 4-36: Part of the bank balance program with a while loop

The program segment begins with the user prompt, "Do you want to see your balance? Y or N". If the user does not reply by typing Y, the loop body never executes. The while loop checks a value at the "top" of the loop before the body has a chance to execute. Sometimes you might need a loop body to execute at least one time. If so, you want to write a loop that checks at the "bottom" of the loop after the first iteration. The **do...while loop** is a loop that checks the bottom of the loop after one repetition has occurred.

Figure 4-37 shows a do...while loop for the bank balance program. The loop starts with the keyword do. The body of the loop follows and is contained within curly brackets. The bankBal variable is output before the user has any option of responding. At the end of the loop, the user is prompted, "Do you want to see next year's balance? Y or N". Now the user has the option of seeing any more balances, but the first prompt was unavoidable. The userResponse is checked at the bottom of the loop. If it is Y, then the loop repeats.

```
do

{

  System.out.println("Bank balance is " + bankBal);

  bankBal = bankBal + bankBal * intRate;

  System.out.println

    ("Do you want to see next year's balance? Y or N");
```

Figure 4-37: Part of the bank balance program with a do...while loop

```
    response = (char)System.in.read();

    System.in.read();   // Absorbs Enter key

} while (response == 'Y');
```

Figure 4-37: Part of the bank balance program with a do...while loop (continued)

In any situation where you want to loop, you never are required to use a do...while loop. Within the bank balance example, you could simply unconditionally display the bank balance once, prompt the user, and then start a while loop that might not be entered. However, when you know you want to perform some task at least one time, the do...while loop is convenient.

Nested Loops

Just as if statements can be nested, so can loops. You can place a while loop within a while loop, a for loop within a for loop, a while loop within a for loop, or any other combination you can think of.

For example, suppose you want to find all the numbers that divide evenly into 100. You can write a for loop that sets a variable to 1 and increments it to 100. Each of the 99 times through the loop, if 100 is evenly divisible by the number (that is, if 100 % num is equivalent to 0), then the program prints the number. Next, you will write a program that determines all the integers that divide evenly into 100.

tip To find all the numbers that divide evenly into 100, you actually have to test divisors only through 50. You cannot divide any number that is more than half of another number evenly into itself.

To write a program that finds the values that divide evenly into 100:

1 Open a new text file.

2 Begin the program named EvenInt by typing the following code to declare an integer variable named num:

```
public class EvenInt
{
    public static void main(String[] args)
    {
        int num;
```

3 Type a statement that explains the purpose of the program:

```
System.out.print("100 is evenly divisible by ");
```

4   Write the `for` loop that varies num from 1 to 99. With each iteration of the loop, test whether `100%num` is 0. If you divide 100 by a number and there is no remainder, then the number goes into 100 evenly.

```
for(num = 1; num < 100; ++num)
  if(100%num == 0)
    System.out.print(num + "  ");
    // Print the number and two spaces
```

5   Add an empty println() statement to advance the cursor to the next line by typing `System.out.println();`.

6   Type the closing curly brackets for the main() method and the EvenInt class.

7   Save the program as **EvenInt.java** in the Chapter.04 folder on your Student Disk. Compile and run the program. The program prints `100 is evenly divisible by 1  2  4  5  10  20  25  50.`

What if you want to know what number goes evenly into 100, but also what every number *up to* 100 can be divided evenly by? You can write 99 more loops, or you can place the current loop inside a different, outer loop, as you will do next.

When you use a loop within a loop, you should always think of the outer loop as the more all-encompassing loop. When you describe the task at hand, you often use the word "each" when referring to the inner loop. If you want to print three mailing labels *each* for 20 customers, the label variable would control the inner loop:

```
for(customer = 1; customer <= 20; ++customer)
  for(label = 1; label <=3; ++label)
    printLabelMethod();
```

If you want to print divisors for *each* number from 1 to 100, then the loop that varies the number to be divided is the outside loop. You need to perform 100 mathematical calculations on each of the numbers, so that constitutes the "smaller" or inside loop.

To create a nested loop to print even divisors for every number up to 100:

1   In the file **EvenInt.java** in your text editor, create an outer loop that uses the variable testNum to test every number from 1 to 100. Position the cursor after the declaration of num but before the semicolon that ends the declaration, and then type a comma and **testNum**.

2   Position the cursor to the right of the line with the variable declarations, press the **Enter** key to start a new line, and then type the other `for` loop:
   `for(testNum = 1; testNum <= 100; ++testNum)`

3   Press the **Enter** key, and then type the opening curly bracket for this loop on the next line.

4   Change the statement that prints "100 is evenly divisible by " to the following:

```
System.out.print(testNum + " is evenly divisible by ");
```

5   Change the `for` statement that varies num from 1 to 100 so it only varies num from 1 to testNum. For example, during each iteration, if testNum is 46, you want to divide it only by numbers that are 45 or less. The code to make this change is as follows:

```
for(num = 1; num < testNum; ++num)
```

6   Change the statement that tests `100 % num` to `if(testNum%num == 0)`.

7   Following the empty println() statement, add the closing curly bracket for the outer `for` loop.

8   Save, compile, and run the program. The output will scroll on the screen. When it stops, it should look similar to Figure 4-38.

```
MS-DOS Prompt                                                              _ | 8 | X
Auto        ▾   [] [] [] [] [] [] A |
77 is evenly divisible by 1   7   11
78 is evenly divisible by 1   2   3    6   13   26   39
79 is evenly divisible by 1
80 is evenly divisible by 1   2   4    5   8    10   16   20   40
81 is evenly divisible by 1   3   9   27
82 is evenly divisible by 1   2   41
83 is evenly divisible by 1
84 is evenly divisible by 1   2   3    4   6    7    12   14   21   28   42
85 is evenly divisible by 1   5   17
86 is evenly divisible by 1   2   43
87 is evenly divisible by 1   3   29
88 is evenly divisible by 1   2   4    8   11   22   44
89 is evenly divisible by 1
90 is evenly divisible by 1   2   3    5   6    9    10   15   18   30   45
91 is evenly divisible by 1   7   13
92 is evenly divisible by 1   2   4   23   46
93 is evenly divisible by 1   3   31
94 is evenly divisible by 1   2   47
95 is evenly divisible by 1   5   19
96 is evenly divisible by 1   2   3    4   6    8    12   16   24   32   48
97 is evenly divisible by 1
98 is evenly divisible by 1   2   7   14   49
99 is evenly divisible by 1   3   9   11   33
100 is evenly divisible by 1  2   4    5   10   20   25   50
A:\Chapter.04>
```

Figure 4-38: Output of the EvenInt program

tip

Depending on your monitor resolution, you may see more lines than shown in Figure 4-38.

When the program executes, 100 lines of output display on the screen. But, as Figure 4-38 shows, the first 76 (or so) lines scroll by so rapidly that you can't read them. It would be helpful if you could stop the output after every 20 lines or so, so that you would have time to read the messages. You can put the modulus operator to use for this task. If you want to stop output when testNum is 20, 40, 60, and 80, then you can test testNum to see if it is evenly divisible by 20. When it is, you can pause program execution by asking the user to press the Enter key and accept keyboard input.

To pause your program after every 20 lines of output:

1 At the end of the EvenInt file and just prior to the closing bracket for the for loop, type the following code to test testNum. If 20 divides into it evenly, then tell the user to press the Enter key and accept an Enter key from the keyboard. There is no need to store the entered key in a variable.

```
if(testNum % 20 == 0)
{
   System.out.println("Press Enter to continue");
   System.in.read(); System.in.read();
}
```

2 Because the program now uses the System.in.read() method, you must position the cursor at the end of the main() method header line and add **throws Exception**.

3 Save, compile, and test the program. It will pause after every 20 lines of output and wait until you press the Enter key before continuing until the program ends.

S U M M A R Y

■ A loop is a structure that allows repeated execution of a block of statements. A loop that never ends is called an infinite loop.

■ Within a looping structure, a boolean expression is evaluated and if it is **true**, a block of statements, called the loop body, executes; then the boolean expression is evaluated again.

■ You can use a **while** loop to execute a body of statements continuously while some condition continues to be **true**.

■ You can break out of an infinite loop by pressing Ctrl + C or Ctrl + Break.

■ To execute a **while** loop, you initialize a loop control variable, test it in a **while** statement, and then alter the loop control variable in the body of the **while** structure.

■ To add one to a variable is to increment the variable. To subtract one is to decrement the variable.

■ The += operator adds and assigns in one operation.

■ The prefix ++ and the postfix ++ increase a variable's value by one.

■ Unary operators are used with one value. Most arithmetic operators are binary operators that operate on two values.

■ When you use the prefix ++, the result is calculated and stored, and then the variable is used. When you use the postfix ++, the variable is used, and then the result is calculated and stored.

■ The shortcut operators +=, -=, *=, and /= perform operations and assign the result in one step.

■ The prefix and postfix decrement operators reduce a variable's value by one.

■ A loop that executes a specific number of times is a definite loop or counted loop.

■ A for loop initializes, tests, and increments in one statement. There are three sections within the parentheses of a for loop that are separated by exactly two semicolons.

■ The do...while loop tests a boolean expression after one repetition has taken place, at the bottom of the loop.

■ You can nest loops.

Q U E S T I O N S

1. A structure that allows repeated execution of a block of statements is a(n) _____ .

   a. cycle
   b. loop
   c. ring
   d. iteration

2. A loop that never ends is a(n) _____ loop.
   a. iterative
   b. infinite
   c. structured
   d. illegal

3. To construct a loop that works correctly, you should initialize a loop control _____ .

   a. variable
   b. constant
   c. structure
   d. condition

4. What is the output of the following code?

```
b = 1;
while (b < 4)
System.out.println(b + "   ");
```

   a. 1
   b. 1   2   3
   c. 1   2   3   4
   d. 1   1   1   1   1   1...

5. What is the output of the following code?

```
b = 1;
while (b < 4)
{
   System.out.println(b + "   ");
   b = b + 1;
}
```

   a. 1
   b. 1   2   3
   c. 1   2   3   4
   d. 1   1   1   1   1...

6. What is the output of the following code?

```
e = 1;
while (e < 4);
System.out.println(e + "   ");
```

   a. 1
   b. 1   1   1   1   1   1...
   c. 1   2   3   4
   d. 4   4   4   4   4   4...

7. If total = 100 and amt = 200, then after the statement total += amt, _____ .

   a. total is equal to 200
   b. total is equal to 300
   c. amt is equal to 100
   d. amt is equal to 300

8. The modulus operator % is a _____ operator.

   a. unary
   b. binary
   c. tertiary
   d. postfix

9. The prefix ++ is a _____ operator.

   a. unary
   b. binary
   c. tertiary
   d. postfix

10. If g = 5, then the value of the expression ++g is _____ .
   a. 4
   b. 5
   c. 6
   d. 7

11. If h = 9, then the value of the expression h++ is _____ .
   a. 8
   b. 9
   c. 10
   d. 11

12. If j = 5 and k = 6, then the value of j++ == k is _____ .
   a. 5
   b. 6
   c. true
   d. false

13. You must always include _____ in a for loop's parentheses.
   a. two semicolons
   b. three semicolons
   c. two commas
   d. three commas

14. The statement for(a = 0; a < 5; ++a) System.out.print(a + " ");
   prints _____ .
   a. 0   0   0   0   0
   b. 0   1   2   3   4
   c. 0   1   2   3   4   5
   d. nothing

15. The statement for(b = 1; b > 3; ++b) System.out.print(b + " ");
   prints _____ .
   a. 1   1   1
   b. 1   2   3
   c. 1   2   3   4
   d. nothing

16. What does the following statement print?
```
for(f = 1, g = 4; f < g; ++f, --g)
System.out.print(f + " " + g + " ");
```
   a. 1   4   2   5   3   6   4   7...
   b. 1   4   2   3   3   2
   c. 1   4   2   3
   d. nothing

17. The loop that performs its conditional check at the bottom of the loop is a
   _____ loop.
   a. while
   b. do...while
   c. for
   d. for...while

18. What does this program segment print?

```
d = 0;
do
{
  System.out.print(d + "  ");
  d++;
} while d < 2;
```

a. 0

b. 0   1

c. 0   1   2

d. nothing

19. What does this program segment print?

```
for(f = 0; f < 3; ++f)
  for(g = 0; g < 2; ++g)
  System.out.print(f + " " + g + " ");
```

a. 0   0   0   1   1   0 1   1   1   0   2   1

b. 0   1   0   2   0   3   1   1   1   2   1   3

c. 0   1   0   2   1   1   1   2

d. 0   0   0   1   0   2   1   0   1   1   1   2   2   0   2   1   2   2

20. What does this program segment print?

```
for(m = 0; m < 4; ++m);
  for(n = 0; n < 2; ++n);
  System.out.print(m + "  " + n + "  ");
```

a. 0   0   0   1   1   0   1   1   2   0   2   1   3   0   3   1

b. 0   1   0   2   1   1   1   2   2   1   2   2

c. 4   2

d. 3   1

E X E R C I S E S

Each of the following exercises describes a program that you *could* write without using a loop—for example, you could alternatively write each program with a series of print statements. However, the purpose of these exercises is for you to practice the looping concepts learned in the chapter. For the following exercises, save each program that you create in the Chapter.04 folder on your Student Disk.

1. Write a program that prints all even numbers from 2 to 100 inclusive. The class name is EvenNums.

2. Write a program that asks a user to type A, B, C, or Q. When the user types Q, the program ends. When the user types A, B, or C, the program displays the message "Good job!" and then asks for another input. When the user types anything else, issue an error message and then ask for another input. The class name is ABCInput.

3. Write a program that prints every integer value from 1 to 20 along with its squared value. The class name is TableOfSquares.

4. Write a program that sums the integers from 1 to 50. The class name is Sum50.

5. Write a program that shows the sum of 1 to *n* for every *n* from 1 to 50. That is, the program prints 1, 3 (the sum of 1 and 2), 6 (the sum of 1, 2, and 3), and so on. The class name is EverySum.

6. Write a program that prints every perfect number from 1 through 1000. A number is perfect if it equals the sum of all the numbers that divide evenly into it. For example, 6 is perfect because 1, 2, and 3 divide evenly into it and their sum is 6. The class name is Perfect.

7. Write a program named Investment.java that calculates the amount of money earned on an investment that includes 12 percent interest. Prompt the user to choose the investment amount from one menu and the number of years for the investment from a second menu. Display the total amount (balance) for each year of the investment. Use a loop instruction to calculate the balance for each year. Use the formula amount = investment * (1 + interest) raised to a power equal to the year to calculate the balance.

8. Write a program named Quiz.java that creates a quiz that contains questions about a hobby, popular music, astronomy, or any other personal interest. After the user selects a topic, display a series of questions. The user should answer the questions with one character for multiple choice, true/false, or yes/no. If the user responds to a question correctly, display an appropriate message. If the user responds to a question incorrectly, display an appropriate response and the correct answer. At the end of the quiz, display the number of correct answers.

9. Write a program named Survey.java that displays a series of survey questions, with one-character answers. At the end of the survey, ask the user if he or she wants to enter another set of responses. If the user responds no, then display the results of the survey for each question. Enter several sets of responses to test the program.

10. Each of the following files in the Chapter.04 folder on your Student Disk has syntax and/or logical errors. In each case, determine the problem and fix the program. After you correct the errors, save each file using the same filename preceded with *Fix*. For example, save DebugFour1.java as FixDebugFour1.java.
    a. DebugFour1.java
    b. DebugFour2.java
    c. DebugFour3.java
    d. DebugFour4.java

CHAPTER 5

Arrays and Strings

case ▶ "I've learned how to create objects and how to use decisions and loops to perform a variety of tasks with those objects," you say as you meet with Lynn Greenbrier, your mentor at Event Handlers Incorporated. "Still, it seems as though I'm doing a lot of work. If I need to check a variable's value against 20 possibilities, it takes me 20 `if` statements or a long `switch` statement to get the job done. I thought computers were supposed to make things easier!"

"I think what you're looking for," Lynn says, "is how to use the power of arrays. Do you have any other concerns?"

"Well, I can write interactive programs that accept a character, but I'd really like to let users enter words or numbers into programs."

"You need to learn about the array's close cousin, the String," Lynn says. "The wide variety of String methods provided with the Java programming language will help you use words and phrases efficiently. You'll even be able to let your users input numbers."

Previewing a Program That Uses Arrays and Strings

The Chap5Events program demonstrates a variety of procedures that rely on arrays or Strings for efficient execution. You will answer questions when prompted, and even play a game.

To preview the Chap5Events program:

1   Start your text editor, open the **Chap5Event.java** file in the Chapter.05 folder on your Student Disk, and examine the code. This program is a simple Event class similar to one you created in Chapter 4.

2   At the command prompt, compile the class with the command `javac Chap5Event.java`.

3   In the text editor, open the **Chap5Events.java** file and examine the code. This program is divided into three parts to demonstrate three of the major concepts you will learn about in this chapter. In the first part of the program, you enter codes for five upcoming events to be handled by Event Handlers Incorporated. The program stores all five events and displays them for you. The program prompts you to specify an Event type by entering a C, P, or N. You can enter any other character, but you must enter five valid characters (C, P, or N) before the program will proceed. After you enter five valid characters, you will see a summary of the five events you selected. The second part of the program will prompt you for the number of guests at your event. If you enter a value over 100, you will see a message regarding a surcharge. The third part of the program will invite you to play a game similar to Hangman, in which you guess the motto of Event Handlers Incorporated.

4   At the command prompt, compile this file with the command `javac Chap5Events.java`. Then run the program with the command `java Chap5Events`. Test the program by following the on-screen directions; you can press Ctrl + C to stop the program at any time.

In this chapter, you will write programs that are similar to the three parts of this program.

Arrays

In this section you will learn how to:

■ Declare an array
■ Initialize an array
■ Use subscripts with an array
■ Declare an array of objects
■ Search an array for an exact match
■ Pass an array to a method
■ Use the length field

Declaring an Array

While completing the first four chapters in this text, you stored values in variables. In the early sections, you simply stored a value and used it. In Chapter 4, you created loops that allowed you to "recycle" variables; that is, after creating a variable, you can assign a value, use the value, and then, in successive cycles through the loop, reuse the variable as it holds different values.

There are times, however, when storing just one value in memory at a time does not fill your needs. For example, a sales manager who supervises 20 employees might want to determine whether each employee has produced sales above or below the average amount. When you enter the first employee's sales figure into a program, you can't determine whether it is above or below average, because you don't know what the average is until you have all 20 figures. Unfortunately, if you assign 20 sales figures to the same variable, when you assign the figure for the second employee, it replaces the figure for the first employee.

A possible solution is to create 20 separate employee sales variables, each with a unique name, so you can store all the sales until you can determine an average. A drawback to this method is that if you have 20 different variable names to be assigned values, then you need 20 separate assignment statements. If you have 20 different variable names, then the statement that calculates total sales will be something unwieldy like `total = firstAmt + secondAmt + thirdAmt + ...` This method might work for 20 salespeople, but what if you have 10,000 salespeople?

The best solution is to create an array. An **array** is a list of data items that all have the same type and the same name. You declare an array variable in the same way as you declare any scalar variable, but you insert a pair of square brackets after the type. For example, to declare an array of double values to hold sales figures for salespeople, you write `double[] salesFigure;`.

> You also can declare an array variable by placing the square brackets after the array name, as in double salesFigure[];. **This format is familiar to C and C++ programmers, but the preferred format among Java programmers is to place the brackets following the variable type and before the variable name, as in** double[] salesFigure;.

After you create an array variable, you still need to create the actual array. You use the same procedure to create an array that you use to create an object. Recall that when you create a class named Employee, you can declare an Employee object with a declaration such as `Employee oneWorker;`, but that declaration does not actually create the oneWorker object. You create the oneWorker object when you use the keyword new and the constructor method, as in `oneWorker = new Employee();`. Similarly, declaring an array and actually reserving memory space for it are two distinct processes. To reserve memory locations for 20 salesFigure objects, you declare the array variable with `double[] salesFigure;`, and then you create the array with `salesFigure = new double[20];`. Just as with objects, you also can declare and create an array in one statement with `double[] salesFigure = new double[20];`.

> Some other languages, such as COBOL, BASIC, and Visual Basic, use parentheses rather than brackets to refer to individual array elements. By using brackets, the creators of Java made it easier for you to distinguish arrays from methods.

The statement `double[] salesFigure = new double[20];` reserves 20 memory locations for 20 salesFigures. You can distinguish each salesFigure from the others with a subscript. A **subscript** is an integer contained within square brackets that indicates one of an array's variables, or **elements**. In the Java programming language, any array's elements are numbered beginning with zero, so you can legally use any subscript from zero through 19 when working with an array that has 20 elements. In other words, the first salesFigure array element is `salesFigure[0]` and the last salesFigure element is `salesFigure[19]`.

It is common to forget that the first element in an array is element zero, especially if you know another programming language in which the first array element is element one. Making this mistake means you will be "off by one" in your use of any array.

> To remember that array elements begin with element zero, it might be helpful to think of the first array element as being "zero elements away from" the beginning of the array, the second element as being "one element away from" the beginning of the array, and so on.

When you work with any individual array element, you treat it no differently than you would treat a single variable of the same type. For example, to assign a value to the first salesFigure in an array, you use a simple assignment statement, such as `salesFigure[0] = 2100.00;`. To print the last salesFigure in an array of 20, you write `System.out.println(salesFigure[19]);`.

Next, you will create a small array to see how arrays are used. The array will hold salaries for four categories of employees.

To create a program that uses an array:

1 Open a new text file in your text editor.

2 Begin the class that will demonstrate array use by typing the following class and main() headers and their corresponding opening curly brackets:

```
public class DemoArray
{
   public static void main(String[] args)
   {
```

3 On a new line, declare and create an array that can hold four double values by typing **double[] salary = new double[4];**.

4 One by one, assign four values to the four salary array elements by typing the following:

```
salary[0] = 5.25;
salary[1] = 6.55;
salary[2] = 10.25;
salary[3] = 16.85;
```

5 To confirm that the four values have been assigned, print the salaries, one by one, using the following code:

```
System.out.println("Salaries one by one are:");
System.out.println(salary[0]);
System.out.println(salary[1]);
System.out.println(salary[2]);
System.out.println(salary[3]);
```

6 Add the two closing curly brackets that end the main() method and the DemoArray class.

7 Save the program as **DemoArray.java** in the Chapter.05 folder on your Student Disk.

8 Compile and run the program. The program's output appears in Figure 5-1.

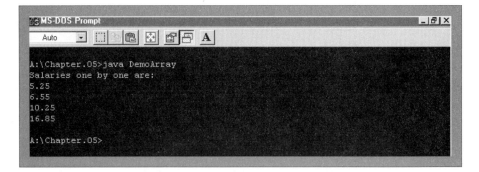

Figure 5-1: Output of the DemoArray program

Initializing an Array

A variable that has a primitive type, such as int, holds a value. A variable with a reference type, such as an array, holds a memory address where a value is stored.

Array names actually represent computer memory addresses; that is, array names are references, as are all Java objects. When you declare an array name, no computer memory address is assigned to it. Instead, the array variable name has the special value **null**, or Unicode value '\u0000'. When you declare int[ ] someNums;, the variable someNums has a value of **null**.

When you define someNums as int someNums = new int[10];, then someNums has an actual memory address value. Each element of someNums has a value of zero because someNums is a numeric array. By default, character array elements are assigned '\u0000'. Boolean array elements are automatically assigned false.

You already know how to assign a different value to a single element of an array, as in someNums[0] = 46;. You also can assign nondefault values to array elements upon creation. To initialize an array, you use a list of values separated by commas and enclosed within curly brackets. For example, if you want to create an array named tenMult and store the first six multiples of 10 within the array, you can declare int tenMult[] = {10, 20, 30, 40, 50, 60};. When you initialize an array by giving it values upon creation, you do not give the array a size—the size will be assigned based on the number of values you place in the initializing list. Also, when you initialize an array, you do not need to use the keyword new; instead, new memory is assigned based on the length of the list of provided values.

tip

In Java, you do not usually use a semicolon after a closing curly bracket, for example, at the end of a method body. However, every statement in Java requires a semicolon, and an array initialization is a statement. Do not forget to type the semicolon after the closing bracket at the end of an array's initialization list.

Next, you will alter your DemoArray program to initialize the array of doubles, rather than declaring the array and assigning values later.

To initialize an array of doubles:

1 Open the **DemoArray.java** file in your text editor, delete the statement that declares the array of four doubles named salary (`double[] salary = new double[4];`), and then replace it with the following initialization statement: `double[] salary = {5.25, 6.55, 10.25, 16.85};`.

2 Delete the following four statements that individually assign the values to the array (`salary[0] = 5.25; salary[1] = 6.55; salary[2] = 10.25; salary[3] = 16.85;`).

3 Save, compile, and test the program. The output is the same as Figure 5-1.

Using Subscripts with an Array

If you treat each array element as an individual entity, then there isn't much of an advantage to declaring an array over declaring individual scalar (primitive) variables, such as int, double, or char. The power of arrays becomes apparent when you begin to use subscripts that are variables rather than subscripts that are constant values.

For example, when you declare an array of five integers, such as `int[] valArray = {2, 14, 35, 67, 85};`, you often want to perform the same operation on each array element. To increase each array element by three, for example, you can write the following:

```
valArray[0] += 3;
valArray[1] += 3;
valArray[2] += 3;
valArray[3] += 3;
valArray[4] += 3;
```

With five array elements, this task is manageable. However, you can shorten the task by using a variable as the subscript. Then you can use a loop to perform arithmetic on each array element in the array, as in the following example:

```
for(sub = 0; sub < 5; ++sub)
  valArray[sub] += 3;
```

The variable sub is set to zero, and then it is compared to five. Because the value is less than five, the loop executes and three is added to valArray[0]. Then the variable sub is incremented and it becomes one, which is still less than five, so when the loop executes again, valArray[1] is increased by three, and so on. A process that took five statements now takes only one. Additionally, if the array had 100 elements, the first method of increasing the array values by three would result in 95 additional statements. The only change required in the `for` loop would be to compare sub to 100 instead of to five.

Next, you will modify the DemoArray program to use a `for` loop with the array.

To use a `for` loop with the array in DemoArray:

1   Open the **DemoArray.java** file in your text editor, and then delete the four println() statements that print the four array values and replace them with the following for loop:

```
for(int x = 0; x < 4; ++x)
   System.out.println(salary[x]);
```

2   Save, compile, and run the program. Again, the output is the same as Figure 5-1.

Declaring an Array of Objects

Just as you can declare arrays of integers or doubles, you can declare arrays that hold elements of any type, including objects. For example, assume you created the Employee class shown in Figure 5-2. This class has two data fields (empNum and empSalary), a constructor, and a get method for each field.

```
public class Employee
{

  private int empNum;

  private double empSalary;

  Employee(int num, double sal)

  {

    empNum = num;

    empSalary = sal;

  }

  public int getEmpNum()

  {

    return empNum;

  }

  public double getSalary()

  {

    return empSalary;

  }

}
```

Figure 5-2: A simple Employee class

You can create separate Employee objects with unique names, such as `Employee painter, electrician, plumber;`, but for many programs it is far more convenient to create an array of Employees. An array named emp that holds seven Employees is defined as `Employee[] emp = new Employee[7];`. This statement reserves enough computer memory for seven Employee objects named emp[0] through emp[6]. However, the statement does not actually construct those Employee objects; instead, you must call the seven individual constructors. According to the class definition shown in Figure 5-2, the Employee constructor requires two arguments: an employee number and a salary. If you want to number your Employees 101, 102, 103, and so on, and start each Employee at a salary of $5.35, then the loop that constructs seven Employee objects is as follows:

```
for(x = 0; x < 7; ++x)
  emp[x] = new Employee(101 + x, 5.35);
```

As x varies from 0 through 6, each of the seven emp objects is constructed with an employee number that is 101 more than x, and each of the seven emp objects holds the same salary of 5.35.

To use a method that belongs to an object that is part of an array, you insert the appropriate subscript notation after the array name and before the dot that precedes the method name. For example, to print data for seven Employees stored in the emp array, you can write the following:

```
for(x = 0; x < 7; ++x)
  System.out.println
    (emp[x].getEmpNum()+ " " + emp[x].getSalary());
```

Pay attention to the syntax of the Employee objects' method calls, such as `emp[x].getEmpNum()`. Although you might be tempted to place the subscript at the end of the expression after the method name, as in `emp.getEmpNum[x]`, you cannot do so—the values in x (0 through 6) refer to a particular emp, each of which has access to a single getEmpNum() method. The placement of the bracketed subscript following emp means the method "belongs" to a particular emp.

Next, you will create an array of Event objects for Event Handlers Incorporated.

To create an array of Event objects:

1 Open the **Event.java** file from the Chapter.05 folder on your Student Disk. This program is the same one that you created in Chapter 4. Examine the code so that you recall that the class contains two data fields: a character representing the type of event, and a double representing the minimum that is charged for the event. The constructor requires values for the two data fields. The class also contains methods to get the field values.

2   Open a new text file in your text editor to create an EventArray program. Type the following class header, the main() method header, and their opening curly brackets:

```
public class EventArray
{
   public static void main(String[] args)
   {
```

3   Declare an array of five Event objects using the following code. You also will declare an integer that can be used as a subscript.

```
Event[] someEvents = new Event[5];
int x;
```

4   Enter the following for loop that calls the Event constructor five times, making each Event type 'X' with a minimum charge of 0.0:

```
for(x = 0; x < 5; ++x)
   someEvents[x] = new Event('X',0.0);
```

5   To confirm that the Event objects have been created, print their values by typing the following:

```
for(x = 0; x < 5; ++x)
   System.out.println(someEvents[x].getEventType() +
      "   " + someEvents[x].getEventMinRate());
```

6   Add the two curly brackets that end the main() method and the class definition.

7   Save the program as **EventArray.java** in the Chapter.05 folder. Compile and run the program. Figure 5-3 shows the program's output.

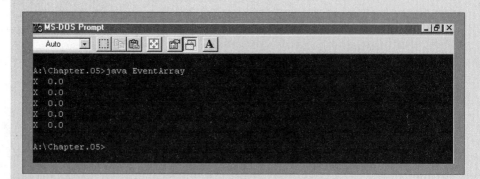

Figure 5-3: Output of the EventArray program

An array of five Event objects—each of which has the same event type and fee—is not very interesting or useful. Next, you will modify the EventArray program so that it creates the events interactively and so each event will possess unique properties.

To create an interactive EventArray program:

1 Open the **EventArray.java** file in your text editor, position the cursor to the right of the opening curly bracket of the EventArray class, press the **Enter** key, and then type the following statements to declare three constants for the corporate, private, and non-profit event rates.

```
static final double CORP_RATE = 75.99;
static final double PRI_RATE = 47.99;
static final double NON_PROF_RATE = 40.99;
```

2 The program will accept keyboard input, so position the cursor to the right of the main() method header and then type **throws Exception**.

3 Just before the for statement that constructs five events, add the following two new variables that will hold an event type and rate and initialize them with dummy values:

```
char event = 'Z';
double rate = 0;
```

4 Within the for loop, remove the line that constructs events with type 'X' and fee 0.0 (someEvents[x] = new Event('X',0.0);), and then replace the line with the following block that prompts the user for one of three event types and constructs an appropriate event based on the value entered:

```
{
  System.out.println("Enter event type");
  System.out.println("C for corporate");
  System.out.println("P for private");
  System.out.println("N for non-profit");
  event = (char)System.in.read();
  System.in.read(); System.in.read();
    // Absorbs Enter key
  if(event == 'C')
    rate = CORP_RATE;
  else if(event == 'P')
    rate = PRI_RATE;
  else rate = NON_PROF_RATE;
  someEvents[x] = new Event(event, rate);
}
```

5 Change the body of the last for loop as follows so it prints an event number along with the event information:

```
System.out.println("Event " + (x + 1) + "   " +
  someEvents[x].getEventType()+ "   " +
  someEvents[x].getEventMinRate());
```

> At this point, when you run the program, if you enter an event type that is not *C* or *P*, the program will assume that the rate is the non-profit rate by default.

6 Save, compile, and run the program several times. Confirm that no matter what combination of *C*, *P*, and *N* you use for data entry, the list of events is stored and displayed correctly.

Searching an Array for an Exact Match

When you want to determine whether some variable holds one of many valid values, one option is to use a series of `if` statements to compare the variable to a series of valid values. For example, suppose that a company manufactures 10 items. When a customer places an order for an item, you need to determine whether the item number on the order form is valid. If valid item numbers are sequential, such as 101 through 110, then the following simple `if` statement that uses a logical AND can verify the order number and set a boolean field to `true`: `if(itemOrdered >= 101 && itemOrdered <= 110) validItem = true;`. If the valid item numbers are nonsequential, however—for example, 101, 108, 201, 213, 266, 304, and so on—you must code the following deeply nested `if` statement or a lengthy OR comparison to determine the validity of an item number:

```
if(itemOrdered == 101)
  validItem = true;
else if(itemOrdered == 108)
  validItem = true;
else if(itemOrdered == 201)
  validItem = true;
// and so on
```

Instead of a long series of `if` statements, a more elegant solution is to compare the itemOrdered variable to a list of values in an array. You can initialize the array with the valid values with the following statement:

```
int[] validValues = {101, 108, 201, 213, 266,
                     304, 311, 409, 411, 412};
```

Then, you can use a `for` statement to loop through the array, and set a boolean variable to `true` when a match is found:

```
for(int x = 0; x < 10; ++x)
{
  if(itemOrdered == validValues[x])
    validItem = true;
}
```

This simple for loop replaces the long series of if statements. Also, if a company carries 1,000 items instead of 10, then the only part of the for statement that changes is the comparison in the middle. As an added bonus, if you set up another parallel array with the same number of elements and corresponding data, you can use the same subscript to access additional information. For example, if the 10 items your company carries have 10 different prices, then you can set up any array to hold those prices: double[] prices = {0.89, 1.23, 3.50, 0.69...};. The prices must appear in the same order as their corresponding item numbers in the validValues array. Now the same for loop that finds the valid item number also finds the price, as shown in Figure 5-4. In other words, if the item number is found in the second position in the validValues array, then you can find the correct price in the second position in the prices array.

tip

If you initialize parallel arrays, it is convenient to use spacing so that the values that correspond to each other visually align on the screen or printed page.

```
int[] validValues = {101,  108,  201,  213,  266,

                     304,  311,  409,  411,  412};

double[] prices =    {0.89, 1.23, 3.50, 0.69, 5.79,

                      3.19, 0.99, 0.89, 1.26, 8.00};

for(int x = 0; x < 10; ++x)

{

  if(itemOrdered == validValues[x])

  {

     validItem = true;

     itemPrice = prices[x];

  }

}
```

Figure 5-4: Accessing information in parallel arrays

tip

In an array with many possible matches, it is most efficient to place the most common items first, so they are matched right away. For example, if item 311 is the most often ordered item, place 311 first in the validValues array, and its price ($0.99) first in the prices array.

Within the code shown in Figure 5-4, you compare every itemOrdered with each of the 10 validValues. Even when an itemOrdered is equivalent to the first value in the validValues array (101), you always make nine additional cycles through the array. On each of these nine additional cycles, the comparison between itemOrdered and validValues[x] is always `false`. As soon as a match for an itemOrdered is found, it is most efficient to break out of the `for` loop early. An easy way to accomplish this is to set *x* to a high value within the block of statements executed when there is a match. Then, after a match, the `for` loop will not execute again because the limiting comparison (x < 10) will have been surpassed. Figure 5-5 shows this program.

```
for(x = 0; x < 10; ++x)

{

  if(itemOrdered == validValues[x])

  {

    validItem = true;

    itemPrice = prices[x];

    x = 10;   // Break out of loop when you find a match

  }

}
```

Figure 5-5: Breaking out of a for loop early

Instead of the statement that sets *x* to 10 when a match is found, you could place a break; statement within the loop in its place.

Some programmers disapprove of breaking out of a for loop early, whether you do it by setting a variable's value or by using a break; statement. If you (or your instructor) agree with this philosophy, then use a method that uses a while statement as described next.

As an alternative, you can choose to forgo the `for` loop entirely, and use a `while` loop to search for a match. Using this approach, you set a subscript to zero and while the itemOrdered is not equal to a value in the array, you increase the subscript and keep looking. You search only while the subscript remains lower than the number of elements in the array. If the subscript increases to 10, then you never found a match in the 10-element array. If the loop ends before the subscript reaches 10, then you found a match and the correct price can be assigned to the itemPrice variable. Figure 5-6 shows this programming approach.

```
x = 0;

while(x < 10 && itemOrdered != validValues[x])

  ++x;

if(x != 10)

{

  validItem = true;

  itemPrice = prices[x];

}
```

Figure 5-6: Searching with a while loop

Next, you will delete the if statements that determine a price for each event at Event Handlers Incorporated and replace them with an array search.

To determine event pricing using parallel arrays:

1 Open the **EventArray.java** file in your text editor, position the cursor to the right of the statement that declares the rate variable (`double rate;`), and then press the **Enter** key to start a new line of text. Then type the following character array to hold the codes for the three allowed event types:
`char[] eventCode = {'C', 'P', 'N'};`

2 Press the **Enter** key, and then on the next line, add the following code to create a double array to hold the rates charged for the three event types:

`double[] eventRate = {CORP_RATE, PRI_RATE, NON_PROF_RATE};`

tip

> Notice that you can use symbolic constants as well as literal constants as array elements. You could even combine the two types of constants within the same array. You can even use variable names as array elements. Don't forget, however, that all elements within a single array must have the same type.

3 Remove the five lines of code (beginning with `if(event == 'C')...`) that constitute the `if...else` structure that determines the event rate. This `if` structure is no longer needed. Replace it with the following `for` loop that searches through the eventCode array, and, upon finding a match, selects a price from the eventRate array:

```
for(int i = 0; i < 3; ++i)
{
  if(event == eventCode[i])
    rate = eventRate[i];
}
```

4 Save, compile, and run the program. Confirm that, just as before, no matter what combination of C, P, and N you use for data entry, the list of events is stored and displayed correctly.

When you run the program, if you enter an invalid event code, an Event object is created and an incorrect rate is assigned to the Event object. Now that you have an array of valid event codes, it is a simple matter to disallow any invalid event codes (those other than C, P, or N).

To force all five Event objects to contain valid codes and rates:

1 Within the EventArray.java program, position the cursor to the right of the `double rate = 0;` variable declaration, press the **Enter** key to start a new line, and then enter the following code to create a boolean variable named codeIsValid: **boolean codeIsValid;**.

2 Position the cursor at the beginning of the for statement that begins the search through the eventCode array (`for(int i = 0; ...)`), and then press the **Enter** key to start a new line. Just before the for loop, you need to ensure that the codeIsValid variable is set to `false` by typing **codeIsValid = false;**.

3 Within the for loop, change the if statement that checks the eventCode array as follows so that if the event variable is equivalent to one of the eventCodes, then a block of two statements will execute—besides setting the rate, the block sets the codeIsValid variable to `true`:

```
if(event == eventCode[i])
{
  rate = eventRate[i];
  codeIsValid = true;
}
```

You can make the program more efficient by breaking out of the for loop early when an event matches an eventCode array element. Set the loop control variable i to a high value when a match is found.

4 Place the cursor to the right of `codeIsValid = true;` and then press the **Enter** key to start a new line. Type **i = 3;** on the new line.

5 Position the cursor at the beginning of the statement that constructs one of the five someEvents objects (`someEvents[x] = new Event(event, rate);`). Press the **Enter** key to start a new line and insert the following condition so the object is created only if the code is valid: **if(codeIsValid)**. To show clearly that the assignment statement depends upon the if, insert two spaces at the beginning of the line containing `someEvents[x] = new Event(event, rate);`.

6   Position the cursor just after `someEvents[x] = new Event(event, rate);` and then press the **Enter** key to start a new line. Enter the following `else` clause that reduces x. Now, for example, if a code is not valid on the third pass through the loop when x is 2, x will be decremented to 1. At the top of the `for` loop (in the third section within the parentheses), x is increased to 2 again for the next pass through the `for` loop. So if the user enters a valid code during this fourth execution of the loop, x still will be 2, and an object will correctly be created at someEvent[2].

```
else
    --x;
```

7   Save, compile, and run the program. Enter as many valid and invalid codes as you like. After five of the codes you enter are identified as valid, the five constructed objects will display.

Searching an Array for a Range Match

Searching an array for an exact match is not always practical. For example, suppose your company gives customer discounts based on the quantity of items ordered. Perhaps no discount is given for any order of fewer than a dozen items, but there are increasing discounts available for orders of increasing quantities, as shown in Figure 5-7.

Total Quantity Ordered	Discount
1 to 12	none
13 to 49	10%
50 to 99	14%
100 to 199	18%
200 or more	20%

Figure 5-7: Discount table for an imaginary company

One awkward option is to create a single array to store the discount rates. You could use a variable named numOfItems as a subscript to the array, but the array would need hundreds of entries—for example, `double[] discount = {0, 0, 0, 0, 0, 0, 0, 0, 0, 0, 0, 0, 0, .10, .10, .10 ...};`. When numOfItems is 3, for example, then discount[numOfItems] or discount[3] is 0.

When numOfItems is 14, then discount[numOfItems] or discount[14] is .10. Because a customer might order thousands of items, the array would need to be ridiculously large.

A better option is to create parallel arrays. One array will hold the five discount rates, and the other array will hold five discount range limits. The Total Quantity Ordered column in Figure 5-7 shows five ranges. If you use only the first figure in each range, you can create an array that holds five low limits: `int[ ] discountRangeLimit = {1, 13, 50, 100, 200};`. A parallel array will hold the five discount rates: `double[ ] discount = {0, .10, .14, .18, .20};`. Then, starting at the last discountRangeLimit array element, for any numOfItems greater than or equal to discountRangeLimit[4], the appropriate discount is discount[4]. In other words, for any numOfItems less than discountRangeLimit[4], you should decrement the subscript and look in a lower range. Figure 5-8 shows the code.

```
int[] discountRangeLimit = {1, 13, 50, 100, 200};

double[] discount =        {0, .10, .14, .18, .20};

double customerDiscount;

int sub = 4;

while(sub >= 0 && numOfItems < discountRangeLimit[sub])

   --sub;

customerDiscount = discount[sub];
```

Figure 5-8: Searching an array of ranges

Passing Arrays to Methods

You already have seen that you can use any individual array element in the same manner as you would use any single variable of the same type. That is, if you declare an integer array as int[] someNums = new int[12];, then you can subsequently print someNums[0] or add one to someNums[1], just as you would for any integer. Similarly, you can pass a single array element to a method in exactly the same manner as you would pass a variable.

Examine the program shown in Figure 5-9. The program creates an array of four integers and prints them. Then the program calls a method, methodGetsOneInt(), four times, passing each element in turn. The method prints the number, changes the number to 999, and then prints the number again. Finally, back in main(), the four numbers are printed again.

```
public class PassArrayElement
{
  public static void main(String[] args)
  {
    int[] someNums = {5, 10, 15, 20};
    int x;
    for(x = 0; x < 4; ++x)
      System.out.println("In main " + someNums[x]);
      for(x = 0; x < 4; ++x)
      methodGetsOneInt(someNums[x]);
    for(x = 0; x < 4; ++x)
      System.out.println("At end of main " + someNums[x]);
  }
  public static void methodGetsOneInt(int one)
  {
    System.out.println("In methodGetsOneInt " + one);
    one = 999;
    System.out.println("After change " + one);
  }
}
```

Figure 5-9: PassArrayElement program

Figure 5-10 shows the program output.

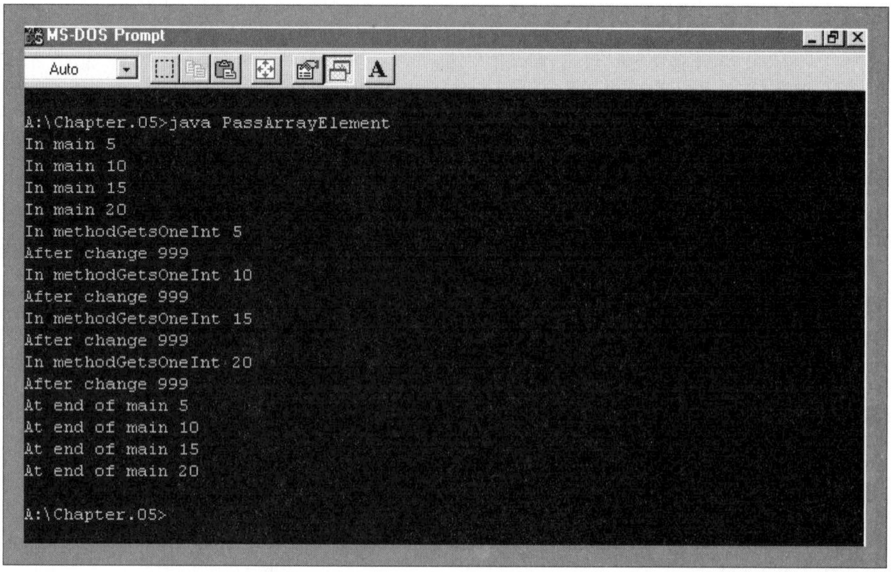

Figure 5-10: Output of the PassArrayElement program

As you can see from Figure 5-10, the four numbers that were changed in the methodGetsOneInt() method remain unchanged back in main(). The variable named one is local to the methodGetsOneInt() method, and any changes to variables passed into the method are not permanent and are not reflected in the array in the main() program. Each variable named one in the methodGetsOneInt() method holds only a copy of the array element passed into the method.

The outcome is quite different when you pass an entire array to a method. Arrays, like all objects, are passed by reference, which, as you will recall from Chapter 3, means that the method receives the actual memory address of the array and has access to the actual values in the array elements. The program shown in Figure 5-11 creates an array of four integers. After the integers print, the entire array is passed to a method named methodGetsArray(). Within the method, the numbers print, which shows that they retain their values from main(), but then the value 888 is assigned to each number. Even though the methodGetsArray() method is a void method (meaning nothing is returned to the main() method), when the program prints the array for the second time within main(), all of the values have been changed to 888, as you can see in Figure 5-12. Because arrays are passed by reference, the methodGetsArray() method "knows" the address of the array declared in main() and makes its changes directly to the original array that was declared in the main() method.

```
public class PassArray
{
  public static void main(String[] args) throws Exception
  {
    int[] someNums = {5, 10, 15, 20};
    int x;
    for(x = 0; x < 4; ++x)
      System.out.println("In main " + someNums[x]);
    methodGetsArray(someNums);
    for(x = 0; x < 4; ++x)
      System.out.println("At end of main " + someNums[x]);
  }
  public static void methodGetsArray(int[] arr)
  {
    for(int y = 0; y < 4; ++y)
    {
      System.out.println("In methodGetsArray " + arr[y]);
      arr[y] = 888;
    }
  }
}
```

Figure 5-11: PassArray program

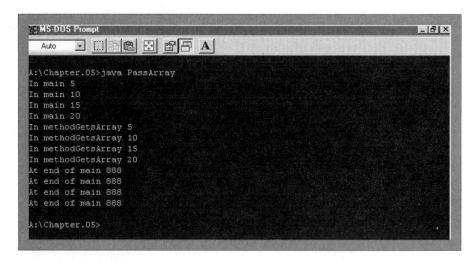

Figure 5-12: Output of the PassArray program

Next, you will add a new method to the Event object class type. Then you will add steps to the EventArray program so you can pass an array of Event objects to a method. This program will demonstrate that changes made within the method affect values in the array permanently.

To add a new method to the Event class:

1 In your text editor, open the **Event.java** file from the Chapter.05 folder on your Student Disk. This text file contains the class definition for Event objects.

2 Add a new setEventMinRate() method that you can use to alter an Event object's eventMinRate. Position the cursor to the left of the final closing curly bracket for the Event class, and then press the **Enter** key to start a new line above the closing bracket. Then enter the following setEventMinRate() method:

```
public void setEventMinRate(double rate)
{
   eventMinRate = rate;
}
```

3 Save the Event.java file, and then compile it from the command line using the command **javac Event.java**.

Next, you will add a method call and a method to the EventArray program. The method will receive an array of Event objects and increase the rate for each event by $5.00.

To add a method call and a method to the EventArray program:

1 Open the **EventArray.java** file in your text editor, position the cursor to the left of the closing curly bracket for the main() method in the EventArray class, and then press the **Enter** key to insert a new blank line above the closing curly bracket.

2 Enter the following method call to a raiseRates() method, which will receive the someEvents array and raise each Event's rate by $5.00:
raiseRates(someEvents);.

3 Press the **Enter** key. To demonstrate that the rates changed as a result of the raiseRates() method, add the following print loop on the new line.

> If you do not want to type this statement, you can simply use your editor's copy function to copy the identical statement that already exists within the program.

```
for(x = 0; x < 5; ++x)
  System.out.println("Event " + (x + 1) + "  " +
    someEvents[x].getEventType()+ "  " +
    someEvents[x].getEventMinRate());
```

4 Place the cursor to the right of the main() method's closing curly bracket, and then press the **Enter** key to start a new blank line before the closing bracket for the EventArray program. Then enter the following raiseRates() method. The method loops through the array five times. With each iteration, the method gets the array element's current rate, stores it in a temporary double variable, and adds $5.00 to the temporary variable. Then the temporary variable value is assigned back into the array object's rate with the setEventMinRate() method.

```
private static void raiseRates(Event[] evnt)
{
  double temp;
  for(int q = 0; q < 5; ++q)
  {
    temp = evnt[q].getEventMinRate();
    temp += 5;
    evnt[q].setEventMinRate(temp);
  }
}
```

> You can replace the three statements temp = evnt[q].getEventMinRate();, temp += 5;, and evnt[q].setEventMinRate(temp); with one statement: evnt[q].setEventMinRate(evnt[q].getEventMinRate() + 5);. If this method call within a method call is clear to you, feel free to use it.

5 Save the program, and then compile and run it. After you answer the prompts to create five events, their old rates and the new increased rates should display on screen. Figure 5-13 shows a sample run.

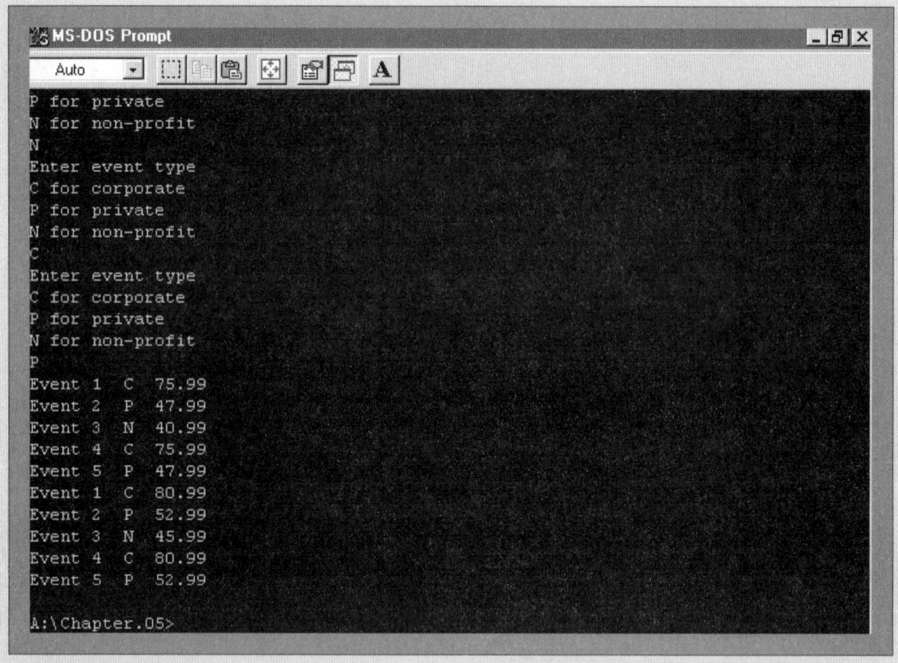

```
MS-DOS Prompt                                                    _ 8 x
 Auto         ▼   [ ]               A
P for private
N for non-profit
N
Enter event type
C for corporate
P for private
N for non-profit
C
Enter event type
C for corporate
P for private
N for non-profit
P
Event 1  C  75.99
Event 2  P  47.99
Event 3  N  40.99
Event 4  C  75.99
Event 5  P  47.99
Event 1  C  80.99
Event 2  P  52.99
Event 3  N  45.99
Event 4  C  80.99
Event 5  P  52.99

A:\Chapter.05>
```

Figure 5-13: Sample output of the EventArray program with the raiseRates() method

Using the Array Length

Every array object that you create is automatically assigned a data field named length. The **length field** contains the number of elements in the array. For example, when you declare double[] salaries = new double[8];, the field salaries.length is assigned the value 8.

When you work with array elements, you must ensure that the subscript you use remains in the range zero through length -1. To access all eight elements of a salaries array, for example, you can code the number 8 explicitly, as in for(x = 0; x < 8; ++x)... If you modify your program to hold more or fewer array elements, you must remember to change every appropriate reference to the array size within the program. Many text editors have a "find and replace" feature that lets you change all the 8s, but you must be careful not to change any 8s that have nothing to do with the array. A better technique is to use salaries.length, as in for(x = 0; x < salaries.length; ++x)... That way, if you change the size of the salaries array, then the array always will use the correct maximum length.

Next, you will remove the explicit 5 you have used in each `for` loop within the EventArray program, and replace each with a reference to the length field.

To use the array length field:

1 Locate the first `for` statement in the main() method of your EventArray program. This loop constructs five Event objects. Delete the 5 in the `for` expression and then replace that number with **someEvents.length**.

2 Locate the next `for` loop in the EventArray program, which checks the event codes entered by a user. Delete the 3 from the `for` loop and replace that number with **eventCode.length**.

3 Locate the next `for` loop, which prints array values. Delete the 5 in the `for` loop and replace that number with **someEvents.length**.

4 The last `for` loop in the main() method of the EventArray program prints the objects. Replace the 5 in this loop with **someEvents.length**.

5 Within the raiseRates() method, locate the `for` loop that raises the rate of each array element. Within the raiseRates() method, the array name is evnt. Replace the 5 in this `for` loop with **evnt.length**.

6 Save, compile, and run the program. The execution of the program should be the same as it was before—five objects are created and three valid event codes are checked.

S U M M A R Y

- An array is a list of variables that all have the same type and same name. You declare an array variable by inserting a pair of square brackets after the type.

- Declaring an array and actually reserving memory space for it are two distinct processes. You use the keyword **new** to reserve memory locations for the array elements.

- A subscript is an integer contained within square brackets that indicates one of an array's variables, or elements. An array's elements are numbered beginning with zero.

- When you work with any individual array element, you treat it no differently than you would a single variable. Array names actually represent computer memory addresses—they are references, as are all Java objects.

- When you declare an array name, it has the value **null**, or Unicode value '\u0000'.

- When you define an array using **new**, the array name takes on a memory address value.

- Each element of a numeric array is automatically set to zero, character array elements are assigned '\u0000', and boolean array elements are automatically assigned the value **false**.

■ To initialize an array, you can use a list of values that are separated by commas and enclosed within curly brackets. When you initialize an array by giving it values upon creation, you do not give the array a size; the size will be assigned based on the number of values you place in the initializing list.

■ The power of arrays becomes apparent when you begin to use subscripts that are variables rather than subscripts that are constant values.

■ Just as you can declare arrays of integers or doubles, you can declare arrays of any type, including objects.

■ You must explicitly call individual constructors for array objects.

■ To use a method that belongs to an object that is part of an array, you insert the appropriate subscript notation after the array name and prior to the dot that precedes the method name.

■ You can find exact matches or range matches for a variable by looping through an array. It is efficient to break out of the loop as soon as a match is found.

■ You can pass a single array element to a method in exactly the same manner you would pass a variable. The array element is passed by value; that is, a copy is made.

■ You can pass an array to a method. Arrays, like all objects, are passed by reference; the method has access to the actual values in the array elements.

■ You can use an array's length field to determine the number of elements in an array.

Q U E S T I O N S

1. A list of variables that all have the same type and same name is a(n) _____.
   a. register
   b. array
   c. list
   d. index

2. When you declare an array variable, you must insert _____ after the type.
   a. a pair of square brackets
   b. a pair of parentheses
   c. a pair of curly brackets
   d. the keyword `array`

3. You reserve memory locations for an array when you _____.
   a. declare the array name
   b. use the keyword `new`
   c. use the keyword `mem`
   d. explicitly store values within the array elements

4. The statement `int[] value = new int[34];` reserves memory for _____ integers.
   a. 0
   b. 33
   c. 34
   d. 35

5. An integer contained within square brackets that indicates one of an array's variables is a(n) _____.
   a. pointer
   b. parameter
   c. argument
   d. subscript

6. If you declare an array as `int[] num = new int[6];`, the first element of the array is _____.
   a. num[0]
   b. num[1]
   c. num[]
   d. impossible to tell

7. If you declare an array as `int[] num = new int[6];`, the last element of the array is _____.
   a. num[5]
   b. num[6]
   c. num[7]
   d. impossible to tell

8. Array names are _____.
   a. values
   b. functions
   c. references
   d. allusions

9. Unicode value '\u0000' also is known as _____.
   a. nill
   b. void
   c. nada
   d. null

10. When you initialize an array by giving it values upon creation, you _____.
    a. do not give the array a size
    b. also must give the array a size
    c. must make all the values zero, blank, or `false`
    d. must make sure each value is different from the others

11. Assume an array is declared as `int[] num = new int[4];`. Which of the following statements correctly assigns the value 100 to each of the four array elements?
    a. `for(x = 0; x < 3; ++x) num[x] = 100;`
    b. `for(x = 0; x < 4; ++x) num[x] = 100;`
    c. `for(x = 1; x < 4; ++x) num[x] = 100;`
    d. `for(x = 1; x < 5; ++x) num[x] = 100;`

12. If a class named Student contains a method setID() that takes an integer argument, and you create an array of 20 Student objects named scholar, which of the following statements correctly assigns an ID number to the first Student scholar?

    a. `Student[0].setID(1234);`

    b. `scholar[0].setID(1234);`

    c. `Student.setID[0](1234);`

    d. `scholar.setID[0](1234);`

13. Assuming `char[] goodResponses = {'Y', 'y', 'N', 'n'};`, which of the following statements tests userEntry and sets the boolean variable goodChoice to `true` if the userEntry is in the goodResponses list?

    a. `for(x = 0; x < 4; ++x)`
       `if(userEntry = goodResponses) goodChoice == true;`

    b. `for(x = 0; x < 4; ++x)`
       `if(userEntry[x] = goodResponses) goodChoice = true;`

    c. `for(x = 0; x < 4; ++x)`
       `if(userEntry = goodResponses[x]) goodChoice == true;`

    d. `for(x = 0; x < 4; ++x)`
       `if(userEntry == goodResponses[x]) goodChoice = true;`

14. Two arrays with the same number of elements and corresponding data are
    _____.

    a. competitive
    b. illegal
    c. identical
    d. parallel

15. Searching through an array for an exact match to some variable is a good idea when
    _____.

    a. no variable values are invalid
    b. the variable values to be matched are sequential
    c. there are relatively few possibilities for the value in the variable
    d. you need to match a variable based on a range of values

16. If a test is graded so that a score of 90 or above is an A, 80 to 89 is a B, and so on, you can create a gradeLimit array (`int[] gradeLimit = {90, 80, 70, 60, 0};`) and a grade array (`char[] grade = {'A', 'B', 'C', 'D', 'F'};`). Which of the following statements assigns the correct grade to a letterGrade variable based on the variable score?

    a. `for(x = 0; x < 4; ++x)`
       `if(score >= gradeLimit[x]) letterGrade = grade[x];`

    b. `for(x = 4; x >= 0; --x)`
       `if(score >= gradeLimit[x]) letterGrade = grade[x];`

    c. `for(x = 0; x < 4; ++x)`
       `if(score >= grade[x]) letterGrade = grade[x];`

    d. `for(x = 4; x >= 0; --x)`
       `if(score <= gradeLimit[x]) letterGrade = grade[x];`

17. When you pass an array element to a method, the method receives _____.
   a. a copy of the array
   b. the address of the array
   c. a copy of the value in the element
   d. the address of the element

18. Arrays are passed by _____.
   a. reference
   b. value
   c. referral
   d. copying

19. When you pass an array to a method, the method receives _____.
   a. a copy of the array
   b. a copy of the first element in the array
   c. the address of the array
   d. nothing

20. If you pass an array from a main() method to a method named changeIt(), and the method changes a value in the array, then _____.
   a. you receive an error message
   b. the original array element in main() changes
   c. the original element in main() remains unchanged
   d. the original element in main() changes only if you return a value from the method

E X E R C I S E S

1. Write a program that can hold five integers in an array. Display the integers from first to last, and then display the integers from last to first.

2. Write a program that prompts the user to make a choice for a pizza size—S, M, L, or X—and then displays the price as $6.99, $8.99, $12.50, or $15.00 accordingly.

3. a. Create a class named Taxpayer. Data fields for Taxpayers include Social Security number (use an int for the type, and do not use dashes within the Social Security number) and yearly gross income. Methods include a constructor that requires values for both data fields, and two get methods that return each of the data field values. Write a program that declares an array of 10 Taxpayer objects. Set each Social Security number to 999999999 and each gross income to zero. Display the 10 Taxpayer objects.

   b. Modify your program so each Taxpayer has a successive Social Security number from 1 through 10, and gross incomes that range from $10,000 to $100,000, increasing by $10,000 for each successive Taxpayer.

4. Create an array that stores 20 prices, such as 2.34, 7.89, 1.34, and so on. Display the sum of all the prices. Display all values less than 5.00. Calculate the average of the prices, and display all values higher than the calculated average value.

5.   a. Write a program that prompts a professor to input grades for five different courses for 10 students. Prompt the professor to enter one grade at a time using the prompt "Enter grades for student #1" and "Enter grade #1". Verify that the professor enters only A, B, C, D, or F. Use variables for the student numbers (1 through 10) and grade numbers (1 through 5). The class name is GradePoint.

      b. Modify the GradePoint program so that it calculates the grade point average (GPA) for each student. A student receives four grade points for an A, three grade points for a B, two grade points for a C, one grade point for a D, and zero grade points for an F. Store the grades and points in parallel arrays. Search the arrays to determine the points for the grade. Store the GPA for each student in another array. (*Hint*: Copy the GPA for each student to a different array by initializing the new array with GPAs from the other array.)

      c. Display the GPA scores from each of the two GPA arrays to verify that the GPAs were copied correctly. Identify which array the scores are from.

6.   a. Write a program that displays a multiple choice quiz of 10 questions with topics related to your favorite hobby. Each question has one correct answer and three possible answers. Verify that the user enters only A, B, or C as the answer. Store the correct answers in an array. Store the user's answers in a second array. If the user responds to a question correctly, display "Correct!"; otherwise display "The correct answer is" and the letter of the correct answer. Determine what to display by comparing the response to the array of correct answers. The class name is Quiz.

      b. Modify your Quiz class so that it displays the number of correct answers after the user answers 10 questions. Determine the score by comparing the two arrays.

7.   a. Write a program that lets the user enter numbers (1 through 9) one at a time, and then prints the numbers that the user entered. Allow the user to enter up to 10 numbers. If the user tries to enter an 11th number, display a message that no more numbers can be entered. Store the numbers in an array. Verify that invalid characters are not entered. The class name is EnterNumbers.

      b. Change the EnterNumbers program so that it lets the user delete or modify a number. Include a menu that shows the options to enter, remove, modify, or display a number, or quit the program. Verify that a correct option is entered. When the user chooses the remove option, prompt the user to specify which number to remove. Verify that the user enters a valid number (1 through 9), and then change that number in the array to 0.

      c. Change the EnterNumbers program so that when the user chooses the modify option, the program prompts the user to specify which number to modify. Verify that the user enters a valid number (1 through 9), ask for the new number, verify that the user enters a valid number, and then change the number in the array.

SECTION B

objectives

In this section you will learn how to:

■ Declare a String object
■ Compare String values
■ Use other String methods
■ Convert Strings to numbers

Strings

Declaring Strings

You learned in Chapter 1 that a sequence of characters enclosed within double quotation marks is a literal string. You have used many literal strings, such as "First Java program", within println() statements. You also can create objects that hold a series of characters and have the type **String**.

••

You also use String **in main() method headers.**

••

The class String is defined in java.lang.String, which automatically is imported into every program you write. You create a String object by using the keyword new and the String constructor method, just as you would create an object of any other type. For example, `String aGreeting = new String("Hello");` is a statement that defines an object named aGreeting, declares it to be of type String, and assigns an initial value of "Hello" to the String. Alternatively, you can declare a String containing "Hello" with `String aGreeting = "Hello";`.

After declaring a String, you can display it in a print() or println() statement, just as you would for any other variable—for example `System.out.println("The greeting is " + aGreeting);`.

Also, as with any other object, you can create an array of Strings. For example, you can store three company department names as `String[] deptName = {"Accounting", "Human Resources", "Sales"};`. You can access these department names like any other array object. For example, to print them, you can use the following code:

```
for(int a = 0; a < deptName.length; ++a)
   System.out.println(deptName[a]);
```

••

Notice that deptName.length; **refers to the length of the array deptName (three elements), and not to the length of any of the String objects stored in the deptName array. Each String object has access to a length() method that returns the length of a String. For example, if deptName[0] is "Accounting", then** deptName[0].length() **is 10.**

••

Next, you will create two arrays to hold event types and manager names for Event Handlers Incorporated. Then, when a user enters an event type, the appropriate event type and manager name will display on the screen.

To add event types and manager names to the EventArray program:

1 Open the **EventArray.java** file in your text editor, position the cursor after the opening curly bracket of the main() method, and then press the **Enter** key to start a new line.

2 Add the array of event types by entering the following:

```
String[] eventType =
  {"Corporate", "Private", "Non-Profit"};
```

3 Press the **Enter** key to start a new line, and then add the following array of manager names:

```
String[] managerName =
  {"Dustin Britt", "Carmen Lindsey", "Robin Armenetti"};
```

4 Locate the for loop that determines if the user entered a valid code. Place the cursor after the statement codeIsValid = true; that appears within the for statement, and then press the **Enter** key to start a new line.

At this point in the program, the variable i indicates the position of a correct event type in the eventCode array. The correct event type is in the same relative position in the eventType array as the correct manager's name is within the managerName array. In other words, managerName[I] "goes with" eventCode[i].

5 Type the following statement that prints the event type and manager's name on the new line:

```
System.out.println("The manager for " + eventType[i]
  + " events is " + managerName[i]);
```

6 To simplify screen output, comment out the call to raiseRate() as well as the lines that print the raised rates. Type // at the beginning of each of these lines.

7 Save, compile, and test the program. Your output should look like Figure 5-14.

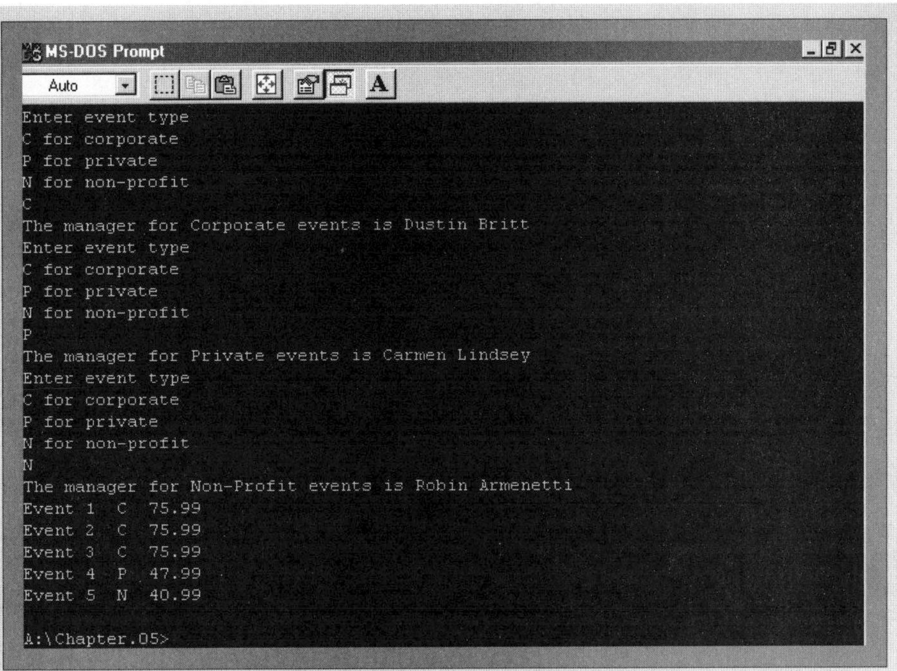

```
MS-DOS Prompt                                              _ |8|X|
Auto      ▼   □  ⊡  ⊞  ⊞  ⊡ ⊟   A
Enter event type
C for corporate
P for private
N for non-profit
C
The manager for Corporate events is Dustin Britt
Enter event type
C for corporate
P for private
N for non-profit
P
The manager for Private events is Carmen Lindsey
Enter event type
C for corporate
P for private
N for non-profit
N
The manager for Non-Profit events is Robin Armenetti
Event 1  C  75.99
Event 2  C  75.99
Event 3  C  75.99
Event 4  P  47.99
Event 5  N  40.99

A:\Chapter.05>
```

Figure 5-14: Output of the EventArray program with event types and manager names

Comparing Strings

A String is an object, like an array. In many programming languages, you create a string by creating an array of characters. In the Java programming language, however, String is a class, and each created String is a class object. Like an array object, or any other object, a String variable name is actually a reference; that is, a String variable name actually refers to a location in memory rather than to a particular value.

The distinction is subtle, but when you declare a variable of a basic, primitive type, such as int x = 10;, the memory address where x is located holds the value 10. If you later assign a new value to x—for example, x = 45;—then the value 45 replaces the 10 at the assigned memory address. When you declare a String as String aGreeting = "Hello";, aGreeting holds a memory address where the characters "Hello" are stored. If you subsequently assign a new value to aGreeting, such as aGreeting = "Bonjour";, then the address held by aGreeting is altered; now aGreeting holds a new address where the characters "Bonjour" are stored. "Bonjour" is an entirely new object created with its own location. The "Hello" String is actually still in memory; it's just that aGreeting isn't holding its address anymore. Eventually, a part of the Java system called the

garbage collector will discard the "Hello" characters. Strings, therefore, are never actually changed; instead, new Strings are created and String variables hold the new addresses. Strings and other objects that can't be changed are known as **immutable**.

Because String variables hold memory addresses, you cannot make a simple comparison to determine whether two String objects are equivalent. For example, if you declare two Strings as `String aGreeting = "Hello";` and `String anotherGreeting = "Hello";`, Java will evaluate a comparison such as `if(aGreeting == anotherGreeting)...` as `false`. When you compare aGreeting to anotherGreeting with the `==` operator, you are comparing their memory addresses, and not their values.

Fortunately, the String class provides you with a number of useful methods. The equals() method evaluates the contents of two String objects to determine if they are equivalent. The method returns `true` if the objects have identical contents. For example, Figure 5-15 shows two String objects and several comparisons. Each of the comparisons in Figure 5-15 is `true`; each comparison results in printing the line "Name's the same".

```
String aName = "Roger";

String anotherName = "Roger";

if(aName.equals(anotherName))

   System.out.println("Name's the same");

if(anotherName.equals(aName))

   System.out.println("Name's the same");

if(aName.equals("Roger");

   System.out.println("Name's the same");
```

Figure 5-15: String comparisons

> The equals() method returns `true` only if two Strings are identical in content. Thus a String holding "Roger " (with a space after the *r*) is *not* equivalent to a String holding "Roger" (with no space after the *r*).

Each String shown in Figure 5-15—aName and anotherName—is an object of type String, so each String has access to the equals() method. The aName object can call equals() with `aName.equals()`, or the anotherName object can call equals() with `anotherName.equals()`. The equals() method can take either a variable String object or a literal String as its argument.

The **equalsIgnoreCase() method** is very similar to the equals() method. As its name implies, it ignores case when determining if two Strings are equivalent. Thus, `aName.equals("roGER")` is `false`, but `aName.equalsIgnoreCase("roGER")` is **true**. This method is very useful when users type responses to prompts in your program. You can never predict when a user might use the Shift key or the Caps Lock key during data entry. The equalsIgnoreCase() method allows you to test entered data without regard to capitalization.

The **compareTo() method** provides additional information. When you use compareTo() to compare two String objects, the method returns zero only if the two Strings hold the same value. If there is any difference between the Strings, a negative number is returned if the calling object is "less than" the argument, and a positive number is returned if the calling object is "more than" the argument. Strings are considered to be "less than" or "more than" each other based on their Unicode values; thus, "a" is less than "b" and "b" is less than "c".

For example, if aName holds "Roger", then the method call `aName.compareTo("Robert")` returns a 5. The number is positive, indicating that "Roger" is more than "Robert". This does not mean that "Roger" has more characters than "Robert"; it means that "Roger" is alphabetically "more" than "Robert". The comparison proceeds as follows:

- The *R* in "Roger" and the *R* in "Robert" are compared, and found to be equal.
- The *o* in "Roger" and the *o* in "Robert" are compared, and found to be equal.
- The *g* in "Roger" and the *b* in "Robert" are compared—they are different. The numeric value of *g* minus the numeric value of *b* is 5 (because *g* is five letters after *b* in the alphabet), so the compareTo() method returns the value 5.

Often, you don't care what the return value of compareTo() is specifically; you simply want to determine if it is positive or negative when, for example, attempting to place two Strings in alphabetical order. For example, you can use a test such as `if(aWord.compareTo(anotherWord)<0)`... to determine whether aWord is alphabetically less than anotherWord. If aWord is a String variable that holds the value "hamster", and anotherWord is a String variable that holds the value "iguana", then the comparison `if(aWord.compareTo(anotherWord)<0)` yields **true**.

Next, you will compare two state names to each element in an array of Strings to determine whether each state name occurs within the array.

To compare a String to each element in an array:

1 Open a new text file in your text editor, and then enter the following opening lines for a FindState class:

```
public class FindState
{
    public static void main(String[] args)
    {
```

2 Enter the following array of String objects that holds the state names where Event Handlers Incorporated has offices:

```
String[] states = {"Alaska", "California", "Illinois",
   "Oregon", "Texas", "Wisconsin", "Wyoming"};
```

3 For testing purposes, assign the following two state names to two String objects named firstState and secondState:

```
String firstState = "Illinois";
   // This state will be found in the list
String secondState = "Ohio";
   // This state will not be found in the list
```

4 Next, declare the following integer variable that you will use as a subscript, and a boolean variable that you will set to `true` when a state name is found in the array:

```
int x;
boolean found = false;
```

5 Enter the following `for` loop that compares the firstState to each state in the array. When a match is found, set the boolean found variable to `true`.

```
for(x = 0; x < states.length; ++x)
  if(firstState.equals(states[x]))
    found = true;
```

6 At the end of the loop, enter the following statements to print a statement indicating whether the firstState was found:

```
if(found)
  System.out.println(firstState + " is in the list");
else
  System.out.println(firstState + " is not in the list");
```

7 Now enter the following statements to reset the variable found to `false` and then repeat the search process for the secondState variable:

```
found = false;
for(x = 0; x < states.length; ++x)
  if(secondState.equals(states[x]))
    found = true;
  if(found)
    System.out.println(secondState + " is in the list");
  else
    System.out.println(secondState + " is not in the list");
```

8 Enter the two closing curly brackets that end the main() method and the FindState class.

9 Save the program as **FindState.java** in the Chapter.05 folder on your Student Disk. Compile and test the program. The program's output appears in Figure 5-16.

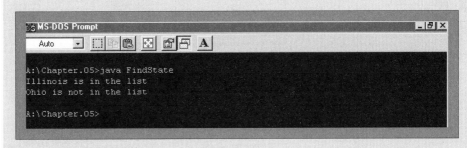

Figure 5-16: Output of the FindState program

Using Other String Methods

A wide variety of additional String methods are available with the String class. The methods toUpperCase() and toLowerCase() convert any String to its uppercase or lowercase equivalent. For example, if you declare a String as `String aWord = "something";`, then `aWord = aWord.toUpperCase` assigns "SOMETHING" to aWord.

The method indexOf() determines whether a specific character occurs within a String. If it does, the method returns the position of the character. String positions, like array positions, begin with zero. The return value is -1 if the character does not exist in the String. For example, for `String myName = "Stacy";`, the value of `myName.indexOf('a')` is 2, and the value of `myName.indexOf('q')` is -1.

The method charAt() requires an integer argument which indicates the position of the character the method returns. For example, if myName is a String holding "Stacy", then the value of myName.charAt(0) is 'S' and myName.charAt(1) is 't'.

The methods endsWith() and startsWith() each take a String argument and return `true` or `false` if a String object does or does not end with or start with the specified argument. For example, if `String myName = "Stacy";`, then `myName.startsWith("Sta")` is `true` and `myName.endsWith("z")` is `false`.

The replace() method allows you to replace all occurrences of some character within a String. For example, if `String yourName = "Annette";`, then `String goofyName = yourName.replace('n', 'X');` assigns "AXXette" to goofyName.

The **toString() method** converts any primitive type to a String. So, if you declare a String as `theString` and an integer as `int someInt = 4;`, then `theString = toString(someInt);` results in the String "4" being assigned to theString. The toString() method is not part of the String class; it is a method included in Java that you can use with any type of object. You actually have been using toString() throughout this book without knowing it. When you use print() and println(), their arguments are converted to Strings automatically if necessary.

You already know that you can join Strings with other Strings or values by using a plus sign (+); you have been using this approach in println() statements since Chapter 1. For example, you can print a firstName, a space, and a lastName with `System.out.println(firstName + " " + lastName);`. Joining Strings is called **concatenation**. Additionally, you can extract part of a String with the substring() method, and use it alone or concatenate it with another String. The substring method takes two arguments—a start position and an end position—that are both based on the fact that a String's first position is position zero. For example, the program segment shown in Figure 5-17 produces the output shown in Figure 5-18.

```
String[] dayOfWeek = {"Monday", "Tuesday",
   "Wednesday", "Thursday", "Friday"};
String sentence;
int x;
for(x = 0; x < dayOfWeek.length; ++x)
{
   sentence = "The abbreviation for " + dayOfWeek[x] + " is " +
      dayOfWeek[x].substring(0,3);
   System.out.println(sentence);
}
```

Figure 5-17: Program segment demonstrating String concatenation

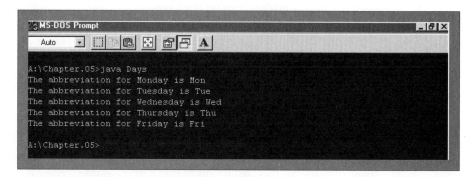

Figure 5-18: Output of the String concatenation code segment

To demonstrate the use of the String methods, you will create a simple guessing game, similar to Hangman. The user will guess letters and attempt to guess the motto of Event Handlers Incorporated.

To create the guessing game:

1 Open a new text file in your text editor. Enter the following first few lines of a SecretPhrase program. The program will contain the target phrase that the user will try to guess ("Plan With Us") as well as a display phrase that is mostly asterisks (with a few hints).

```
public class SecretPhrase
{
  public static void main(String[] args) throws Exception
  {
    String targetPhrase = "Plan With Us";
    String displayPhrase = "P*** W*** U*";
```

2 Add the following variables that will hold the user's guess and the position of a guess that is found within the phrase:

```
char guess;
int position;
```

3 Next, add the following brief instruction:

```
System.out.println("Play our game - guess our motto");
```

4 Enter the statement to display the hint phrase:

```
System.out.println(displayPhrase);
```

5 Add the following loop that continues while asterisks remain in the displayPhrase. The user will enter a letter. You will use the indexOf() method to determine whether the guessed letter appears in the targetPhrase. If it does not, then ask the user to guess again. If the guessed letter appears in the phrase, you reconstruct the display phrase with the following:

■ The substring of characters in the display phrase that comes before the correct guess.
■ The correct guess.
■ The substring of characters in the display phrase that appears after the correct guess; in other words, the correct letter replaces the appropriate asterisk.

```
while(displayPhrase.indexOf('*') != -1)
{
  System.out.println("Enter a letter");
  guess = (char)System.in.read();
```

```
System.in.read(); System.in.read();
   // Absorbs Enter key
position = targetPhrase.indexOf(guess);
   // Determines position of guess
if(position == -1) // If guess is not in target phrase
   System.out.println("Sorry - guess again");
else // If guess is in target phrase
{
   displayPhrase = displayPhrase.substring(0,position) +
      guess + displayPhrase.substring
         (position+1,displayPhrase.length());
   System.out.println(displayPhrase);
}
}
```

6 The while loop will continue until all the asterisks in the targetPhrase are replaced by correct letters. Therefore, after the closing curly bracket for the while loop, enter **System.out.println("Congratulations!");**.

7 Type the closing curly brackets for the main() method and for the SecretPhrase class.

8 Save the program as **SecretPhrase.java** in the Chapter.05 folder on your Student Disk, and then compile and run the program. Make sure you understand how all the String methods contribute to the success of this program.

Converting Strings to Numbers

If a String contains all numbers, as in "649", you can convert it from a String to a number so you can use it for arithmetic, or use it like any other number. To convert a String to an integer, you use the **Integer** class, which is part of java.lang, and therefore automatically is imported into programs you write. A method of the Integer class is parseInt(), which takes a String argument and returns its integer value. For example, `int anInt = Integer.parseInt("649");` stores the numeric value 649 in the variable anInt. You can then use the integer value just as you would any other integer.

> **tip**
>
> The word *parse* in English means "to resolve into component parts," as when you "parse a sentence." In Java, to **parse** a String means to break its separate characters into a numeric format.

It is only slightly more difficult to convert a String object to a double value. You must use the **Double** class, which, like the Integer class, also is imported into your programs automatically. Conversion to a double variable is a two-step process:

- You use the Double.valueOf() method to convert a String into a Double (with an uppercase *D*) object.
- You use the doubleValue() method to convert the Double to a double variable.

For example, to convert a String containing "147.82" to a double, you can use the following code:

```
String stringValue = new String("147.82");
Double tempValue = Double.valueOf(stringValue);
double doubleValue = doubleValue(tempValue);
```

The stringValue is passed to the Double.valueOf() method, which returns a Double object. The Double object, tempValue, is passed to the doubleValue() method, which returns a double variable.

tip

The Double and Integer classes are examples of wrappers. A **wrapper** is a class or object that is "wrapped around" a simpler thing. You use the Double (uppercase *D*) class to make it convenient to work with primitive double (lowercase *d*) variables.

When planning an event, Event Handlers Incorporated needs to know how many guests to expect. Next, you will prompt the user for the number of guests, read characters from the keyboard, store the characters in a String, and then convert the String to an integer.

To create a program that accepts integer input:

1   Open a new text file in your text editor, and then enter the following first few lines of a NumInput class that will accept numeric input:

```
public class NumInput
{
  public static void main(String[] args) throws Exception
  {
```

2   Declare the following variables to hold the input String, each character of input, and the resulting integer:

```
String inputString = new String();
char newChar;
int inputNumber;
```

3   Prompt the user for the number of guests and read in the first character by entering the following lines:

```
System.out.println
  ("Enter the number of guests at your event");
newChar = (char)System.in.read();
```

4 Enter the following `while` loop that continues while you continue to enter digits. Within the loop, you will take the current input String and concatenate each new character to it. Then read another new character before looping back to check if the next character is a digit.

```
while(newChar >= '0' && newChar <= '9')
{
   inputString = inputString + newChar;
   newChar = (char)System.in.read();
}
```

5 When the `while` loop ends, add the following read() statement to absorb the Enter key: `System.in.read();`.

6 Use the following Integer.parseInt() method to convert the input String to an integer. Then use the integer in a numeric decision.

```
inputNumber = Integer.parseInt(inputString);
if(inputNumber > 100)
   System.out.println("A surcharge will apply!");
```

7 Enter the final two closing brackets to the program.

8 Save the program as **NumInput.java** in the Chapter.05 folder on your Student Disk, and then compile and test the program.

S U M M A R Y

■ A sequence of characters enclosed within double quotation marks is a literal string.

■ You create a String object by using the keyword new and the String constructor method.

■ Each String is a class object and a String variable name is actually a reference. Strings, therefore, are never actually changed; they are immutable.

■ The equals() method evaluates the contents of two String objects to determine whether they are equivalent, and then returns a boolean value.

■ The equalsIgnoreCase() method determines if two Strings are equivalent without considering case.

■ The compareTo() method returns zero if two String objects hold the same value. A negative number is returned if the calling object is "less than" the argument, and a positive number is returned if the calling object is "greater than" the argument.

■ The methods toUpperCase() and toLowerCase() convert any String to its uppercase or lowercase equivalent.

- The method indexOf() determines whether a specific character occurs within a String. If it does, the method returns the position of the character. The return value is -1 if the character does not exist in the String.

- The methods endsWith() and startsWith() each take a String argument and return `true` or `false` if a String object does or does not end with or start with the specified argument.

- The replace() method allows you to replace all occurrences of some character within a String.

- The toString() method converts any primitive type to a String.

- You can join Strings with other Strings or values by using a plus sign (+); this process is called concatenation.

- You can extract part of a String with the substring() method, which takes two arguments—a start position and an end position—that are both based on the fact that a String's first position is position zero.

- If a String contains all numbers, you can convert it to a number.

- The method parseInt() takes a String argument and returns its integer value.

- The method Double.valueOf() converts a String to a Double object; the doubleValue() method converts a Double object to a double variable.

Q U E S T I O N S

1. A sequence of characters enclosed within double quotation marks is a _____.
   a. symbolic string
   b. literal string
   c. prompt
   d. command

2. To create a String object, you can use the keyword _____.
   a. `object`
   b. `create`
   c. `char`
   d. `new`

3. A String variable name is a _____.
   a. reference
   b. value
   c. constant
   d. literal

4. Objects that cannot be changed are _____.
   a. irrevocable
   b. nonvolatile
   c. immutable
   d. stable

5. If you declare two String objects as `String word1 = new String("happy");` and `String word2 = new String("happy");`, then the value of `word1 == word2` is _____.
   a. `true`
   b. `false`
   c. illegal
   d. unknown

6. If you declare two String objects as `String word1 = new String("happy");` and `String word2 = new String("happy");`, then the value of `word1.equals(word2)` is _____.
   a. `true`
   b. `false`
   c. illegal
   d. unknown

7. The method that determines whether two objects are equivalent without regard to case is _____.
   a. equalsNoCase()
   b. toUpperCase()
   c. equalsIgnoreCase()
   d. equals()

8. If a String is declared as `String aStr = new String("lima bean");`, then `aStr.equals("Lima Bean");` is _____.
   a. `true`
   b. `false`
   c. illegal
   d. unknown

9. If you create two String objects using `String name1 = new String("Jordan");` and `String name2 = new String("Jore");`, then `name1.compareTo(name2)` has a value of _____.
   a. `true`
   b. `false`
   c. -1
   d. 1

10. If `String myFriend = new String("Ginny");`, then which of the following has the value 1?
   a. `myFriend.compareTo("Gabby");`
   b. `myFriend.compareTo("Gabriella");`
   c. `myFriend.compareTo("Ghazala");`
   d. `myFriend.compareTo("Hammie");`

11. If `String movie = new String("West Side Story");`, then the value of `movie.indexOf('s')` is _____.
    a. `true`
    b. `false`
    c. 2
    d. 3

12. The replace() method replaces _____.
    a. a String with a character
    b. one String with another String
    c. one character in a String with another character
    d. every occurrence of a character in a String with another character

13. The toString() method converts any _____ to a String.
    a. character
    b. integer
    c. float
    d. of the preceding

14. Joining Strings is called _____.
    a. chaining
    b. joining
    c. linking
    d. concatenation

15. The first position in a String _____.
    a. must be alphabetic
    b. must be uppercase
    c. is position zero
    d. is ignored by the compareTo() method

16. The substring() method requires _____ arguments.
    a. no
    b. one
    c. two
    d. three

17. The method parseInt() converts a(n) _____.
    a. integer to a String
    b. integer to a Double
    c. Double to a String
    d. String to an integer

18. The difference between int and Integer is _____.
    a. int is a primitive type, whereas Integer is a class
    b. int is a class, whereas Integer is a primitive type
    c. nonexistent; they both are primitive types
    d. nonexistent; both are classes

E X E R C I S E S

1. Write a program that stores vowels (*a*, *e*, *i*, *o*, and *u*) in an array. Ask the user to enter a character. Then the program should indicate whether the entered character is a vowel.

2. Store 40 characters in an array, such as `1234%$#@UHGF...` Write a program that produces a count of how many of the characters are letters in the English alphabet, and how many of the characters are not letters.

3. Write a program that prompts the user for a first name. Print a greeting to the person using the name, such as `Hello Kimberly!`.

4. Store 20 integer employee ID numbers in an integer array, and 20 corresponding employee last names in a String array. When a user inputs an ID number, print the appropriate last name.

5. Create an array of Strings containing the days of the week ("Sunday" through "Saturday"). Review the use of the Date class in Chapter 3. The Date class contains a method getDay() that returns an integer value zero through six that represents Sunday through Saturday. Write a program in which you create a Date object, assign it a value, and then print a day that corresponds to the Date.

6. Create an array of Strings, each containing one of the top 10 reasons that you like Java. Prompt a user to enter a number, convert the number to an integer, and then use the integer to print one of the reasons for the user.

7. Create an array of five Strings containing the first names of people in your family. Write a program that counts and displays the number of vowels in the Strings that you entered, without regard to case (uppercase versus lowercase letters). The class name is Vowels.

8. Write a program that lets the user enter a student ID number with nine numbers and then displays the student's first name and grade point average. The class name is StudentId.

9. Write a program that changes the phone number for a person in a phone directory based on the person's ID number. The user should be able to enter an ID number (with nine digits) and then change the phone number for that person. To verify that the change was made correctly, display the person's name and new phone number. The class name is PhoneNumber.

In this section you will learn:

■ How to sort primitive array elements

■ How to sort object array elements

■ How to sort String array elements

■ How to use two-dimensional arrays

■ About multidimensional arrays

■ About the StringBuffer class

Advanced Array Techniques

tip

This section presents additional array and String methods and techniques. Your instructor might omit this section; however, you will not suffer any loss in continuity.

Sorting Primitive Array Elements

Sorting is the process of arranging a series of objects in some logical order. When you place objects in order beginning with the object with the lowest value, you are sorting in **ascending** order; conversely, when you start with the object that has the largest value, you are sorting in **descending** order.

The simplest possible sort involves two values that are out of order. To place the values in order, you must swap the two values. For example, suppose that you have two variables valA and valB, and further suppose that `valA = 16` and `valB = 2`. To exchange the values of the two variables, you cannot simply use the following code:

```
valA = valB; // 2 goes to valA
valB = valA; // 2 goes to valB
```

If valB is 2, then after you execute `valA = valB;`, both variables hold the value 2. The value 16 that was held in valA is lost. When you execute the second assignment statement, `valB = valA;`, each variable still holds the value 2.

The solution that allows you to retain both values is to employ a variable to hold valA's value temporarily during the swap:

```
temp = valA; // 16 goes to temp
valA = valB; // 2 goes to valA
valB = temp; // 16 goes to valB
```

Using this technique, valA's value (16) is assigned to the temp variable. The value of valB (2) is then assigned to valA, so valA and valB are equivalent. Then the temp value (16) is assigned to valB, so the values of the two variables finally are swapped.

If you want to sort any two values, valA and valB, in ascending order so that valA is always the lower value, then you use the following `if` statement to make the decision whether to swap. If valA is more than valB, you want to switch the values. If valA is not more than valB, you do not want the values to switch.

```
if(valA > valB)
{
  temp = valA;
  valA = valB;
  valB = temp;
}
```

Sorting two values is a fairly simple task; sorting more values (valC, valD, valE, and so on) is more complicated. Without the use of an array, sorting a series of numbers would be a daunting task; the task becomes manageable when you know how to use an array.

As an example, you might have a list of five numbers that you want to place in ascending numeric order. One approach is to use a method popularly known as a **bubble sort**. To use a bubble sort, you place the original, unsorted values in an array, such as `int[] someNums = {88, 33, 99, 22, 54};`. After a series of comparisons and swaps, the numbers eventually will be placed in order within the array. You compare the first two numbers; if they are not in ascending order, you swap them. You compare the second and third numbers; if they are not in ascending order, you swap them. You continue down the list. Generically, for any someNums[x], if the value of someNums[x] is larger than someNums[x + 1], then you want to swap the two values.

With the numbers 88, 33, 99, 22, and 54, the process proceeds as follows:

- Compare 88 and 33. They are out of order. Swap them. The list becomes 33, 88, 99, 22, 54.
- Compare the second and third numbers in the list—88 and 99. They are in order. Do nothing.
- Compare the third and fourth numbers in the list—99 and 22. They are out of order. Swap them. The list becomes 33, 88, 22, 99, 54.
- Compare the fourth and fifth numbers—99 and 54. They are out of order. Swap them. The list becomes 33, 88, 22, 54, 99.

When you reach the bottom of the list, the numbers are not in ascending order, but the largest number, 99, has moved to the bottom of the list. It is because of this feature that the bubble sort gets its name—the "heaviest" value has sunk to the bottom of the list as the "lighter" values have bubbled up to the top.

Assuming b and temp both have been declared as integer variables, the code so far is as follows:

```
for(b = 0; b < 4; ++b)
  if(someNums[b] > someNums[b + 1])
  {
    temp = someNums[b];
    someNums[b] = someNums[b + 1];
    someNums[b + 1] = temp;
  }
```

Notice that the `for` statement tests every value of b from zero through three. The array someNums contains five integers. The subscripts in the array range in value from zero through four. Within the `for` loop, each someNums[b] is compared to someNums[b + 1], so the highest legal value for b is three when array element b (3) is compared to array element b + 1 (4). For a sort on any size array, the value of b must remain less than the array's length minus one.

The list of numbers that began as 88, 33, 99, 22, 54 is currently 33, 88, 22, 54, 99. Although the largest value is at the end of the list now, the list is still not in order. You must perform the entire comparison-swap procedure again.

- Compare the first two values—33 and 88. They are in order; do nothing.
- Compare the second and third values—88 and 22. They are out of order. Swap them so the list becomes 33, 22, 88, 54, 99.
- Compare the third and fourth values—88 and 54. They are out of order. Swap them so the list becomes 33, 22, 54, 88, 99.
- Compare the fourth and fifth values—88 and 99. They are in order; do nothing.

After this second pass through the list, the numbers are 33, 22, 54, 88, and 99—close to ascending order, but not quite. You can see that with one more pass through the list, the values 22 and 33 would swap and the list finally would be placed in order. With the worst case list, one in which the original numbers were descending (as "out of ascending order" as they could possibly be), you would need to go through the list four times making comparisons and swaps. You always, at most, need to pass through the list as many times as its length minus one. Figure 5-19 shows the entire procedure.

```
for(a = 0; a < (someNums.length - 1); ++a)

  for(b = 0; b < (someNums.length - 1); ++b)

    if(someNums[b] > someNums[b + 1])

    {

      temp = someNums[b];

      someNums[b] = someNums[b + 1];

      someNums[b + 1] = temp;

    }
```

Figure 5-19: Ascending sort of the someNums array

....

To place the list in descending order, you need to make only one change in the method in Figure 5-19: You change the greater than sign (>) in `if(someNums[b] > someNums[b + 1])` to a less than sign (<).

....

Next, you will write a program that includes a method that sorts characters that you enter from the keyboard.

To write a program that sorts characters:

1 Open a new file in your text editor, and then type the following class header and main() method header for a SortCharArray program:

```
public class SortCharArray
{
  public static void main(String[] args) throws Exception
  {
```

2 Enter the following code to declare a character array that can hold 10 characters, and an integer x to use as a subscript with the array:

```
char[] someChars = new char[10];
int x;
```

3 Enter the following `for` loop that allows the user to enter 10 characters from the keyboard:

```
for(x = 0; x < someChars.length; ++x)
{
  System.out.print("Enter a character ");
  someChars[x] = (char)System.in.read();
  System.in.read(); System.in.read();
}
```

4 Enter the following `for` loop that displays the characters as originally entered:

```
System.out.println("Before sort");
for(x = 0; x < someChars.length; ++x)
  System.out.print(someChars[x] + " ");
```

5 Call a method named bubbleSort(). You will pass two arguments to bubbleSort(): the array, and the length of the array.

```
bubbleSort(someChars, someChars.length);
```

6 Add a loop that prints the characters after the sort has executed:

```
System.out.println("\nAfter sort");
for(x = 0; x < someChars.length; ++x)
  System.out.print(someChars[x] + " ");
```

tip

> When you sort a series of numbers, you place them in arithmetic order. Characters are sorted by their numeric Unicode value.

7 Add a final println() statement to the program, as well as a closing curly bracket for the main() method:

```
System.out.println();
}
```

8 Save the file as **SortCharArray.java** in the Chapter.05 folder on your Student Disk. You cannot compile the file yet because you have not written the bubbleSort() method.

Next, you will add the bubbleSort() method to the SortCharArray program. An advantage of creating the sort as a method that is separate from the main() method is that you might want to use this method with other programs. The bubbleSort() method will sort any size array of characters; you might be able to use it in any application in which you have a number of characters to sort.

To write the bubbleSort() method:

1 Below the main() method in the existing SortCharArray program, write the header for a bubbleSort() method that takes a character array and an integer length as arguments, and then press the **Enter** key and type the method's opening curly bracket:

```
public static void bubbleSort(char[] array, int len)
{
```

2 Type the following code to declare two integers, a and b, to use in the method's for loops. Additionally, declare a temporary character variable.

```
int a,b;
char temp;
```

3 The two for loops you need to sort the array each must execute len minus one times. If you place the subtraction calculation within each for statement, as in for(a = 0; a < (len – 1); ++a), then the subtraction is performed on each cycle through the loop. It is more efficient to calculate len – 1 once, store the value in a variable, and use the new variable in the for loops. Figure 5-20 shows this process. Add this code to your program.

```
int highSubscript = len - 1;

for(a = 0; a < highSubscript; ++a)

{

  for(b = 0; b < highSubscript; ++b)

    if(array[b] > array[b + 1])

    {

      temp = array[b];

      array[b] = array[b + 1];

      array[b + 1] = temp;

    }

}
```

Figure 5-20: Portion of the sort process

4   Add the closing curly bracket for the bubbleSort() method and the closing curly bracket for the SortCharArray class.

5   Save, compile, and execute the program. Figure 5-21 shows a typical program run.

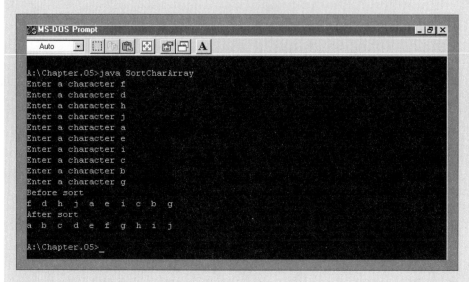

Figure 5-21: Output of the SortCharArray program

When you use a bubble sort to sort any array into ascending order, the largest value "falls" to the bottom of the array after you have compared each pair of values in the array one time. The second time you go through the array making comparisons, there really is no need to check the last pair of values. The largest value is guaranteed to be at the bottom of the array already. You can make the sort process even more efficient by using a new variable for the inner `for` loop and reducing the value by one on each cycle through the array.

To make the array more efficient:

1 Within the bubbleSort() method in the SortCharArray.java file, position your cursor after the statement `int highSubscript = len - 1;`, and then press the **Enter** key to start a new line.

2 Declare a variable that holds the number of comparisons to make by typing the following:

```
int compsToMake = len - 1;
```

3 Replace the inner, b-loop statement, `for(b = 0; b < highSubscript; ++b)`, with **`for(b = 0; b < compsToMake; ++b)`**.

4 Position the cursor after the closing curly bracket in the `if` block, and then press the **Enter** key to start a new line.

5 Type the statement that reduces compsToMake by one on each cycle through the array by typing **`--compsToMake;`**. Make sure that this statement is between the closing curly bracket of the inner `for` loop and the closing curly bracket of the outer `for` loop.

6 Save, compile, and run the program. The program executes exactly as before; however, it is more efficient. When you sort an array with 10 or 20 elements, you will not notice any improved efficiency. However, if you need to sort an array with thousands of elements, the program will run much faster if you employ this technique to reduce unnecessary comparisons.

Sorting Arrays of Objects

You can sort arrays of objects in much the same way that you sort arrays of primitive types. The major difference occurs when you make the comparison that determines whether you want to swap two array elements. When you construct an array of the primitive element type, you compare the two array elements to determine whether they are out of order. When array elements are objects, you usually want to sort based on a particular field of the object.

For example, assume you have created a simple Employee class as shown in Figure 5-22. The class holds two data fields, a constructor, and get and set methods for the fields.

```
public class Employee
{
  private int empNum;
  private double empSal;
  public Employee(int e, double s)
  {
    empNum = e;
    empSal = s;
  }
  public int getEmpNum()
  {
    return empNum;
  }
  public double getEmpSal()
  {
    return empSal;
  }
  public void setEmpSal(double r)
  {
    empSal = r;
  }
}
```

Figure 5-22: Employee class

You can write a program that contains an array of Employee objects using the statement `Employee[] someEmps = new Employee[5];`. After you assign employee numbers and salaries to the Employee objects, you want to sort the Employees in empSal order. You can pass the array and its length to a bubbleSort() method that is prepared to receive Employee objects. Figure 5-23 shows the method.

```
public static void bubbleSort(Employee[] array, int len)
{
  int a,b;
  Employee temp;
  int highSubscript = len - 1;
  for(a = 0; a < highSubscript; ++a)
    for(b = 0; b < highSubscript; ++b)
      if(array[b].getEmpSal() > array[b + 1].getEmpSal())
      {
        temp = array[b];
        array[b] = array[b + 1];
        array[b + 1] = temp;
      }
}
```

Figure 5-23: The bubbleSort() method for Employee objects

If you examine Figure 5-23 carefully, you might notice that it is very similar to a sort method you use for an array of any primitive type, but with three major differences:

- The bubbleSort() method header shows it receives an array of type Employee.
- The temp variable created for swapping is type Employee.
- The comparison for swapping uses the method call getEmpSal() to compare the salary for each Employee object in the array with the salary of the adjacent Employee object.

tip

It is important to note that even though only Employee salaries are compared, you do not swap Employee salaries. You do not want to substitute one Employee's salary for another's. Instead, you swap the entire Employee object so that each Employee object's empNum and empSal are swapped as a unit.

Sorting Strings

When you sort an array of Strings, you must remember that String names are addresses. Therefore, you cannot determine whether two String objects require swapping by comparing their names. Instead, you must use the compareTo() method. Next, you will sort a list of Strings.

To sort an array of String objects:

1 Open a new file in your text editor, and then enter the first few lines of a program that will sort String objects:

```
public class SortStrings
{
  public static void main(String[] args)
  {
```

2 Use the following code to declare an array of student names and an integer variable to use as a subscript:

```
String[] students =
  {"Kim", "Ken", "Tom", "Kathy", "Brad"};
int x;
```

3 Write the code that prints the list of Strings, passes the list to a sortStrings() method, and prints the list again:

```
System.out.println("Before sort");
for(x = 0; x < 5; ++x)
  System.out.println(students[x]);
sortStrings(students, students.length);
System.out.println("\nAfter sort");
for(x = 0; x < 5; ++x)
  System.out.println(students[x]);
```

4 Add the closing curly bracket for the main() method.

5 Enter the sortStrings() method shown in Figure 5-24. The method uses the compareTo() method to determine whether two Strings should be swapped. Recall that when the compareTo() method returns a value greater than zero, then the first String is larger than (that is, out of order with) the second String.

```
public static void sortStrings(String[] array, int len)
{
  int a,b;
  String temp;
  int highSubscript = len - 1;
  for(a = 0; a < highSubscript; ++a)
    for(b = 0; b < highSubscript; ++b)
      if(array[b].compareTo(array[b + 1]) > 0)
      {
        temp = array[b];
        array[b] = array[b + 1];
        array[b + 1] = temp;
      }
}
```

Figure 5-24: The sortStrings() method

6 Add the closing curly bracket for the SortStrings class.

7 Save the program as **SortStrings.java** in the Chapter.05 folder on your Student Disk and compile. When you run the program, the output appears similar to Figure 5-25.

Figure 5-25: Output of the SortStrings program

Using Two-dimensional Arrays

When you declare an array such as `int[] someNumbers = new int[3];`, you can envision the three declared integers as a column of numbers in memory, as shown in Figure 5-26. In other words, you can picture the three declared numbers stacked one on top of the next. An array that you can picture as a column of values is a **one-dimensional** or **single-dimensional** array.

someNumbers[0]
someNumbers[1]
someNumbers[2]

Figure 5-26: Single-dimensional array

tip

You can think of the single dimension of a single-dimensional array as the height of the array.

The Java programming language also supports two-dimensional arrays. **Two-dimensional arrays** have more than one column of values, as shown in Figure 5-27. It is easiest to picture two-dimensional arrays as having both rows and columns. When mathematicians use a two-dimensional array, they often call it a **matrix**; you might have used a two-dimensional array called a spreadsheet.

`int[][] someNumbers = new int[3][4];`

someNumbers[0][0]	someNumbers[0][1]	someNumbers[0][2]	someNumbers[0][3]
someNumbers[1][0]	someNumbers[1][1]	someNumbers[1][2]	someNumbers[1][3]
someNumbers[2][0]	someNumbers[2][1]	someNumbers[2][2]	someNumbers[2][3]

Figure 5-27: Two-dimensional array

tip

You can think of the two dimensions of a two-dimensional array as height and width.

When you declare a one-dimensional array, you type a set of square brackets after the array type. To declare a two-dimensional array, you type two sets of brackets after the array type. For example, `int[][] someNumbers = new int[3][4];` declares an array named someNumbers that holds three rows and four columns.

Just as with a one-dimensional array, if you do not provide values for the elements in a two-dimensional numeric array, the values default to zero. You can assign values to the array elements later. For example, `someNumbers[0][0] = 14;` assigns the value 14 to the element of the someNumbers array that is in the first column of the first row. Alternatively, you can initialize a two-dimensional array with values when it is created. For example, the following code assigns values to someNumbers when it is created:

```
int[][] someNumbers =
{       {8, 9, 10, 11},
        {1, 3, 12, 15},
        {5, 9, 44, 99}  };
```

The someNumbers array contains three rows and four columns. You contain the entire set of values within a pair of curly brackets. The first row of the array holds the four integers 8, 9, 10, and 11. Notice that these four integers are placed within their own set of curly brackets to indicate that they constitute one row, or the first row, which is row zero. Similarly, 1, 3, 12, and 15 make up the second row, which you reference with the subscript 1, and 5, 9, 44, and 99 are the values in the third row, which you reference with the subscript 2. The value of someNumbers[0][0] is 8. The value of someNumbers[0][1] is 9. The value of someNumbers[2][3] is 99. The value within the first bracket following the array name always refers to the row; the value within the second bracket refers to the column.

As an example, assume you own an apartment building with four floors—a basement which you refer to as floor zero, and three other floors numbered one, two, and three. Additionally, each of the floors has studio (with no bedroom) and one- and two-bedroom apartments. The monthly rent for each type of apartment is different—the higher the floor, the higher the rent (the view is better), and with more bedrooms, the rent is higher. Figure 5-28 shows the rental amounts.

Floor	Zero Bedrooms	One Bedroom	Two Bedrooms
0	400	450	510
1	500	560	630
2	625	676	740
3	1000	1250	1600

Figure 5-28: Rents charged

To determine a tenant's rent, you need to know two pieces of information: the floor on which the tenant rents an apartment, and the number of bedrooms in the apartment. Within a Java program, you can declare an array of rents using the following code:

```
int[][] rents =
{       {400, 450, 510},
        {500, 560, 630},
        {625, 676, 740},
        {1000, 1250, 1600}  };
```

Assuming you declare two integers to hold the floor number and bedroom count as int floor, bedrooms;, then any tenant's rent is rents[floor][bedrooms].

To demonstrate the use of a two-dimensional array, you can create a short demonstration program. You will create a teacher's classroom seating chart that holds four rows and three columns. Then you will search for a particular student's location.

To write a program that uses a two-dimensional array to create a student seating chart:

1　Open a new text file in your text editor.

2　Enter the following class header and main() method header for a FindStudent class:

```
public class FindStudent
{
  public static void main(String[] args) throws Exception
  {
```

3　Create a two-dimensional String array that holds the names of 12 students who sit in four rows. For convenience, assign each student a name with a unique initial. That way, you can search for a student's position using an initial.

```
String[][] students =
    {       {"Dave", "Bonnie", "Hannah"},
            {"Iris",  "Keith", "Carl"},
            {"Amy", "Jessica", "Francis"},
            {"Ellen", "George", "Lydia"}  };
```

4　You will use a character variable to hold an initial input from the keyboard, and two integer variables to hold the row and column position of the student whose initial matches the input initial:

```
char stu;
int r, c;
```

5 Add the following statements to prompt the user for an initial and read the character from the keyboard:

```
System.out.print("Enter student initial ");
stu = (char)System.in.read();
```

6 You will use two nested `for` loops to test each combination of row and column position. When the character input at the keyboard matches the character in the first position of any of the Strings in the two-dimensional array, print the row and column position. Enter the following `for` loops:

```
for(r = 0; r < 4; ++r)
   for(c = 0; c < 3; ++c)
      if(stu == students[r][c].charAt(0))
         System.out.println("Student is in row " + r +
            " and column " + c);
```

7 Add the closing curly bracket for the main() method and the closing curly bracket for the class.

8 Save the program as **FindStudent.java** in the Chapter.05 folder on your Student Disk. Compile the program, and then execute it several times. Confirm that with each initial you type, the correct row and column positions are located. Figure 5-29 shows a sample program run.

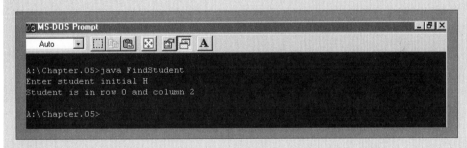

Figure 5-29: Output of the FindStudent program

Understanding Multidimensional Arrays

The Java programming language supports **multidimensional arrays,** or arrays of more than two dimensions. For example, if you own an apartment building with a number of floors and different numbers of bedrooms available in apartments on each floor, you can use a two-dimensional array to store the rental fees. If you own several apartment buildings, you might want to employ a third dimension to store the building number. An expression such as `rents[building][floor][bedrooms]` refers to a specific rent figure for a building whose building number is stored in the building variable and whose floor and bedroom numbers are stored in the floor and bedrooms variables. Specifically, `rents[5][1][2]` refers to a two-bedroom apartment on the first floor of building 5.

When you are programming in Java, you can use four, five, or more dimensions in an array. As long as you can keep track of the order of the variables needed as subscripts, and as long as you don't exhaust your computer's memory, Java will let you create arrays of any size.

Using StringBuffer

A limitation of the String class is that the value of a String is fixed after the String is created; that is, Strings are immutable. When you write `someString = "Hello";` and follow it with `someString = "Goodbye";`, you have not actually changed the contents of computer memory at someString, nor have you eliminated the characters "Hello". Instead, you have stored "Goodbye" at a new computer memory location and stored the new address in the someString variable. If you want to modify someString from "Goodbye" to "Goodbye Everybody", you cannot actually add a space and "Everybody" to the someString that contains "Goodbye". Instead, you must create an entirely new String "Goodbye Everybody" and assign it to the someString address.

To circumvent these limitations, you can use the StringBuffer class. **StringBuffer** is an alternative to the String class, and can usually be used anywhere you would use a String. StringBuffer is more flexible than String in that you can insert or append new contents into a StringBuffer. The StringBuffer class provides you with three constructors:

- `public StringBuffer()`, which constructs a StringBuffer with no characters in it and a default size of 16 characters.
- `public StringBuffer(int length)`, which constructs a StringBuffer with no characters, and a capacity specified by length.
- `public StringBuffer(String s)`, which contains the same characters as are stored in the String object s. The capacity of the StringBuffer is the length of the String argument you provide, plus 16 additional characters.

Every StringBuffer object has a maximum capacity or size, but if you add additional characters to a StringBuffer so as to exceed the capacity, Java automatically provides a larger capacity.

The **append() method** lets you add characters to the end of a StringBuffer object. For example, if a StringBuffer is declared as `StringBuffer someBuffer = new StringBuffer("Happy");`, then the statement `someBuffer.append (" birthday")` alters someBuffer to hold "Happy birthday".

The **insert() method** lets you add characters at a specific location within a StringBuffer object. For example, if someBuffer holds "Happy birthday", then `someBuffer.insert(6, "30th ");` alters the StringBuffer to contain "Happy 30th birthday". The first character in the StringBuffer object occupies position zero. To alter just one character in a StringBuffer, you can use the setCharAt() method. This method requires two arguments, an integer position, and a character. If someBuffer holds "Happy 30th birthday", then `someBuffer.setCharAt(6,'4');` changes the someBuffer value into a 40th birthday greeting.

Next, you will use StringBuffer methods.

To use StringBuffer methods:

1 Open a new text editor file and type the following first lines of a DemoStringBuffer class:

```
public class DemoStringBuffer
{
   public static void main(String[] args)
   {
```

2 Use the following code to create a StringBuffer variable, and then call a print() method (that you will create in Step 7) to print the StringBuffer:

```
StringBuffer str = new StringBuffer("singing");
print(str);
```

3 Enter the following append() method to add characters to the existing StringBuffer and print it again:

```
str.append(" in the dead of ");
print(str);
```

4 Enter the following insert() method to insert characters, print, insert additional characters, and print the StringBuffer again:

```
str.insert(0, "Black");
print(str);
str.insert(5, "bird ");
print(str);
```

5 Add one more append() and print() combination:

```
str.append("night");
print(str);
```

6 Add a closing curly bracket for the main() method.

7 Enter the following print() method that prints StringBuffer objects:

```
public static void print(StringBuffer s)
{
   System.out.println(s);
}
```

8 Type the closing curly bracket for the class, then save the file as **DemoStringBuffer.java** in the Chapter.05 folder on your Student Disk. Compile and execute. Compare your output to Figure 5-30 and make sure you understand the effect of each program statement.

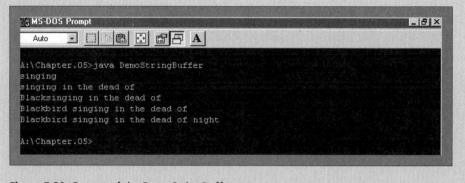

Figure 5-30: Output of the DemoStringBuffer program

 # S U M M A R Y

- Sorting is the process of arranging a series of objects in some logical order. When you place objects in order beginning with the object with the lowest value, you are sorting in ascending order; when you start with the object that has the largest value, you are sorting in descending order.

- To sort any two values in ascending order, you use an `if` statement to make the decision whether to swap the positions of the two values.

- To use a bubble sort, you place the original, unsorted values in an array, compare pairs of values, and then if they are not in ascending order, swap them. To use a bubble sort, you always, at most, need to pass through a list as many times as its length minus one.

- You can sort arrays of objects you usually want to sort based on a particular field of the object.

- You must use the compareTo() method when sorting Strings.

- An array that you can picture as a column of values is a one-dimensional or single-dimensional array.

- The Java programming language supports multidimensional arrays, or arrays of more than two dimensions.

- To circumvent some limitations of the String class, you can use the StringBuffer class. You can insert or append new contents into a StringBuffer.

 **Q U E S T I O N S**

1. When you place objects in order beginning with the object with the lowest value, you are sorting in _____ order.
   a. acquiescing
   b. ascending
   c. demeaning
   d. descending

2. Which of the following lists is in descending order?
   a. 19, 14, 8, 3, 1
   b. 4, 6, 8, 99
   c. 2, 7, 1, 9
   d. 4, 4, 3, 4

3. Using a bubble sort involves _____.
   a. comparing parallel arrays
   b. comparing each array element to the average
   c. comparing each array element to the adjacent array element
   d. swapping every array element with its adjacent element

4. When you use a bubble sort to sort numbers in ascending order, at the end of the first pass through the array, the _____ number is at the bottom of the array.
   a. smallest
   b. largest
   c. originally first
   d. originally last

5. Which array types cannot be sorted?
   a. Arrays of characters
   b. Arrays of Strings
   c. Arrays of objects
   d. You can sort all of these array types.

6. Which list is in ascending order?
   a. d, f, m, y
   b. Z, T, S, F
   c. a, A, b, B
   d. z, y, x, Z

7. When array elements are objects, you usually want to sort based on a particular _____ of the object.
   a. field
   b. method
   c. name
   d. type

8. When you compare two Strings for sorting, you use the _____ .
   a. String() method
   b. equals sign
   c. compareTo() method
   d. SortString() method

9. The array `int[ ] values = new int[10];` is a _____ array.
   a. one-dimensional
   b. two-dimensional
   c. multidimensional
   d. nondimensional

10. If you declare an array as `int[ ][ ] values = new int[6][3];`, the array has _____ rows.
   a. two
   b. three
   c. five
   d. six

11. If you declare an array as `int[ ][ ] values = new int[6][3];`, then the array has _____ columns.
   a. two
   b. three
   c. five
   d. six

12. If you declare an array as `double[ ][ ] money = new double[10][5];`, then the last value in the first row is _____ .
   a. money[0][4]
   b. money[0][5]
   c. money[9][0]
   d. money[10][0]

13. If you declare an array as `char[ ][ ] codes[5][6];`, which of the following statements is invalid?
   a. codes[3][3]
   b. codes[4][5]
   c. codes[0][0]
   d. codes[5][4]

14. Using Java, you can create an array with a maximum of _____ dimensions.
   a. two
   b. three
   c. four
   d. virtually unlimited

15. For an alternative to the String class, you can use
   a. char
   b. StringHolder
   c. StringBuffer
   d. StringMerger

16. The default capacity for a StringBuffer object is ─────────── characters.

    a. zero

    b. two

    c. 16

    d. 32

17. The StringBuffer method you use to add characters at the end of a StringBuffer is ───────────.

    a. add()

    b. adjust()

    c. append()

    d. attach()

18. If aStringBufObject holds "abcdefg", then `aStringBufObject.insert(2,"XXX")` results in aStringBufObject holding ───────────.

    a. `XXX`

    b. `aXXXbcdefg`

    c. `abXXXcdefg`

    d. `aXXXefg`

E X E R C I S E S

Save each of the following programs in the Chapter.05 folder of your Student Disk.

1.   a. Write a program containing an array of 15 double values. Include a method to sort the values in ascending order. Display the results. The class name is SortDouble.

    b. Add a method to SortDouble to sort in descending order. Display the results.

2.   a. Create a class for services offered by a hair styling salon. Data fields include a String to hold the service description (for example, "Cut", "Shampoo", or "Manicure"), a double to hold the price, and an integer to hold the average minutes it takes to perform the service. The class name is HairSalon. Include a constructor that requires arguments for all three data fields and three get methods that each return one of the data field's values.

    b. Write a program named SortSalon that contains an array to hold six HairSalon objects and fill it with data. Include a method to sort the array in ascending order by price of service. Call the method and display the results.

    c. Add a method to the SortSalon program that sorts the HairSalon objects in descending order by time to perform the service. Call the method and display the results.

    d. Add a method to the SortSalon program that sorts the HairSalon objects in alphabetical order by service description. Call the method and display the results.

    e. Add a prompt to the SortSalon program giving the user three choices: sort by description, price, or time. Depending on the user's input, call one of the three sort methods and display the results.

3. Create a class that holds three initialized StringBuffer objects: your first name, middle name, and last name. Create three new StringBuffer objects as follows:

   ■ An object named EntireName that holds your three names, separated by spaces
   ■ An object named LastFirst that holds your last name, a comma, a space, and your first name, in that order
   ■ An object named Signature that holds your first name, a space, your middle initial (not the entire name), a period, a space, and your last name

   Display all three objects.

4. Write a program that allows the user to enter a course ID number and then displays the course name (such as "CIS 110") and the day of the week and time that the course is held (such as "Th 3:30"). Store the course name and day/time in a two-dimensional array. The class name is Schedule.

5. Write a program that stores an array of video titles (such as "True Grit") and their corresponding ID numbers in inventory (such as "145"). Display the list before it is sorted, and then display a list sorted by inventory ID number. Use two single-dimensional arrays—one for the titles and one for the scores. The class name is Video.

6. Write a program that stores the name, title, and hourly wage of people employed by a grocery store. The data are: Ollie Regan, manager, $18/hour; William Sherman, assistant manager, $16/hour; Maureen Mooney, produce manager, $15/hour; Marty Sharik, bakery manager, $15.25/hour; and Marcella Riley, cashier manager, $13/hour. List the employee name and job title for employees who earn more than $15 per hour. Store the names and titles for each employee in a two-dimensional array, and store the rate in a single-dimensional array. The class name is Rate.

7. Each of the following files in the Chapter.05 folder on your Student Disk has syntax and/or logical errors. In each case, determine the problem and fix the program. After you correct the errors, save each file using the same filename preceded with *Fix*. For example, DebugFive1.java will become FixDebugFive1.java.
   a. DebugFive1.java
   b. DebugFive2.java
   c. DebugFive3.java
   d. DebugFive4.java

Applets

case ▶ "It seems like I've learned a lot," you tell Lynn Greenbrier
during a coffee break at Event Handlers Incorporated. "I can
use variables, make decisions, write loops, and use arrays."

"You've come a long way," Lynn agrees.

"But," you continue, "it also seems like I know nothing!
When I visit the simplest Web site, it looks far more sophisticated than my most advanced application. There is color and
movement. There are buttons to click and boxes into which I
can type responses to questions. Nothing I've done even
approaches that."

"But you have a good foundation in Java programming," Lynn says. "Now you can put all that knowledge to work. By adding a few new objects to your repertoire, and by learning a little about applets, you can comfortably enter the world of interactive Web programming."

Previewing the PartyPlanner Applet

The Chap6PartyPlanner applet lets potential Event Handlers Incorporated customers calculate the cost of a planned event based on the number of guests they intend to invite. You now can use a completed version of the applet that is saved in the Chapter.06 folder on your Student Disk.

To run the Chap6PartyPlanner applet:

1   Go to the command prompt for the Chapter.06 folder on your Student Disk (A:\Chapter.06>), type **appletviewer Chap6Plan.html**, and then press the **Enter** key. It might take a few minutes for the Applet Viewer window to open. See Figure 6-1.

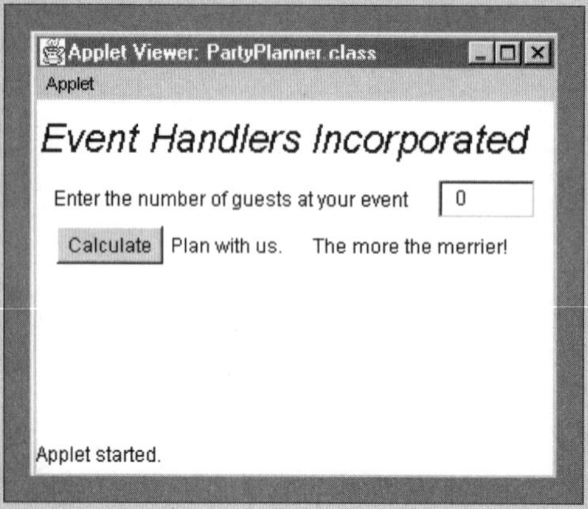

Figure 6-1: Chap6PartyPlanner applet

2 Use the applet as if you were a customer of Event Handlers Incorporated. Use the text box to enter any number of guests you want to invite to a hypothetical event. Then, either press the **Enter** key or click the **Calculate** button to view the results. The applet will quote you a per-person price as well as a price for the entire event. Enter a new number of guests, and then press the **Enter** key or click the **Calculate** button; then the applet will recalculate the rates.

3 Close the Applet Viewer by clicking the **Close** button ☒ in the upper-right corner of the Applet Viewer window.

In this section you will learn:

- How to write an HTML document to host an applet
- How to write a simple applet using a Label
- How to change a Label's font
- How to add TextFields and Buttons to applets
- About event-driven programming
- How to add output to an applet

HTML and Applet Basics

Writing an HTML Document to Host an Applet

You have written many Java applications. When you write a Java application, you do the following:

- Write the application in the Java programming language, and then save it with a .java file extension.
- Compile the application into bytecode using the `javac` command. The bytecode is stored in a file with a .class file extension.
- Use the `java` command to interpret and execute the .class file.

Applications are stand-alone programs. In contrast, **applets** are programs that are called from within another application. You run applets within a page on the Internet, or within another program called **appletviewer**, which comes with the Java Developer's Kit. An applet must be called from within another document written in HTML, or Hypertext Markup Language. **HTML** is a simple language used to create Web pages for the Internet. When you create an applet, you do the following:

- Write the applet in the Java programming language, and save it with a .java file extension, just as when you write an application.
- Compile the applet into bytecode using the `javac` command, just as when you write an application.
- Write an HTML document that includes a statement to call your compiled Java class.
- Load the HTML document into a Web browser (such as Netscape Navigator or Microsoft Internet Explorer), or run the Applet Viewer program, which, in turn, uses the HTML document.

Java, in general, and applets, in particular, are popular topics among programmers, mostly because users can execute applets using a Web browser on the Internet. A **Web browser** is a program that allows you to display HTML documents on your computer screen. Web documents often contain Java applets.

HTML contains many commands that allow you to format text on a Web page, import graphic images, and link your page to other Web pages. Fortunately, to run a Java applet, you don't need to learn the entire HTML language; you need to learn only two pairs of HTML commands, called **tags**.

The tag that begins every HTML document is **<HTML>**. Like all tags, this tag is surrounded by angle brackets. HTML is an HTML keyword that specifies that what follows the keyword is an HTML document. The tag that ends every HTML document is **</HTML>**. The insertion of the backslash before any tag indicates the tag is the ending half of a pair of tags. The following is the simplest HTML document you can write:

```
<HTML>
</HTML>
```

Unlike the Java programming language, HTML is not case-sensitive, so you can use <html> in place of <HTML>. However, using uppercase letters for HTML tags is conventional.

As with the Java programming language, HTML generally ignores whitespace, so you can write the HTML document on one line as <HTML></HTML>.

This simple document begins and ends and does nothing in the process; you can create an analogous situation in a Java method by typing an opening curly bracket and following it immediately with the closing curly bracket. Usually, of course, HTML documents contain more statements. For example, to run an applet from within an HTML document, you add an **<APPLET>** and **</APPLET>** tag pair. Usually, you place three attributes within the **<APPLET>** tag: CODE, WIDTH, and HEIGHT. Note the following example:

```
<APPLET CODE = "aClass.class" WIDTH = 300 HEIGHT = 200>
```

The following are the three parts of the APPLET tag:

■ CODE = and the name of the compiled applet you are calling
■ WIDTH = and the width of the applet on the screen
■ HEIGHT = and the height of the applet on the screen

The name of the applet you call must be a compiled Java applet (with a .class file extension). The width and height of an applet are measured in pixels. **Pixels** are the *pic*ture *ele*ments, or tiny dots of light that make up the image on your video monitor. Many monitors display 640 pixels horizontally and 480 pixels vertically, so a statement such as WIDTH = 300 HEIGHT = 200 will create an applet that occupies a little less than a quarter of most screens (half the height and half the width).

A VGA monitor displays 640 x 480 pixels. A Super VGA monitor displays up to 1280 x 1024 pixels. In general, the maximum size of your applets should be approximately 600 x 400 pixels to make sure that most people will be able to see the entire applet. Keep in mind that the browser's menu bar and screen elements (such as the toolbar and the scrollbars) will take up some of the screen viewing area for an applet.

Next, you will create a simple HTML document that you will use to display the applet that you will create in the next section. You will name the applet Greet, and it will occupy a screen area of 450 x 200 pixels.

To create a simple HTML document:

1 Open a new file in your text editor.

2 Type the opening HTML tag, **<HTML>**.

3 On the next line, type the opening APPLET tag that contains the applet's name and dimensions: **<APPLET CODE = "Greet.class" WIDTH = 450 HEIGHT = 200>**.

4 On the next line, type the applet's closing tag: **</APPLET>**.

5 On the next line, type the closing HTML tag: **</HTML>**.

6 Save the file as **Test.html** in the Chapter.06 folder on your Student Disk. Just as when you create a Java application, make sure that you save the file as text only. The .html file extension is not required, but makes the file easy to identify as an HTML file. If you are using Notepad or another text editor, enclose the filename in quotation marks to save the .html file extension, as in "A:\Chapter.06\Test.html".

Writing a Simple Applet Using a Label

Writing an applet involves learning only a few additions and changes to writing a Java application. To write an applet, you must do the following:

■ Add some import statements
■ Learn to use some Windows components and applet methods
■ Learn to use the keyword extends

In Chapter 2, you used an import statement to access classes such as java.util.Date within your application. The purpose of importing the Date class was to avoid having to write common date-handling routines that already exist in Java. Similarly, Java's creators created a variety of classes to handle common applet needs. Most applets contain at least two import statements: import java.applet.*; and import java.awt.*;. The java.applet package contains a class named Applet—every applet you create is based on this class. The java.awt package is the **Abstract Windows Toolkit**, or **AWT**. It contains commonly used Windows **components** such as Labels, Menus, and Buttons. You import java.awt so you don't have to "reinvent the wheel" by creating these components yourself. A Java applet isn't required to contain Windows components, but it almost always does.

For example, one of the simplest Window components is a Label. **Label** is a built-in class that holds text that you can display within an applet. The Label class also contains fields that indicate appearance information, such as font and alignment. As with other objects, you can declare a Label without allocating memory, as in `Label greeting;`, or you can call the Label constructor without any arguments, as in `Label greeting = new Label();`. You can assign some text to the Label with the **setText() method**, as in `greeting.setText("Hi there");`. Alternatively, you can call the Label constructor and pass it a String argument so the Label is initialized upon construction, as in `Label greeting = new Label("Hello. Who are you?");`.

The method you use to add a component to an applet window is **add()**. For example, if a Label was defined as `Label greeting = new Label("Hello. Who are you?");`, then you can place a greeting within an applet using the command `add(greeting);`.

....

The object of the add() method is the applet itself, so when you add a component to a window, you could write `this.add();` **in place of** `add();`. **You learned about the** `this` **reference in Chapter 3.**

....

When you create an application, you follow any needed import statements with a class header such as `public class aClass`. Applets begin the same way as Java applications, but they also must include the words `extends Applet`. The keyword **extends** indicates that your applet will build upon, or **inherit**, the traits of the Applet class defined in the java.applet package.

The Applet class provides a general outline used by any Web browser when it runs an applet. In an application, the main() method calls other methods that you write. With an applet, the browser calls many methods automatically. The following four methods are included in every applet:

- `public void init()`
- `public void start()`
- `public void stop()`
- `public void destroy()`

If you fail to write one or more of these methods, Java creates them for you. The methods Java creates have opening and closing curly brackets only—in other words, they are empty. To create a Java program that does anything useful, you must code at least one of these methods.

The init() method is the first method called in any applet. You use the method to perform initialization tasks, such as setting variables to initial values or placing applet components on the screen. You must code init()'s header as `public void init()`.

Figure 6-2 shows the program to create an applet that displays "Hello. Who are you?" on the screen.

```
import java.applet.*;

import java.awt.*;

public class Greet extends Applet

{

  Label greeting = new Label("Hello. Who are you?");

  public void init()

  {

    add(greeting);

  }

}
```

Figure 6-2: Greet applet

Next, you will create and compile the Greet applet.

To create and run the Greet applet:

1 Open a new text file in your text editor.
2 Enter the code shown in Figure 6-2.
3 Save the file as **Greet.java** in the Chapter.06 folder on your Student Disk.
4 Compile the program with the command **javac Greet.java**.
5 If necessary, correct any errors, and then compile again.

To run the Greet applet, you can use your Web browser or the `appletviewer` command. In the following steps, you will do both.

To run the applet using your Web browser:

1 Open any Web browser, such as Microsoft Internet Explorer or Netscape Navigator. You do not have to connect to the Internet; you will be using the browser locally.

help

You can start your Web browser by double-clicking the shortcut icon on the desktop or by using the Start button. If you have problems starting your Web browser, ask your instructor or technical support person for help.

help

If you do not have a Web browser installed on your computer, skip to the end of Step 3.

2 Click **File** on the menu bar, and then click **Open** or **Open Page**. Then type
A:\Chapter.06\Test.html, which is the complete path for the HTML
document that you created to access Greet.class, and then press the **Enter**
key. The applet appears on your screen, as shown in Figure 6-3.

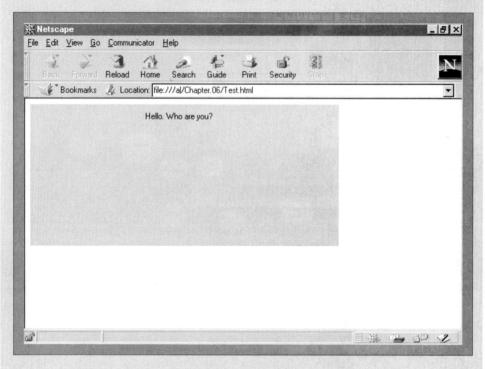

Figure 6-3: Test.html page in a Web browser

3 Close your Web browser by clicking the **Close** button ⊠ in the upper-right
corner of the browser's program window.

You also can view your applet using the `appletviewer` command, as you
will see next. In this book, you will test your applets using the `appletviewer`
command.

Some applets will not work correctly using your browser. Java was designed with a
number of security features, so when an applet displays on the Internet, the applet cannot perform malicious tasks such as deleting a file from your hard drive. If an applet
does nothing to compromise security, then testing it using the Web browser or the
`appletviewer` command will achieve the same results. For now, you can get your
applets to perform better by using the Applet Viewer window.

To run the applet using the `appletviewer` **command:**

1 At the command line, type **`appletviewer test.html`**, and then press the **Enter** key. After a few moments, the Applet Viewer window opens and displays the applet, as shown in Figure 6-4.

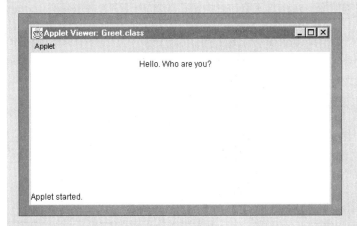

Figure 6-4: Output of the Greet.java program in the Applet Viewer window

2 Use the mouse pointer to drag any corner of the Applet Viewer window to resize it. Notice that if you widen the window by dragging its right border to the right, the window is redrawn on the screen and the Label is automatically repositioned to remain centered within the window. If you narrow the window by dragging its left border to the left, the Label eventually becomes partially obscured when the window becomes too narrow for the display.

3 Close the Applet Viewer window by clicking the **Close** button ☒.

Changing a Label's Font

If you use the Internet and a Web browser to visit Web sites, you probably are not very impressed with your Greet.java applet. You might think that the string, "Hello. Who are you?" is pretty plain and lackluster. Fortunately, Java provides you with a **Font** object that holds typeface and size information. The **setFont() method** requires a Font object argument. To construct a Font object, you need three arguments: typeface, style, and point size.

The **typeface** is a String representing a font. Common fonts are Arial, Helvetica, Courier, and TimesRoman. The typeface is only a request; the system on which your applet runs might not have access to the requested font and therefore might substitute a default font. The **style** applies an attribute to displayed text and is one of three arguments, Font.PLAIN, Font.BOLD, or Font.ITALIC. The **point size** is an integer that represents 1/72 of an inch. Normal printed text is usually about 12 points; a headline might be 30 points.

To give a Label object a new font, you create the Font object, as in `Font headlineFont = new Font("Helvetica", Font.BOLD,36);`, and then you use the setFont() method to assign the font to a Label with the statement `greeting.setFont(headlineFont);`.

▶ **tip**

The typeface name is a String, so you must enclose it in double quotation marks when you use it to declare the Font object.

Next, you will change the font of the text in your Greet applet.

To change the appearance of the greeting in the Greet applet:

1 Open the **Greet.java** file in your text editor.

2 Position the cursor at the end of the line that declares the greeting Label, and then press the **Enter** key to start a new line of text.

3 Declare a Font object named bigFont by typing the following:

```
Font bigFont = new Font("TimesRoman", Font.ITALIC,24);
```

4 Place the cursor to the right of the opening curly bracket of the init() method, and then press the **Enter** key to start a new line.

5 Set the greeting font to bigFont by typing `greeting.setFont(bigFont);`.

6 Save the file using the same filename (**Greet.java**).

7 At the command line, compile the program with the command **javac Greet.java**.

8 Run the applet using the HTML document created earlier by executing the **appletviewer test.html** command at the command prompt. Figure 6-5 shows the output.

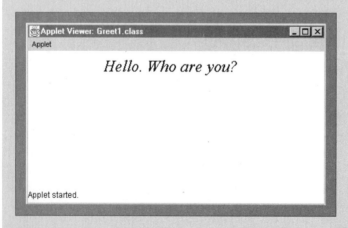

Figure 6-5: Output of the Greet.java program using bigFont

9 Close the Applet Viewer window.

Adding TextField and Button Components to an Applet

In addition to including Labels, applets often contain other window features such as TextFields and Buttons. A **TextField** is a Windows component into which a user can type a single line of text data. (Text data includes any characters you can enter from the keyboard, including numbers and punctuation.) Typically, a user types a line into a TextField and then presses the Enter key on the keyboard or clicks a button with a mouse to enter the data. You can construct a TextField object using one of several constructors:

- `public TextField()`, which creates an empty TextField with an unspecified length
- `public TextField(int numColumns)`, where numColumns specifies a width for the field
- `public TextField(String initialText)`, where initialText provides some initial text within the TextField
- `public TextField(String initialText, int numColumns)`, which specifies both initial text and width

For example, to provide a TextField for a user to answer the "Who are you?" question, you can code `TextField answer = new TextField(10);` to provide a TextField that is empty and displays approximately 10 characters. To add the TextField named answer to an applet, you write `add(answer);`.

The number of characters a TextField can actually display depends on the font being used and the actual characters typed. For example, in most fonts, *w* is wider than *i*, so a TextField of size 10 using Arial font can display 24 *i* characters but only eight *w* characters.

Try to anticipate how many characters your users will enter when you create a TextField. Even though the user can enter more characters than the number that display, the characters scroll out of view. It can be disconcerting to try to enter data into a field that is not large enough.

Several other methods are available for use with TextFields. The **setText() method** allows you to change the text in a TextField that already has been created, as in `answer.setText("Thank you");`. The **getText() method** allows you to retrieve the String of text in a TextField, as in `String whatDidTheySay = answer.getText();`.

When a user encounters a TextField you have placed within an applet, the user must position the mouse pointer in the TextField and click to get a cursor. When the user clicks within the TextField, the TextField has **keyboard focus**, which means that the next entries from the keyboard will be entered at that location. When you want the cursor to appear automatically within the TextField without requiring the user to click in it first, you can use the **requestFocus() method**. For example, if you have added a TextField named answer to an applet, then `answer.requestFocus()` causes the cursor to appear within the TextField, and the user can begin typing immediately without moving the mouse.

In addition to saving the user some time and effort, requestFocus() is useful when you have several TextFields and you want to direct the user's attention to a specific one. At any time, only one component within a window can have the keyboard focus.

When a TextField has the capability of accepting keystrokes, the TextField is **editable**. If you do not want the user to be able to enter data in a TextField, you can use the **setEditable() method** to change the editable status of a TextField. For example, if you want to give a user only one chance to answer a question correctly, then you can prevent the user from replacing or editing the characters in the TextField by using the code `answer.setEditable(false);`. If conditions change, and you want the user to be able to edit the TextField, use the code `answer.setEditable(true);`.

A Button is even easier to create than a TextField. There are only two Button constructors:

- `public Button()`, which you use to create an unlabeled Button
- `public Button(String label)`, which you use to create a labeled Button

For example, to create a Button with the label "Press when ready", you write `Button readyButton = new Button("Press when ready");`. To add the Button to an applet, you write `add(readyButton);`. You can change a Button's Label with the **setLabel() method**, as in `readyButton.setLabel("Don't press me again!");`, or get the Label and assign it to a String object with the **getLabel() method**, as in `String whatsOnButton = readyButton.getLabel();`.

Make sure that the Label on your Button describes its function for the user.

As with TextField components, you can use the requestFocus() method with Button components. The surface of the Button that has the keyboard focus appears with an outline so it stands out from the other Buttons.

Next, you will add a TextField and a Button to your applet.

To add a TextField and a Button to the Greet.java applet:

1 Open the **Greet.java** text file in your text editor.

2 Position the cursor at the end of the line that defines the Font bigFont object, and then press the **Enter** key to start a new line of text.

3 Declare a Button with the Label "Press Me" and an empty TextField by typing the following:

```
Button pressMe = new Button("Press Me");
TextField answer = new TextField("",10);
```

4 Position the cursor at the end of the add() statement that adds the greeting to the applet, and then press the **Enter** key to start a new line.

5 Add the TextField and the Button to the applet by typing the following:

```
add(answer);
add(pressMe);
```

6 On the next line, request focus for the answer by typing the following:

```
answer.requestFocus();.
```

7 Save the file and compile with the **javac Greet.java** command.

8 Run the applet with the **appletviewer test.html** command. Confirm that you can type characters into the TextField and that you can click the Button using the mouse. You haven't coded any action to take place as a result of a Button click yet, but the components should be functional.

9 Close the Applet Viewer window.

Event-driven Programming

An **event** occurs when someone using your applet takes action on a component, such as clicking the mouse on a Button object. The programs you have written so far in this text have been **procedural**—in other words, you dictated the order in which events occurred. You retrieved user input, wrote decisions and loops, and created output. When you retrieved user input, you had no control over how much time the user took to enter a response to a prompt, but you did control the fact that processing went no further until the input was completed. In contrast, with **event-driven programs**, the user might initiate any number of events in any order. For example, if you use a word-processing program, you have dozens of choices at your disposal at any moment in time. You can type words, select text with the mouse, click a button to change text to bold, click a button to change text to italics, choose a menu item, and so on. With each word-processing document you create, you choose options in any order that seems appropriate at the time. The word-processing program must be ready to respond to any event you initiate.

Within an event-driven program, a component on which an event is generated is the **source** of the event. A Button that a user can click is an example of a source; a TextField that a user can use to enter text is another source. An object that is interested in an event is a **listener**. Not all objects can receive all events—you probably have used programs in which clicking on many areas of the screen has no effect at all. If you want an object, such as your applet, to be a listener for an event, you must register the object as a listener for the source.

Newspapers around the world register with news services, such as the Associated Press or United Press International. The news service maintains a list of subscribers, and sends each one a story when important national events occur. Similarly, a Java component source object (such as a Button) maintains a list of registered listeners and notifies all registered listeners (such as an applet) when any event occurs, such as a mouse click. When the listener "receives the news," an event-handling method that is part of the listener object responds to the event.

> A source object and a listener object can be the same object. For example, a Button can change its Label when a user clicks it.

To respond to user events within any applet you create, you must do the following:

- Prepare your applet to accept event messages
- Tell your applet to expect events to happen
- Tell your applet how to respond to any events that happen

Preparing Your Applet to Accept Event Messages

You prepare your applet to accept mouse events by importing the java.awt.event package into your program and adding the phrase `implements ActionListener` to the class header. The java.awt.event package includes event classes with names such as ActionEvent, ComponentEvent, and TextEvent. ActionListener is an **interface**, or a set of specifications for methods that you can use with Event objects. Implementing ActionListener provides you with standard event method specifications that allow your applet to work with ActionEvents, which are the types of events that occur when a user clicks a button.

> You can identify interfaces such as ActionListener by the fact that they are "implemented," and not "imported" (by writing `import java.applet.*)` or "extended" (by writing `extends Applet`).

Telling Your Applet to Expect Events to Happen

You tell your applet to expect ActionEvents with the **addActionListener() method**. If you have declared a Button named aButton, and you want to perform an action when a user clicks aButton, then aButton is the source of a message, and you can think of your applet as a **target** to which to send a message. You learned in Chapter 3 that the `this` reference is used to mean "this current method," so `aButton.addActionListener(this);` causes any ActionEvent messages (Button clicks) that come from aButton to be sent to "this current applet."

> Not all Events are ActionEvents with an addActionListener() method. For example, TextEvents have an addTextListener() method.

Telling Your Applet How to Respond to Any Events That Happen

The ActionListener interface contains the **actionPerformed(ActionEvent e) method** specification. When an applet has registered as a listener with a Button, and a user clicks the Button, the actionPerformed() method will execute. You must write the actionPerformed() method, which contains a header and a body like all methods. You use the header `public void actionPerformed(ActionEvent e)`, where e is any name you choose for the Event (the Button click) that initiated the notification of the ActionListener (the applet). The body of the method contains any statements that you want to execute when the action occurs. You might want to perform some mathematical calculations, construct new objects, produce output, or execute any other operation. For example, Figure 6-6 shows an actionPerformed() method that produces a line of output at the operating system prompt.

```
public void actionPerformed(ActionEvent someEvent)

{

  System.out.println

    ("I'm inside the actionPerformed() method!");

}
```

Figure 6-6: The actionPerformed() method that produces a line of output

Next, you will make your applet an event-driven program by adding functionality to your applet's Button and TextField. When the user enters a name and clicks the Button, the applet will display a greeting on the command line.

To add functionality to your applet:

1 Open the **Greet.java** file in your text editor.

2 For the third import statement in your program, add **import java.awt.event.*;**.

3 Position the cursor at the end of the class header (`public class Greet extends Applet`), press the **Spacebar**, and then type **implements ActionListener**.

4 Position the cursor at the end of the statement in the init() method that adds the pressMe button to the applet, and then press the **Enter** key. Prepare your applet for Button-source events by typing the statement **pressMe.addActionListener(this);**.

5 Position the cursor to the right of the closing curly bracket for the init() method, and then press the **Enter** key. Add the following actionPerformed() method after the init() method but before the closing bracket for the Greet class. This method declares a String that will hold the user's name, uses the getText() method on the answer TextField to retrieve the String, and then displays an on-screen message to the user.

```
public void actionPerformed(ActionEvent thisEvent)
{
  String name = answer.getText();
  System.out.println("Hi there " + name);
}
```

6 Save and compile the program. Execute the test.html program using the `appletviewer test.html` command at the command prompt.

7 Type your name in the TextField and then click the **Press Me** button. Examine your command-prompt screen. The personalized message ("Hi there" and your name) appears on the command prompt screen.

help

> You might need to drag the Applet Viewer window to a new position so you can see the output on the command line.

8 Use the mouse to highlight the name in the TextField in the Applet Viewer window, and then type a new name. Click the **Press Me** button. A new greeting appears on the command line screen.

9 Close the Applet Viewer window.

In most applets that contain a TextField, there are two ways to get the applet to accept user input. Usually, you can enter text and click a Button, or you can enter text and press the Enter key. If your applet needs to receive an event message from a TextField, then you need to make your applet a registered Event listener with the TextField.

To add the ability to press the Enter key from within the TextField for input:

1 In the **Greet.java** text file, position the cursor at the end of the statement `pressMe.addActionListener(this);` and then press the **Enter** key.

2 Make the answer field accept input by typing:

```
answer.addActionListener(this);.
```

3 Save and compile the program. Run the test.html program using the **appletviewer test.html** command at the command prompt. Confirm that you can input a name in the TextField either by clicking the **Press Me** button or by pressing the **Enter** key.

4 Close the Applet Viewer window.

Adding Output to an Applet

An applet that produces output on the command line screen is not very exciting. Naturally, you will want to make changes within your applet as various events occur. For example, rather than using System.out.println() to send a greeting to the command line screen, it would be nice to add a greeting to the applet itself. One approach to this task is to create a new Label that gets added to the applet with the add() method after the user enters a name. You can declare a new, empty Label with the statement `Label personalGreeting = new Label("");`. After the name is retrieved, you can use the setText() method to set the Label text for personalGreeting to `"Hi there " + name`.

To add a personalGreeting Label to the applet:

1 Within the **Greet.java** text file, remove the System.out.println() statement from the actionPerformed() method.

2 Add the following statements to the actionPerformed() method to declare a new Label named personalGreeting, to set the text of the personalGreeting, and then to add the personalGreeting to the applet:

```
Label personalGreeting = new Label("");
personalGreeting.setText("Hi " + name);
add(personalGreeting);
```

3 Save and compile the program, and then run the applet using the **appletviewer** command. Try typing a name in the TextField and then press the **Enter** key or click the **Press Me** button. When you type a name in the TextField and then press the Enter key, nothing happens. When you enter a name in the TextField and click the Press Me button, nothing happens.

4 Now use the mouse to resize the Applet Viewer window by dragging one of its borders, or by minimizing it and then restoring it. The personalGreeting appears.

5 Close the Applet Viewer window.

Your applet does not display the personalGreeting because it is added to the applet too late. The init() method lays out all the applet components when the applet starts, and the **add(personalGreeting);** statement is not part of the init()

method. The applet screen is drawn only when it is created or when the applet is out of date. When you minimize or resize an applet, it "knows" it must be redrawn to accommodate the new size. Similarly, if you open another application so all or part of your applet screen is hidden, when you close the window that appears on top, the underlying applet "knows" it must be redrawn. However, when you use add() to place a new component on the screen, the applet does not "realize" it is out of date.

You can cause the applet to know it is out of date by using the **invalidate()** **method**, which marks the window so it knows that it is not up to date with recent changes. Then, you can cause the changes to take effect by using the **validate()** **method**, which redraws any invalid window.

To redraw your Applet Viewer window after adding the personalGreeting:

1 Within the actionPerformed() method of the Greet.java file, position the cursor at end of the `add(personalGreeting);` statement, and then press the **Enter** key. Then add the following statements:

```
invalidate();
validate();
```

2 Save, compile, and run the applet. The greeting now displays immediately after you type a name and press the Enter key or click the Press Me button.

3 Close the Applet Viewer window.

If you can add components to an applet, you should also be able to remove them; you do so with the **remove() method**. For example, after a user enters a name into the TextField, you might not want the user to use the TextField or its Button again, so you can remove them from the applet. You use the remove() method by placing the component's name within the parentheses. As with add(), you must redraw the applet after remove() to display the effects.

To remove the TextField and Button from the Greet applet:

1 Place the cursor at the end of the `add(personalGreeting);` statement in the actionPerformed() method of the Greet.java text file, and then press the **Enter** key. Then enter the following statements:

```
remove(answer);
remove(pressMe);
```

2 Save, compile, and run the applet. When you enter a name and either press the Enter key or click the Press Me button, the TextField and the Button disappear from the screen.

3 Close the Applet Viewer window, and then close your text editor.

 # S U M M A R Y

- Applets are programs that are called from within another application. You run applets within a Web page, or within another program called appletviewer, which comes with the Java Developer's Kit.

- An applet must be called from within an HTML (Hypertext Markup Language) document.

- A Web browser is a program that allows you to display HTML documents on your computer screen; such documents often contain Java applets.

- HTML commands are called tags. Tags usually come in pairs. The tag that begins every HTML document is `<HTML>` and the tag that ends every HTML document is `</HTML>`.

- To run an applet from within an HTML document, you add the `<APPLET>` and `</APPLET>` tags to your HTML document.

- You can place three attributes within the `<APPLET>` tag: `CODE`, `WIDTH`, and `HEIGHT`.

- Most applets contain at least two import statements: `import java.applet.*;` and `import java.awt.*;`. The java.awt package is the Abstract Windows Toolkit, or AWT. It contains commonly used Windows components such as Labels, Menus, and Buttons.

- Label is a built-in class that holds text that can be displayed within an applet. The setText() method assigns text to a Label or any other component.

- You use the add() method to add a component to an Applet Viewer window.

- Applet class headers include the words `extends Applet`.

- Four methods that are included in every applet are `public void init()`, `public void start()`, `public void stop()`, and `public void destroy()`.

- The init() method is the first method called in any applet. You use this method to perform initialization tasks, such as setting variables to initial values or placing applet components on the screen.

- A Font object holds typeface and size information. To construct a Font object, you need three arguments: typeface, style, and point size. The typeface is a String representing a font. Common fonts are Arial, Helvetica, Courier, and TimesRoman. The style applies an attribute to displayed text and is one of three arguments: Font.PLAIN, Font.BOLD, or Font.ITALIC. The point size is an integer that represents 1/72 of an inch.

- To give a Label object a new Font, you create the Font and then use the setFont() method to assign the Font to a Label.

- A TextField is a Windows component into which a user can type a single line of text data. Typically, a user types a line into a TextField and then inputs the data by pressing the Enter key on the keyboard or clicking a Button with the mouse.

- You can create a TextField with or without initial text, and with or without a specified size.

- The setText() method allows you to change the text in a TextField that has already been created. The getText() method allows you to retrieve the String of text in a TextField.

- You can create a Button with or without a label. You can change a Button's Label with the setLabel() method, or get the Label and assign it to a String object with the getLabel() method.

- An event occurs when your applet's user takes action on a component, such as using the mouse to click a Button object. In event-driven programs, the user might initiate any number of events in any order.

- Within an event-driven program, a component on which an event is generated is the source of the event. An object that is interested in an event is a listener.

- To respond to user events within any applet you create, you must prepare your applet to accept event messages, tell your applet to expect events to happen, and then tell your applet how to respond to any events that happen.

- Adding `implements ActionListener` to an applet's class header prepares an applet to receive event messages.

- An interface is a set of specifications for methods that you can use with events.

- An ActionEvent is the type of event that occurs when a user clicks a Button. You tell your applet to expect ActionEvents with the addActionListener() method. The ActionListener interface contains the `actionPerformed(ActionEvent e)` method specification. In the body of the method, you write any statements that you want to execute when an action takes place.

- You can alert the applet when it is out of date by using the invalidate() method, which marks the window as not up to date with recent changes. Using the validate() method redraws any invalid window.

Q U E S T I O N S

1. Applets are _____ .
   a. stand-alone programs
   b. Web pages
   c. called from within another application
   d. written in HTML

2. Which of the following is true about `appletviewer`?
   a. It is a method.
   b. You must code it yourself.
   c. It comes with the Java Developer's Kit.
   d. It must be called from within an HTML document.

3. HTML stands for _____
   a. Hypertext Markup Language
   b. Hash Table Management Language
   c. Heap Task Monitoring List
   d. How To Make a Lasting Impression

4. When you write a Java applet, you save the code with the _____ file extension.
   a. .app
   b. .html
   c. .java
   d. .class

5. Java applications and Java applets are similar because both _____.
   a. are compiled using the `javac` command
   b. are executed using the `java` command
   c. are executed from within an HTML document
   d. have a main() method

6. To use an applet within an HTML document, you include the name of the _____.
   a. .java source code file
   b. .class compiled file
   c. .exe executable file
   d. Web site from which the applet will be run

7. A program that allows you to display HTML documents on your computer screen is a _____.
   a. search engine
   b. compiler
   c. browser
   d. server

8. HTML commands also are called _____.
   a. instructions
   b. regulations
   c. tips
   d. tags

9. All HTML commands are surrounded by _____.
   a. parentheses
   b. curly brackets
   c. dots
   d. angle brackets

10. The ending half of any HTML tag pair is preceded with a _____.
    a. dot
    b. forward slash
    c. backslash
    d. colon

11. The name of any applet called using CODE within an HTML document must use the _____ extension.
    a. .exe
    b. .code
    c. .java
    d. .class

12. Usually, you should create your applets to run on a monitor that measures _____ pixels so most users can see the entire applet.
    a. 100 x 100
    b. 220 x 360
    c. 640 x 480
    d. 2200 x 100

13. Labels and Buttons are _____ .
    a. components
    b. containers
    c. applets
    d. constituents

14. The method that places a value within a previously constructed Label is _____ .
    a. getValue()
    b. setText()
    c. fillLabel()
    d. setValue()

15. The add() method _____ .
    a. adds two integers
    b. adds two numbers of any data type
    c. places a component within an Applet Viewer window
    d. places a text value within an applet component

16. Which of the following methods is *not* included in every applet?
    a. init()
    b. add()
    c. stop()
    d. destroy()

17. The first method called in any applet is _____ .
    a. main()
    b. start()
    c. init()
    d. whatever method appears first within the applet

18. A Font object contains all of the following arguments except _____ .
    a. language
    b. typeface
    c. style
    d. point size

19. A Windows component into which a user can type a single line of text data is a(n) _____ .

    a. InputArea

    b. DataField

    c. TextField

    d. Label

20. The constructor `public Button("4")` creates _____ .

    a. an unlabeled Button

    b. a Button four pixels wide

    c. a Button four characters wide

    d. a Button with a "4" on it

21. You can change a Button's label using the _____ method.

    a. setText()

    b. getText()

    c. setLabel()

    d. getLabel()

22. A user might initiate any number of events in any order in _____ program.

    a. an event-driven

    b. a procedural

    c. a random

    d. any Java

23. ActionListener is an example of a(n) _____ .

    a. import

    b. applet

    c. interface

    d. component

24. When an applet is registered as a listener with a Button, if a user clicks the Button, the method that executes is _____ .

    a. buttonPressed()

    b. addActionListener()

    c. start()

    d. actionPerformed()

25. You alert an applet when it is out of date by using the _____ method.

    a. date()

    b. change()

    c. invalidate()

    d. validate()

E X E R C I S E S

For the following exercises, save each program that you create in the Chapter.06 folder on your Student Disk.

1. Create an applet with a Button labeled "Who's the greatest?" When the user clicks the button, display your name in a large font.

2. a. Create an applet that asks a user to enter a password into a TextField and then press the Enter key. Compare the password to "Rosebud"; if they match, display "Access Granted"; if not, display "Access Denied".

    b. Modify the password applet in Exercise 2a to ignore differences in case between the typed password and "Rosebud".

    c. Modify the password applet in Exercise 2b to compare the password to a list of five valid passwords: "Rosebud", "Redrum", "Jason", "Surrender", or "Dorothy".

3. Create an applet with a Button. Display your name in an 8-point font. Every time the user clicks the Button, increase the font size for the displayed name by four points. Remove the Button when the font size exceeds 24 points.

4. Create an applet that displays the date and time in a TextField with the Label "Today is" when the user clicks a Button.

5. Create an applet that displays an employee's title in a TextField when the user types the employee's first and last names (separated by a space) in another TextField. Include Labels for each TextField. You can use arrays to store the employees' names and titles.

6. Create an applet that displays an employee's title in a TextField when the user types an employee's first and last names (separated by a space) in another TextField, or displays an employee's name in a TextField when the user types an employee's title in a TextField. Include a Label for each of the TextFields. Add a Label at the top of the applet with the text "Enter a name or a title". You can use arrays to store the employees' names and titles.

In this section you will learn:

- About the applet life cycle
- How to create a more sophisticated interactive applet
- How to use the setLocation() method
- How to disable a component
- How to get help

The Applet Life Cycle and More Sophisticated Applets

The Applet Life Cycle

Applets are popular because they are easy to use in a Web page. Because applets execute in a browser, the Applet class contains methods that automatically are called by the browser. In Section A, you learned the names of four of these methods: init(), start(), stop(), and destroy().

You already have written your own init() methods. When you write a method that has the same method header as an automatically provided method, you replace or **override** the original version. Every time a Web page containing an applet is loaded in the browser, or when you run the `appletviewer` command with an HTML document that calls an applet, if you have written an init() method for the applet, that method executes; otherwise the automatically provided init() method executes. You should write your own init() method when you have any initialization tasks to perform, such as setting up user interface components.

> Overriding a method means creating your own version that Java will use instead of using the automatically supplied version with the same name. It is not the same as *overloading* a method, which means writing several methods that have the same name but take different arguments. You learned about overloading methods in Chapter 3.

The start() method executes after the init() method, and it executes again every time the applet becomes active after it has been inactive. For example, if you run an applet using the `appletviewer` command, if you minimize the Applet Viewer window, the applet becomes inactive. When you restore the window, the applet becomes active again. On the Internet, users can leave a Web page, visit another page, and then return to the first site. Again, the applet becomes inactive, and then active. You write your own start() method if there are any actions you want to take when a user revisits an applet; for example, you might want to resume some animation that you suspended when the user left the applet.

When a user leaves a Web page, perhaps by minimizing a window or traveling to a different Web page, the stop() method is invoked. You override the existing empty stop() method only if you want to take some action when an applet is no longer visible. You usually don't need to write your own stop() methods.

The destroy() method is called when the user closes the browser or Applet Viewer. Closing the browser or Applet Viewer releases any resources the applet might have allocated. As with stop(), you usually do not have to write your own destroy() methods.

> Advanced Java programmers override the stop() and destroy() methods when they want to add instructions to "suspend a thread," or stop a chain of events that were started by an applet, but which are not yet completed.

In summary, every applet has the same life cycle outline, as shown in Figure 6-7. When any applet executes, the init() method runs, followed by start(). If the user leaves the applet's page, stop() executes. When the user returns, start() executes. The stop()-and-start() sequence might continue any number of times, until the user closes the browser (or Applet Viewer) and the destroy() method is invoked.

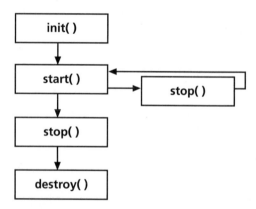

Figure 6-7: Applet life cycle outline

To demonstrate an applet's life cycle methods in action, you can write an applet that overrides all four methods and count the number of times each method executes.

To demonstrate the life cycle of an applet:

1 Open a new text file in your text editor, and then type the following import statements that you will need for the applet:

```
import java.applet.*;
import java.awt.*;
import java.awt.event.*;
```

2 Type the following header for a LifeCycle applet. The applet will include a Button that the user can click, so the ActionListener will be implemented. (You can type the header all on one line, if you want. It is written on two lines here to fit on the book page.)

```
public class LifeCycle
   extends Applet implements ActionListener
```

3 Press the **Enter** key, type the opening curly bracket for the class, and then press the **Enter** key again to start a new line.

4 Declare the following six Label objects that you will use to display the names of each of six methods that will execute during the lifetime of the applet:

```
Label messageInit = new Label("init ");
Label messageStart = new Label("start ");
Label messageDisplay = new Label("display ");
Label messageAction = new Label("action ");
Label messageStop = new Label("stop ");
Label messageDestroy = new Label("destroy");
```

5 Declare a Button by typing the following:

```
Button pressButton = new Button("Press");
```

6 Declare six integers that will hold the number of occurrences of each of the six methods by typing the following code on one line:

```
int countInit, countStart, countDisplay, countAction,
   countStop, countDestroy;.
```

7 Add the following init() method, which adds one to countInit, places the components within the applet, and then calls the display() method.

```
public void init()
{
   ++countInit;
   add(messageInit);
   add(messageStart);
   add(messageDisplay);
   add(messageAction);
   add(messageStop);
   add(messageDestroy);
   add(pressButton);
   pressButton.addActionListener(this);
   display();
}
```

8 Add the following start() method, which adds one to countStart and calls display():

```
public void start()
{
  ++countStart;
  display();
}
```

9 Add the following display() method, which adds one to countDisplay and then displays the name of each of the six methods with the current count and indicates how many times the method has executed:

```
public void display()
{
  ++countDisplay;
  messageInit.setText("init " + countInit);
  messageStart.setText("start " + countStart);
  messageDisplay.setText("display " + countDisplay);
  messageAction.setText("action " + countAction);
  messageStop.setText("stop " + countStop);
  messageDestroy.setText("destroy " + countDestroy);
}
```

10 Add the following stop() and destroy() methods, which each add one to the appropriate counter and call display():

```
public void stop()
{
  ++countStop;
  display();
}
public void destroy()
{
  ++countDestroy;
  display();
}
```

11 When the user clicks pressButton, the following actionPerformed() method will execute; it adds one to countAction and displays it. Enter the method:

```
public void actionPerformed(ActionEvent e)
{
  ++countAction;
  display();
}
```

12 Add the closing curly bracket for the class. Save the class as **LifeCycle.java** in the Chapter.06 folder on your Student Disk. If necessary, compile, correct any errors, and compile again.

Take a moment to examine the code you created for LifeCycle.java. Each of the methods adds one to one of the six counters, but you never explicitly call any of the methods except display(); each of the other methods will be called automatically. Next, you will create an HTML document so you can test LifeCycle.java.

To create an HTML document to test LifeCycle.java:

1 Open a new text file in your text editor.

2 Enter the following HTML document:

```
<HTML>
<APPLET CODE="LifeCycle.class" WIDTH = 460 HEIGHT = 200>
</APPLET>
</HTML>
```

3 Save the file as **life.html** in the Chapter.06 folder on your Student Disk.

4 Run the HTML document using the command **appletviewer life.html**. Figure 6-8 shows the output. When the applet begins, the init() method is called, so one is added to countInit. The init() method calls display(), so one is added to countDisplay. Immediately after the init() method executes, the start() method is executed, and one is added to countStart. The start() method calls display() so one more is added to countDisplay. The first time you see the applet, countInit is 1, countStart is 1, and countDisplay is 2. The methods actionPerformed(), stop(), and destroy() have not yet been executed.

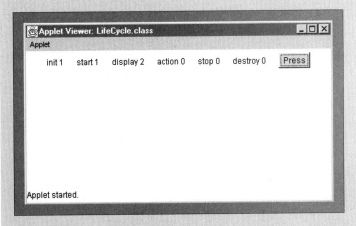

Figure 6-8: LifeCycle applet after startup

5   Minimize the Applet Viewer window by clicking the **Minimize** button ▬|, and then restore it. The applet now looks like Figure 6-9. The init() method still has been called only once, but when you minimized the applet, the stop() method executed, and when you restored it, the start() method executed. Therefore, countStop is now 1 and countStart has increased to 2. Additionally, both start() and stop() call display(), so countDisplay() is increased by two, and it now holds the value 4.

Figure 6-9: LifeCycle applet after being minimized and restored

6   Minimize and maximize the Applet Viewer window again. Now the stop() method has executed twice, the start() method has executed three times, and the display() method has executed a total of six times. See Figure 6-10.

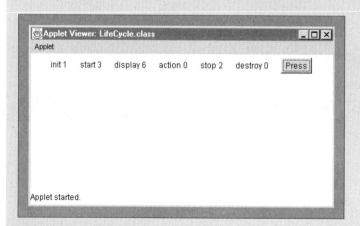

Figure 6-10: LifeCycle applet after being minimized and restored twice

7   Click the **Press** button. The count for the actionPerformed() method now is 1, and actionPerformed() calls display(), so countDisplay() is up to 7, as shown in Figure 6-11.

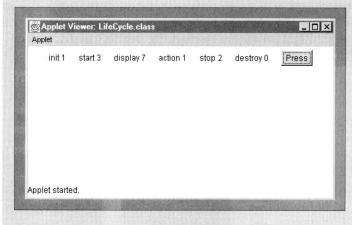

Figure 6-11: LifeCycle applet after you click the Press button

8 Continue to minimize, maximize, and press the button, and note the changes that occur with each activity until you can correctly predict the outcome. Notice that the destroy() method is not executed until you close the applet, and then it is too late to observe an increase in countDestroy.

A Complete Interactive Applet

You are now able to create a fairly complex application or applet. Next, you will create an applet that contains several components, receives user input, makes decisions, uses arrays, performs output, and reacts to the applet life cycle.

The PartyPlanner applet lets its user estimate the cost of an event hosted by Event Handlers Incorporated. Event Handlers uses a sliding fee scale so the per-guest cost decreases as the total number of invited guests increases. Figure 6-12 shows the fee structure.

Number of Guests	Cost per Guest
1 to 24	$27
25 to 49	$25
50 to 99	$22
100 to 199	$19
200 to 499	$17
500 to 999	$14
1000 and over	$11

Figure 6-12: Cost per guest for events

The applet lets the user enter a number of anticipated guests. The user can press the Enter key or click a Button to perform the fee lookup and event cost calculation. Then the applet displays the cost per person as well as the total cost for the event. The user can continue to request fees for a different number of guests and view the results for any length of time before making another request or leaving the page. If the user leaves the page, however, you want to erase the last number of requested guests and make sure the next user starts fresh with zero guests.

To begin to create an interactive party planner applet:

1 Open a new text file in your text editor.

2 Type the following import statements, the PartyPlanner class header, and the opening curly bracket for the class:

```
import java.applet.*;
import java.awt.*;
import java.awt.event.*;
public class PartyPlanner
   extends Applet implements ActionListener
{
```

3 You will need several components: a Label for the company name, a Button the user can click to perform a calculation, a prompt for the Button, a TextField in which the user can enter the number of invited guests, and two more Labels to display output. Add the following code to implement these components:

```
Label companyName =
   new Label("Event Handlers Incorporated");
Button calcButton = new Button("Calculate");
Label prompt =
   new Label("Enter the number of guests at your event");
TextField numGuests = new TextField(5);
Label perPersonResult = new Label("Plan with us.");
Label totalResult = new Label("The more the merrier!");
```

4 Additionally, for appearance, create a Font by typing the following:

```
Font bigFont = new Font("Helvetica", Font.ITALIC, 24);
```

5 You can use the init() method to place components within the applet screen and prepare the Button and text-entry field to receive action messages by typing the following:

```
public void init()
{
  companyName.setFont(bigFont);
  add(companyName);
  add(prompt);
  add(numGuests);
  add(calcButton);
  calcButton.addActionListener(this);
  numGuests.addActionListener(this);
  add(perPersonResult);
  add(totalResult);
}
```

6 Add the following start() method, which executes when the user leaves the applet and resets the result Labels and the data-entry TextField:

```
public void start()
{
  perPersonResult.setText("Plan with us.");
  numGuests.setText("0");
  totalResult.setText("The more the merrier!");
  invalidate();
  validate();
}
```

7 Save the partially completed applet as **PartyPlanner.java** in the Chapter.06 folder on your Student Disk.

You finished the init() and start() methods for the PartyPlanner applet, placed each component in the applet, and reinitialized each component each time a user returns to the applet after leaving. At this point, the applet doesn't actually do anything; most of the applet's work is contained in the actionPerformed() method, which is the most complicated method in this applet. Next, you will create the actionPerformed() method. You will begin by declaring two parallel arrays—one array will hold guest limits for each of six event rates, and the other array will hold the actual rates.

To complete the PartyPlanner applet:

1 Enter the following method header for actionPerformed() and declare two arrays for guest limits and rates:

```
public void actionPerformed(ActionEvent e)
{
  int[] guestLimit =  { 0, 25, 50,100,200,500,1000};
  int[] ratePerGuest = {27, 25, 22, 19, 17, 14, 11};
```

2 Next, add the following variable to hold the number of guests. The user will enter text into a TextField, but you need an integer to perform calculations, so you can use the parseInt() method.

```
int guests = Integer.parseInt(numGuests.getText());
```

You learned about the parseInt() method in Chapter 5.

3 You need two variables that will hold the individual, per-person fee for an event, and the fee for the entire event. Enter the following variables:

```
int individualFee = 0, eventFee = 0;
```

4 Enter the following variables to use as subscripts for the arrays:

```
int x = 0, a = 0;
```

There are a number of ways to search through the guestLimit array to discover the appropriate position of the per-person fee in the ratePerGuest array. One possibility is to use a `for` loop and vary a subscript from five down to zero. If the number of guests is greater than or equal to any value in the guestLimit array, then the corresponding per-person rate in the ratePerGuest array is the correct rate. After finding the correct individual rate, you determine the price for the entire event by multiplying the individual rate by the number of guests. After finding the appropriate individual fee for a given event, you do not want to search through the guestLimit array any longer, so you set the subscript *x* equal to zero to force an early exit from the `for` loop.

5 Enter the following `for` loop:

```
for(x = 5; x >= 0; --x)
   if(guests >= guestLimit[x])
     {
        individualFee = ratePerGuest[x];
        eventFee = guests * individualFee;
        x = 0;
     }
```

6 The only tasks that remain in the actionPerformed() method involve producing output for the user. Enter the following code to accomplish this processing:

```
perPersonResult.setText
   ("$" + individualFee + " per person");
totalResult.setText("Event cost $" + eventFee);
```

7 Add two closing curly brackets: one for the actionPerformed() method, and one for the entire PartyPlanner applet.

8 Save the file and then compile it at the command prompt.

9 Open a new text file in your text editor, and then create the following HTML document to test the applet:

```
<HTML>
<APPLET CODE="PartyPlanner.class"
    WIDTH = 320 HEIGHT = 200>
</APPLET>
</HTML>
```

10 Save the HTML document as **PartyPlan.html** in the Chapter.06 folder on your Student Disk. Then use the `appletviewer` command to execute the file. Your output should look like Figure 6-1 at the beginning of this chapter. Test the applet with different guest numbers until you are sure that the per-person rates and event rates are correct. Minimize and restore the Applet Viewer window and observe that any calculated fees are replaced with start() messages. For example, if you enter 100 guests, then your output resembles Figure 6-13.

Figure 6-13: PartyPlanner applet

11 Close the Applet Viewer window.

Using the setLocation() Method

A serious shortcoming of the objects you have written so far is that you have not been able to choose the location of the Label and Button objects you place within your applets. When you use the add() method to add a component to an applet, it seems to have a mind of its own as to where it is physically placed. Although you need to learn more about the Java programming language before you can change where components are placed initially when you use the add() method, you can use the setLocation() method to change the location of a component at a later time. The **setLocation() method** allows you to place a component at a specific location within the Applet Viewer window.

Any applet window consists of a number of horizontal and vertical pixels on the screen. You set the pixel values in the HTML document you write to test the applet. Any component you place on the screen has a horizontal, or **x-axis**, position as well as a vertical, or **y-axis**, position in the window. The upper-left corner of any display is position 0,0. The first, or **x-coordinate**, value increases as you travel from left to right across the window. The second, or **y-coordinate**, value increases as you travel from top to bottom. Figure 6-14 illustrates the screen coordinate positions.

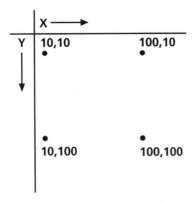

Figure 6-14: Screen coordinate positions

For example, to position a Label object named someLabel at the top-left corner of a window, you write `someLabel.setLocation(0,0);`. If a window is 200 pixels wide and 100 pixels tall, then you can place a Button named pressMe in the approximate center of the window with the statement `pressMe.setLocation(100,50);`.

> **tip**
>
> •••
> You can picture a coordinate as an infinitely thin line that lies between the pixels of the output device.
> •••

> **tip**
>
> •••
> When you use setLocation(), the top-left corner of the component is placed at the specified x- and y-coordinates. If a window is 100 by 100 pixels, then `aButton.setLocation(100,100);` places the Button outside the window, where you cannot see the component.
> •••

Next, you will create a Label that changes its location with each Button click.

To create a moving Label:

1 Open a new text file in your text editor, and then type the following import statements that you will need:

```
import java.applet.*;
import java.awt.*;
import java.awt.event.*;
```

2 Type the following class header and opening curly bracket for a class named MoveLabel. The applet will use the mouse, so it must implement ActionListener.

```
public class MoveLabel
   extends Applet implements ActionListener
{
```

3 Declare the following Label, Button, and two integers that will hold the horizontal and vertical coordinates of the Label:

```
Label movingMsg = new Label("Event Handlers Inc.");
Button pressButton = new Button("Press");
int xLoc = 20, yLoc =20;
```

4 Enter the following init() method to add the components to the applet screen and prepare the Button to receive messages:

```
public void init()
{
  add(movingMsg);
  add(pressButton);
  pressButton.addActionListener(this);
}
```

5 When the user clicks the Button, the message will move 10 pixels to the right and 10 pixels down. In other words, it will appear to move across the screen at a downward angle. Enter the following actionPerformed method() to do this:

```
public void actionPerformed(ActionEvent e)
{
   movingMsg.setLocation(xLoc+=10, yLoc+=10);
}
```

6 Add the closing curly bracket to the class.

7 Save the file as **MoveLabel.java** in the Chapter.06 folder on your Student Disk, and then compile it.

8 Open a new file in your text editor, and then create the following HTML document to test the applet:

```
<HTML>
<APPLET CODE="MoveLabel.class" WIDTH = 460 HEIGHT = 300>
</APPLET>
</HTML>
```

9 Save the HTML document as **move.html** in the Chapter.06 folder on your Student Disk. Then run the file using the `appletviewer` command at the command prompt. Observe how the Label moves each time you click the **Press Me** button.

10 Close the Applet Viewer window.

Using the setEnabled() Method

You probably have used computer programs in which a component becomes disabled or unusable. For example, a Button might become dim and unresponsive when the programmer no longer wants you to have access to the Button's functionality. You can use the **setEnabled() method** with a component to make it unavailable and, in turn, to make it available again. The setEnabled() method takes an argument of `true` if you want to enable a component, or `false` if you want to disable a component.

When you create a component, it is enabled by default.

For example, in the MoveLabel applet, a user can continue to click the Button until the Label moves completely off the screen. If you want to prevent this from happening, you can disable the Button after the Label has advanced as far as you want it to go. Next, you will stop the Label from moving after it reaches a y-coordinate of 280.

To disable the Button:

1 Open the **MoveLabel.java** file in your text editor.

2 Position the cursor at the end of the statement in the actionPerformed() method, and then press the **Enter** key to start a new line of text. Then add the following statement to disable the Button when the message has moved to a y-coordinate of 280:

```
if(yLoc==280)
    pressButton.setEnabled(false);
```

3 Save the program, compile, and run the move.html file using the **appletviewer** command. Click the **Press** button until the Button is disabled and the Label cannot descend any farther.

4 Close the Applet Viewer window, and then close your text editor.

Getting Help

Now your Java programs are becoming more sophisticated—each program you write contains several methods and many individual statements. As you continue to learn about programming, many Java applications and applets you write easily could become 20 times larger than the ones you are writing now. There are hundreds of additional Java methods that you have not learned yet, and developers are creating new objects daily for you to use. With all that programming code to write and all those methods to understand, it is easy to get lost. Fortunately, a few sources of help are available to you.

A wealth of material exists at the Sun Microsystems Web site, at http://java.sun.com. Of particular interest are the **FAQs (Frequently Asked Questions)** and the Help file to which you can link from the java.sun home page.

Some Java newsgroups on the Web are summarized in Figure 6-15. While you are still a novice programmer, it's a good idea to read the messages that are posted at these newsgroups. Reserve adding comments of your own until you are sure you are not asking a question that has been asked dozens of times before.

```
comp.lang.java.advocacy

comp.lang.java.announce

comp.lang.java.api

comp.lang.java.beans

comp.lang.java.gui

comp.lang.java.help

comp.lang.java.misc

comp.lang.java.programmer

comp.lang.java.security

comp.lang.java.setup

comp.lang.java.softwaretools

comp.lang.java.tech
```

Figure 6-15: Java newsgroups

S U M M A R Y

■ When you write a method that has the same method header as an automatically provided method, you replace or override the original version.

■ The start() method executes after the init() method and every time the applet becomes active after it has been inactive. You write your own start() method if there are any actions you want to take when an applet is revisited.

■ When a user moves off the page, perhaps by minimizing a window or traveling to a different Web page, the stop() method is invoked.

■ The destroy() method is called when the user closes the browser or Applet Viewer; this releases any resources the applet may have allocated.

■ When you use the add() method to add a component to an applet, you do not determine the physical location of the component. The setLocation() method allows you to place a component at a specific location within an Applet Viewer window.

- Any Applet Viewer window consists of a number of horizontal and vertical pixels on the screen, called the x-axis positions and y-axis positions, respectively.

- The upper-left corner of any display is position 0,0. The first or x-coordinate value increases as you travel from left to right across the window. The second or y-coordinate value increases as you travel from top to bottom.

- When you use setLocation(x,y), the top-left corner of the component is placed at the specified x- and y-coordinates.

- You can use the setEnabled() method with a component to make it unavailable and, in turn, to make it available again. The setEnabled() method takes an argument of `true` if you want to enable a component, or `false` if you want to disable a component.

- When you are writing Java programs, you can get help from the Sun Microsystems Web site or from Java newsgroups.

Q U E S T I O N S

1. When you write a method that has the same method header as an automatically provided method, you _____ the original version.
   a. destroy
   b. override
   c. call
   d. copy

2. If you do not write an init() method for an applet, then _____ .
   a. your program will not compile
   b. your program will compile but not run
   c. you must write a main() method
   d. an automatically provided init() method executes

3. The method that executes immediately after init() is _____ .
   a. main()
   b. begin()
   c. start()
   d. stop()

4. The start() method executes _____ .
   a. after the init() method
   b. every time the applet becomes active after it has been inactive
   c. both of these
   d. none of these

5. The method that executes when a user leaves a page is _____ .
   a. stop()
   b. destroy()
   c. kill()
   d. finish()

6. The destroy() method is called when the user _____ .
   a. closes the browser or Applet Viewer window
   b. minimizes the Applet Viewer window
   c. leaves the page
   d. shuts down the computer

7. The stop()-and-start() sequence _____ within an applet.
   a. must not occur more than once
   b. might occur any number of times
   c. must never occur
   d. does not usually occur

8. Which of the following statements creates a Label that says "Welcome"?
   a. `Label = new Label("Welcome");`
   b. `Label aLabel = Label("Welcome");`
   c. `aLabel = new Label("Welcome");`
   d. `Label aLabel = new Label("Welcome");`

9. Which of the following statements correctly creates a Font object?
   a. `Font aFont = new Font("TimesRoman", Font.ITALIC, 20);`
   b. `Font aFont = new Font(30, "Helvetica", Font.ITALIC);`
   c. `Font aFont = new Font(Font.BOLD,"Helvetica", 24);`
   d. `Font aFont = new Font(22, Font.BOLD,"TimesRoman";`

10. The method that positions a component within an applet is _____ .
    a. position()
    b. setPosition()
    c. location()
    d. setLocation()

11. The y-axis position within a window refers to _____ .
    a. horizontal position
    b. vertical position
    c. font size
    d. order of operations

12. The upper-left corner of a display that is 100 x 100 pixels is position _____ .
   a. 0,0
   b. 0,100
   c. 100,0
   d. 100,100

13. The upper-right corner of a display that is 100 x 100 pixels is position _____ .
   a. 0,0
   b. 0,100
   c. 100,0
   d. 100,100

14. In a window that is 200 x 200 pixels, position 10,190 is nearest to the _____ corner.
   a. top-left
   b. top-right
   c. bottom-left
   d. bottom-right

15. You use the setEnabled() method to make a component _____ .
   a. available
   b. unavailable
   c. both of these
   d. none of these

16. Which of the following statements disables a component named someComponent?
   a. `someComponent.setDisabled();`
   b. `someComponent.setDisabled(true);`
   c. `someComponent.setEnabled(false);`
   d. `someComponent.setEnabled(true);`

E X E R C I S E S

For the following exercises, save each program that you create in the Chapter.06 folder on your Student Disk.

1. Create an applet named DoubleInteger that allows the user to enter an integer. When the user clicks a Button, the integer is doubled and the answer is displayed.

2. Create an applet named SumIntegers that allows the user to enter two integers into two separate TextFields. When the user clicks a Button, the sum of the integers is displayed.

3   a. Create an applet named DivideTwo that allows the user to enter two integers in two separate TextFields. The user can click a Button to divide the first integer by the second integer and display the result.

     b. Modify the DivideTwo applet created in Exercise 3a so that if a user enters zero for the second integer, when the user clicks the Button to divide, the applet displays the message "Division by zero not allowed!"

4.   a. Create a payroll applet named CalcPay that allows the user to enter two double values—hours worked and hourly rate. When the user clicks a Button, gross pay is calculated.

     b. Modify the payroll applet created in Exercise 4a so that federal withholding tax is subtracted from gross pay based on the following table:

Income—$	Withholding—%
0 to 99.99	10
100.00 to 299.99	15
300.00 to 599.99	21
600.00 and up	28

5. Create a conversion applet named ConvertMiles that lets the user enter a distance in miles in a TextField, and then converts miles to kilometers and displays the result in a TextField. Each TextField should have a Label. You can use the formula miles *1.6 to convert miles to kilometers.

6. Create an applet named CalculateBalance that calculates the current balance in a checking account in a TextField. The user enters the beginning balance, check amount, and deposit amount in separate TextFields with the appropriate Labels. After the applet calculates the current balance, reposition the TextFields and Labels so that the beginning balance appears on the first line, the check and deposit amounts appear on the second line, and the new balance appears on the third line.

7. Create an applet named FamilyRecord that displays two of your family members' names, relationships to yourself, and ages in TextFields when you click a Button. Each TextField should have a Label. After clicking the Button, reposition the TextFields and Labels so that your family members' names appear on the second line, and the family members' relationships to you and ages appear on the third line.

8. Each of the following files in the Chapter.06 folder on your Student Disk has syntax and/or logical errors. In each case, determine the problem and fix the program. After you correct the errors, save each file using the same filename preceded with *Fix*. For example, DebugSix1.java will become FixDebugSix1.java. You can test each of these applets with the testDebug.html file on the Student Disk. Remember to change the Java class file referenced in the HTML document so it matches the DebugSix applet you are working on.

    a. DebugSix1.java
    b. DebugSix2.java
    c. DebugSix3.java
    d. DebugSix4.java

Index

Java™ Development Kit Version 1.1.6 Binary Code License

This binary code license ("License") contains rights and restrictions associated with use of the accompanying software and documentation ("Software"). Read the License carefully before installing the Software. By installing the Software you agree to the terms and conditions of this License. 1. Limited License Grant. Sun grants to you ("Licensee") a non-exclusive, non-transferable limited license to use the Software without fee for evaluation of the Software and for development of Java™ compatible applets and applications. Licensee may make one archival copy of the Software and may re-distribute complete, unmodified copies of the Software to software developers within Licensee's organization to avoid unnecessary download time, provided that this License conspicuously appear with all copies of the Software. Except for the foregoing, Licensee may not re-distribute the Software in whole or in part, either separately or included with a product. Refer to the Java Runtime Environment Version 1.1.6 binary code license (http://java.sun.com/products/JDK/1.1/index.html) for the availability of run-time code which may be distributed with Java compatible applets and applications. 2. Java Platform Interface. Licensee may not modify the Java Platform Interface ("JPI", identified as classes contained within the "java" package or any subpackages of the "java" package), by creating additional classes within the JPI or otherwise causing the addition to or modification of the classes in the JPI. In the event that Licensee creates any Java-related API and distributes such API to others for applet or application development, Licensee must promptly publish an accurate specification for such API for free use by all developers of Java-based software. 3. Restrictions. Software is confidential copyrighted information of Sun and title to all copies is retained by Sun and/or its licensors. Licensee shall not modify, decompile, disassemble, decrypt, extract, or otherwise reverse engineer Software. Software may not be leased, assigned, or sublicensed, in whole or in part. Software is not designed or intended for use in on-line control of aircraft, air traffic, aircraft navigation or aircraft communications; or in the design, construction, operation or maintenance of any nuclear facility. Licensee warrants that it will not use or redistribute the Software for such purposes. 4. Trademarks and Logos. This License does not authorize Licensee to use any Sun name, trademark or logo. Licensee acknowledges that Sun owns the Java trademark and all Java-related trademarks, logos and icons including the Coffee Cup and Duke ("Java Marks") and agrees to: (i) to comply with the Java Trademark Guidelines at http://java.sun.com/trademarks.html; (ii) not do anything harmful to or inconsistent with Sun's rights in the Java Marks; and (iii) assist Sun in protecting those rights, including assigning to Sun any rights acquired by Licensee in any Java Mark. 5. Disclaimer of Warranty. Software is provided "AS IS," without a warranty of any kind. ALL EXPRESS OR IMPLIED REPRESENTATIONS AND WARRANTIES, INCLUDING ANY IMPLIED WARRANTY OF MERCHANTABILITY, FITNESS FOR A PARTICULAR PURPOSE OR NON-INFRINGEMENT, ARE HEREBY EXCLUDED. 6. Limitation of Liability. SUN AND ITS LICENSORS SHALL NOT BE LIABLE FOR ANY DAMAGES SUFFERED BY LICENSEE OR ANY THIRD PARTY AS A RESULT OF USING OR DIS-TRIBUTING SOFTWARE. IN NO EVENT WILL SUN OR ITS LICENSORS BE LIABLE FOR ANY LOST REVENUE, PROFIT OR DATA, OR FOR DIRECT, INDIRECT, SPECIAL, CONSEQUENTIAL, INCIDENTAL OR PUNITIVE DAM-AGES, HOWEVER CAUSED AND REGARDLESS OF THE THEORY OF LIABILITY, ARISING OUT OF THE USE OF OR INABILITY TO USE SOFTWARE, EVEN IF SUN HAS BEEN ADVISED OF THE POSSIBILITY OF SUCH DAMAGES. 7. Termination. Licensee may terminate this License at any time by destroying all copies of Software. This License will terminate immediately without notice from Sun if Licensee fails to comply with any provision of this License. Upon such termination, Licensee must destroy all copies of Software. 8. Export Regulations. Software, including technical data, is subject to U.S. export control laws, including the U.S. Export Administration Act and its associated regulations, and may be subject to export or import regulations in other countries. Licensee agrees to comply strictly with all such regulations and acknowledges that it has the responsibility to obtain licenses to export, re-export, or import Software. Software may not be downloaded, or otherwise exported or re-exported (i) into, or to a national or resident of, Cuba, Iraq, Iran, North Korea, Libya, Sudan, Syria or any coun-try to which the U.S. has embargoed goods; or (ii)to anyone on the U.S. Treasury Department's list of Specially Designated Nations or the U.S. Commerce Department's Table of Denial Orders. 9. Restricted Rights. Use, duplication or disclosure by the United States government is subject to the restrictions as set forth in the Rights in Technical Data and Computer Software Clauses in DFARS 252.227-7013(c) (1) (ii) and FAR 52.227-19(c) (2) as applicable. 10. Governing Law. Any action related to this License will be governed by California law and controlling U.S. federal law. No choice of law rules of any jurisdiction will apply. 11. Severability. If any of the above provisions are held to be in violation of applicable law, void, or unenforceable in any jurisdiction, then such provisions are herewith waived to the extent necessary for the License to be otherwise enforceable in such jurisdiction. However, if in Sun's opinion deletion of any provisions of the License by operation of this paragraph unreasonably compromises the rights or increase the liabilities of Sun or its licensors, Sun reserves the right to terminate the License and refund the fee paid by Licensee, if any, as Licensee's sole and exclusive remedy.